DIRECTORS' CUTS

1 0 JUN 2024

Other titles in the Directors' Cuts series:

the cinema of
ROMAN POLANSKI

dark spaces of the world

edited by john orr & elżbieta ostrowska

WALLFLOWER PRESS LONDON & NEW YORK

First published in Great Britain in 2006 by
Wallflower Press
6a Middleton Place, Langham Street, London W1W 7TE
www.wallflowerpress.co.uk

A catalogue record for this book is available from the British Library

ISBN 1-904764-75-4 (paperback)
      1-904764-76-2 (hardback)

Book design by Rob Bowden Design

Printed in Great Britain by Antony Rowe Ltd, Chippenham, Wiltshire

CONTENTS

ACKNOWLEDGEMENTS

We wish to thank Adam Wyżyński from the National Film Archive, Poland, for supplying the stills from *Knife in the Water* and *When Angels Fall*, and Zbigniew Stanek from SF 'Oko' and Jarosław Czembrowski from Polish Film School for their permission to reproduce the materials. We also wish to thank Joel Finler for permissions for stills from *Repulsion*, *Cul-de-Sac*, *Chinatown*, *The Tenant* and *Bitter Moon*.

NOTES ON CONTRIBUTORS

Paul Coates is Professor of Film Studies at the University of Western Ontario. His publications include *The Story of the Lost Reflection* (Verso, 1985), *The Gorgon's Gaze: German Cinema, Expressionism, and the Image of Horror* (Cambridge University Press, 1991), *Lucid Dreams: The Films of Krzysztof Kieslowski* (as editor) (Flicks Books, 1999), *Cinema, Religion and the Romantic Legacy* (Ashgate, 2003) and *The Red and the White: The Cinema of People's Poland* (Wallflower Press, 2005).

Mark Cousins is a film writer, producer and director. He is the author of *The Story of Film* (Pavilion, 2004) and *Scene by Scene* (Laurence King, 2004), and co-editor of *Imagining Reality: The Faber Book of Documentary* (Faber, 1997). He was Director of the Edinburgh International Film Festival in 1996 and 1997 and writes regularly for *Prospect*, *The Times*, *The Scotsman*, *Scotland on Sunday* and the *Sunday Herald*. He has directed documentaries for the BBC and Channel Four on neo-Nazism, the Gulf War, Ian Hamilton Finlay, Powell and Pressburger and Iranian Cinema. Through his company 4 Way Pictures, he is currently producing *Meat Trade* and *The Man Who Walks*.

Herbert J. Eagle is Associate Professor in the Slavic Languages and Literatures Department at the Residential College where he also headed the Program in Film and Video Studies from 1981 to 1988. He is the editor of *Russian Formalist Film Theory* (Oxon Publishing, 1981) and, with Anna Lawton, of *Russian Futurism Through its Manifestos* (Cornell University Press, 1988). He has also written on many Russian and East Central European filmmakers in books and journals, including *Wide Angle*, *Periphery: Journal of Polish Affairs* and *Cross Currents: A Yearbook of Central European Culture*.

Lucy Fischer is Professor of Film Studies and English at the University of Pittsburgh where she serves as Director of the Film Studies Program. She is the author of *Jacques Tati* (G. K. Hall, 1983), *Shot/Countershot: Film Tradition and Women's Cinema* (Princeton University Press, 1989), *Imitation of Life* (Rutgers University Press, 1991), *Cinematernity: Film, Motherhood, Genre* (Princeton University Press, 1996), *Sunrise* (British Film Institute, 1998), *Designing Women: Art Deco, Cinema and the Female Form*

(Columbia University Press, 2003) and co-editor, with Marcia Landy, of *Stars: The Film Reader* (Routledge, 2004.) She is currently editing *American Film in the 1920s: Themes and Variations* for Rutgers University Press. She has also published widely in journals such as *Screen, Sight and Sound, Camera Obscura, Wide Angle, Cinema Journal, Journal of Film and Video, Film Criticism, Women and Performance, Frauen und Film, Biography* and *Film Quarterly*. She has also served as president of the Society for Cinema and Media Studies.

Helena Goscilo is UCIS Research Professor/Professor of Slavic at the University of Pittsburgh. She has authored and edited more than a dozen volumes on gender and culture, among them *Dehexing Sex: Russian Womanhood During and After Glasnost* (Michigan University Press, 1996), *Russian Culture in the 1990s* (Studies in 20th Century Literature, 2000), *Politicizing Magic: An Anthology of Russian and Soviet Fairy Tales*, with M. Balina and M. Lipovetsky (Northwestern University Press, 2005), *Gender and National Identity in 20th Century Russian Culture*, with Andrea Lanoux (Northern Illinois University Press, 2006) and the *Encyclopedia of Contemporary Russian Culture*, with T. Smorodinskaya and K. Evans-Romaine (Routledge, 2006). She is currently completing a volume entitled *Fade From Red: Screening the Ex-Enemy During the Nineties*, with Bożenna Goscilo, and a volume on post-Soviet celebrities, with Vladimir Strukov.

Izabela Kalinowska is Assistant Professor in the Department of European Languages, Literatures, and Cultures at Stony Brook University. She is the author of *Between East and West: Polish and Russian Nineteenth-Century Travel to the Orient* (University of Rochester Press, 2004) and of several articles dealing with various aspects of Polish cinema. She is currently working on an annotated translation of Andrzej Wajda's autobiography.

Tony McKibbin teaches film in Open Studies at the University of Edinburgh. He has written numerous articles for film and literary magazines (*Film West, Film Ireland, Cencrastus* and *Hard Times*), listings magazines (*The List*), academic journals such as *Studies in French Cinema* and internet magazines, including *Senses of Cinema*.

Maximilian Le Cain is a filmmaker and critic based in Cork, Ireland. His short films include *Kingdom of the Shadows* (2001), *Dead Time* (2003) and *Another Last Glimpse* (2004) made for Cork Capital of Culture 2005. He is a regular contributor to *Senses of Cinema* and has also written for, among others, *Rouge* and *Film Ireland*. He is currently writing a book on the cinema of James Fotopoulos.

John Orr is Emeritus Professor at the University of Edinburgh. He is the author of *Cinema and Modernity* (Edinburgh University Press, 1993), *Contemporary Cinema* (Edinburgh University Press, 1998), *The Art and Politics of Film* (Edinburgh University Press, 2000) and *Hitchcock and Twentieth-Century Cinema* (Wallflower Press, 2005), and the editor of *Cinema and Fiction*, with Colin Nicholson (Edinburgh University

Press, 1992), *Post-war Cinema and Modernity: A Film Reader*, with Olga Taxidou (New York University Press, 2000) and *The Cinema of Andrzej Wajda: The Art of Irony and Defiance*, with Elżbieta Ostrowska (Wallflower Press, 2003).

Elżbieta Ostrowska currently teaches film at the University of Alberta, Canada. She is the author of *Przestrzeń filmowa* (Rabid 2000) and *Women in Polish Cinema*, with Ewa Mazierska (Berghahn, 2006), and the editor of *Kino ma sto lat*, with Jan Rek (Wydawnictwo Uniwersytetu Łódzkiego 1998), *Gender in Film and the Media: East-West Dialogues*, with Elżbieta H. Oleksy and Michael Stevenson (Peter Lang, 2000), *Gender-Film-Media*, with Elżbieta H. Oleksy (Rabid, 2001), *Gender w kinie europejskim i mediach* (Rabid, 2001), *The Cinema of Andrzej Wajda: The Art of Irony and Defiance*, with John Orr (Wallflower Press, 2003) and *Gender: wizerunki kobiet i mężczyzn w kulturze*, with Elżbieta Durys (Rabid, 2005).

Dana Polan teaches in the Cinema Studies program of the Tisch School of the Arts at New York University. He is the author of five books in film and media studies, including *Pulp Fiction* (British Film Institute, 2000) and *Jane Campion* (British Film Institute, 2001). Two additional volumes are forthcoming: *Scenes of Instructions: The Beginning of the U.S. Study of Film* (University of California Press) and *The Sopranos* (Duke University Press). His current project is a study of Julia Child's TV show, *The French Chef*.

Michael Stevenson teaches in the Department of Film, Theatre and Television at the University of Reading, UK. He is the co-editor of *Gender in Film and the Media: East-West Dialogues*, with Elżbieta H. Oleksy and Elżbieta Ostrowska (Peter Lang, 2000). Recent publications include articles on the representation of the Holocaust in the films of Andrzej Wajda and on contemporary Polish cinema.

Polanski's Fourth Wall Aesthetic

Mark Cousins

It is more than twenty years since François Truffaut's book-length interview with Alfred Hitchcock (Truffaut 1984) convinced film historians and critics of the value of reading closely a director's comments on his or her own work. Before that, volumes such as Joseph von Sternberg's *Fun in a Chinese Laundry* (1965) and Robert Bresson's *Notes on Cinematography* (1977) had shown that certain filmmakers were interested in the lexicon of cinema criticism but, on the whole, Hawksian disingenuousness was the norm. Where artists in other fields – notably Paul Klee in his diaries – showed an ability to describe the mental processes behind their work, the majority of film-makers have been unwilling or unable to do so. Paul Schrader, Bernardo Bertolucci, Abbas Kiarostami and Hou Hsiao-Hsien are notable exceptions to this, but in general the ambiguous commerciality of cinema as well as the massive amount of technical process, which lies between a creative thought and its realisation in the completed work, have meant that most directors talk mostly about business or equipment.

His gripping, ghosted autobiography notwithstanding, Roman Polanski has followed suit in this regard. For more than three decades he has deflected questions about the meanings of his films and the human and aesthetic ideas they evince. Asked to justify the position or angle of his camera, for example, he answers with variations on 'It is there because it felt right' or 'because that's where I would watch the action from'. At times he has shown contempt even for the idea of such enquiry. Asked why Françoise Dorléac's character in *Cul-de-Sac* (1966) dresses her husband

Donald Pleasance in women's clothes (Cousins 2000) his complete response was a single, wordless snore.

Of course it is the critic's job, not Polanski's, to describe the genesis and operation of his films, and he is at liberty to ridicule their attempts to do so, but despite the director's manifest reluctance to analyse, it would be a mistake not to attend to what he says about his work. This is the case for three related reasons. Firstly, he is bracingly intelligent. Secondly, he talks at length about the meanings, not just the techniques, of other art forms, such as the paintings of Balthus; not only is he not one of those directors whose visual abilities come at the expense of verbal ones, but he accepts the idea of semantic analysis. From this we can conclude that, thirdly, and as a direct result of such articulacy, even his deflections and generalisations might reveal more than those of other directors.

This seems to be the case. Take, for example, this from a four-hour television interview, conducted for the BBC in March 2000 in Paris. Asked why he was so influenced by Laurence Olivier's film *Hamlet*, made in Britain in 1948 for the J. Arthur Rank Films, Polanski commented:

> I loved everything about it … first of all the atmosphere … I liked films which made you feel that you are actually inside an interior, feeling virtually the fourth wall behind you. Like in Dutch paintings! *Hamlet* was one of them. It was somehow romantic … this mysterious geography … you could not determine the shape of the castle … the camera gliding though these corridors. (Cousins 2002: 98)

There is the seed of something very interesting here. Olivier's film is seldom considered a landmark one, especially when compared to his conceptually more daring *Henry V*, made four years earlier. Whereas the latter ventilated Shakespeare by moving from interior theatrical to exteriors, it is Olivier's failure to extend *Hamlet*, his refusal of the infinite spatial possibilities afforded by editing, its ability to make him feel enclosed by it, which seems to excite Polanski. The reference to Vermeer, whose people are almost always inside, whose vanishing points can sometimes be glimpsed through open doors giving onto other rooms or exteriors but whose backgrounds are largely obscured by walls, emphasises the point. Poussin's deliberate restriction of renaissance space, by depicting events in frieze-like foregrounds backed by heavy curtains in some of his paintings, has a similar effect. In each case there is a denial of exteriority. Though Polanski has always admired Shakespeare, it is not the human or thematic elements of *Hamlet* that he mentions, but the confined spatial ones. He is responding to a theatrical effect, which if one goes further and sees theatre and movie space as opposed, could be considered anti-cinematic. That his favourite film of all time is Carol Reed's studio bound and claustrophobic *Odd Man Out* (1947), made the year before Olivier's film, also for Britain's J. Arthur Rank Films, strengthens the point. The spatial confinement in both these films is present throughout Polanski's work. *Cul-de-Sac* (1966), *The Fearless Vampire Killers* (1967), *Macbeth* (1971) and *The Ninth Gate* (1999) are totally or partially set in, and employ the 'mysterious geography' of, castles. *Knife in the*

Water (1962), *Pirates* (1986) and *Bitter Moon* (1992) each take place on boats. *Repulsion* (1965), *Rosemary's Baby* (1968), *The Tenant* (1976) and *Death and the Maiden* (1994) are almost entirely set in apartments whose back walls press against the backs of their protagonists. And *Knife in the Water*, *Cul-de-Sac*, *Bitter Moon* and *Death and the Maiden* are all versions of the same story, a couple discomforted by the presence of a third person who gets too close.

Aesthetically speaking, what makes Polanski stand out from his art-house contemporaries such as Truffaut, Ingmar Bergman, Michelangelo Antonioni and Federico Fellini is that despite the trendiness of the times he lived through, his interest in unified, enclosed space meant that he was never a modernist. This is remarkable. Rather than indulging in fancy editing or flashy camerawork, he applied the studio bound classicism of his favourite films – *Odd Man Out* and *Hamlet* – to his central theme: human claustrophobia and unease.

If the bleakness in Polanski's work comes from his life, it is surely the case that his interest in spatial confinement does too. But anti-modernism also derives directly from another element dealt to him by fortune: his technical talent. Whereas Truffaut and the like had their films shot roughly, with few lights, Polanski's collaborators on *Rosemary's Baby*, his first American film, were astonished at his exacting camera requirements and precise understanding of the optics and geometry of lenses. New Wave filmmakers loved the flickering aspect of films but the causticity of *Chinatown* (1974), *Cul-de-Sac*, *Repulsion* and *The Tenant* – and the reason they prevail – is that they do *not* flicker. At the human and technical level, they are devastatingly clear.

This, then, rather than his extraordinary biography, is the lasting significance of a director who is cited today as a major influence by filmmakers such as the brothers Coen and Wachowski and who, at the age of 73, is still boyish, arrogant and full of energy. Ever the anti-modernist his most recent movie, filmed in the Barrandov studios in Prague, is a faithful adaptation of *Oliver Twist* (2005). Those of us who felt that *The Pianist* (2002) was a disappointment, that in the light of *Schindler's List* (1993) – which Spielberg offered Polanski – it looked unconvincing, will be encouraged by the prospect of a retreat back into the world of the film studio and claustrophobic space. Polanski is quite simply the master of such space. In the age of the Danish film movement Dogme95, of handheld shooting and digital imagery, he once again looks like one of the most distinctive filmmakers of the last half-century.

CHAPTER ONE

Polanski: The Art of Perceiving

John Orr

Wrongly neglected by many critics has been the central role that perception plays in the development of Roman Polanski's cinema, how it informs his narratives, his style of filming and the impact that his films have had on his audiences down the years. In different decades three films that engage the cinematic art of perception stand out for different reasons: *Repulsion*, *Chinatown* and *The Ninth Gate*. Before examining them in detail we have to outline the general contours of the art of perceiving that run throughout Polanski's work, and also place him in the history of cinema itself.

Without doubt, Polanski has been one of the great directors of his generation. Now into his seventies and still making big movies, as *Oliver Twist* succeeds the box-office triumph of *The Pianist*, he shot his first films in Poland at the age of 24 and his first feature, *Knife in the Water* (*Nóż w wodzie*) at 28. His career has thus spanned several generations of cinema since it began in the late 1950s. At the same time he has endured great vicissitudes in personal fortune: last-ditch escape from Nazi terror in the Cracow ghetto and from attempted murder in post-war Cracow; the trauma of Sharon Tate's brutal killing in Hollywood; the criminal charges that ended his career in the United States. Many argue over the exact impact of survivor's guilt on his work, a very dense and difficult project, but one thing is clear: Polanski has a deep sense of the tragic missing from most British and American cinema, yet offset by a brilliant streak of humour that comes from his close observing of life in all its frail vanities. The latter is true of his underrated films, often dismissed as self-indulgent. *What?* (1972) and

Bitter Moon are darkly funny, astute fables about contemporary life: some have taken short-cuts by deeming them models of Polanski's sexual obsession in his personal life. Others have pigeonholed *Repulsion* and *Rosemary's Baby* as cult 'horror' movies and worshipped them accordingly. True, George A. Romero, the cult horror specialist who should know, has named *Repulsion* his favourite horror film of all time (2002: 49). But generally the label is a short cut, for more is at stake than mere horror. Polanski at his best is discomforting for another reason. He explores without preconception the encounters of cold evil and human fallibility in modern times.

Although he has been called a modernist (Wexman 1985) and been seen as part of the 1960s European cinema that contained the French New Wave, Bergman and Buñuel, Fellini and Antonioni, his work is really at a tangent to all of them. Ironically, colleague Jerzy Skolimowski who co-wrote *Knife in the Water* was much closer to the abstract, experimental forms that came in the new modernist wave of Western Europe, but proved less successful, commercially speaking, in his journey West. Polanski's route was different, arising at first out of the Polish cinema of Andrzej Wajda and Andrzej Munk, with Munk's sense of irony the more dominant force, and then more tellingly, the American examples of Orson Welles and Alfred Hitchcock. He has also expressed his admiration for key films in post-war British cinema, Carol Reed's *Odd Man Out* (1947), Laurence Olivier's *Hamlet* (1948) and Michael Powell's *Peeping Tom* (1960) released only five years before his own British debut, *Repulsion*. Polanski's main inspiration is thus Polish and Anglo-American. Add to this the impact on the young Polanski of Central European masters like Witold Gombrowicz and Franz Kafka and we have a starting point that is quite unique. Polanski is never easily placed. He is not a great style-experimenter, nor is he a committed realist even though his location shooting is always bold and risk-taking, embellishing his strong naturalistic sense of place. Often, he makes great use of subjective camera; but he is never overly empathic. His black humour has a surreal edge that places it close to Buñuel, but unlike the Spanish director his continuity editing presents us with a knowable world even when true knowledge evades us. This plasticity leads to only one conclusion: Polanski is a law unto himself.

The legacy of Gombrowicz, one of Poland's key modernist writers, can also be used to quash some of the myth-making surrounding Polanski's sexual notoriety. The cinematic encounters of young girls and older men are sometimes seen as a reflection of the director's sexual appetite. But Gombrowicz's fiction fascinated a Pole who as a wartime fugitive was forced to grow old too early and too quickly in desperate circumstances, and who by the war's end felt himself still a child and yet prematurely an old man. The major fiction, especially *Ferdydurke* (1937) and *Pornografia* (1960) often deals with the encounter of youth and age as a highly existential and sexualised chemistry of fascination. The former is a pre-war fable of a young Polish gentleman transformed by an insane professor into a schoolchild so that treated like a child by others he lives out their version of his identity; the latter is a story of two ageing men in wartime Poland fascinated, voyeuristically, by the flowering of a youthful teenage passion. Both feature an exchange between young and old that can be described as mutual vampirism in which characters of different generations feed off one another voraciously, though it is the old who have a greater need for the verve and immaturity of youth than the young have a need for the maturity of age. In *Pornografia* the urge of the two old men to spoil the innocence of the young couple is the dominant and triumphant force.

The age motif is firmly embedded in Polanski's own work, through the picaresque encounters of the naïve young Nancy (Sydne Rome) in *What?* culminating in the hilarity of her peepshow for the villa's reclusive ageing millionaire (Hugh Griffith) who dies happy; but also through the destructive marriages of *Cul-de-Sac* and *Bitter Moon*, those two fractious encounters between jaundiced, middle-aged husbands and beautiful girl-brides. In *Rosemary's Baby* the encounter of the young newlyweds with their sinister ageing neighbours (who might be witches) adds a new frisson to Polanski's work in which Rosemary feels herself the victim of diabolic seduction. In *Chinatown*, with the patriarchal figure of Noah Cross (John Huston) and the incest motif spread over three generations, it assumes its darkest hue. With *Tess* (1979) Polanski, now in French exile not just from Poland but also from the United States, explored similar themes courtesy of Thomas Hardy's classic novel of tragic destiny, using Normandy locations for Hardy's imaginary Wessex. In all these features there is a misconceived exchange between youth and maturity that goes eerily wrong and in which one will devour the other. Polanski thus explores, either as fate or tragedy or both, this interchange of generations.

Because of Polanski's strong sense of place and the entrapments of place, and his tight focus on a cinema of intimacy – often between generations – there are few self-conscious embellishments, no new wave flourishes. With the exception of *Bitter Moon* his features are chronological, no voice-over, flashbacks or flash-forwards. Narrative is usually compact; there are few digressions. Yet his narratives have a double structure of line and cycle. Places and objects repeat themselves: things appear to progress yet always return to their starting-point. In his 'apartment-trilogy' – *Repulsion*, *Rosemary's Baby* and *The Tenant* – his troubled subjects move forward to tragic nemesis but never break free of the space that encloses them and recurs to haunt them. In his 'water-trilogy' – *Knife in the Water*, *Cul-de-Sac* and *What?* – action more or less ends physically where it began: narrative returns to its spatial origin, its first place of encounter. In his 'quest-trilogy' – *Chinatown*, *Frantic* (1988) and *The Ninth Gate* – there is also a return of sorts amidst the cut and thrust of hard-nosed detection. In *Frantic* Harrison Ford as Dr Richard Walker is finally reunited with his kidnapped wife while *Chinatown*'s Jack Nicholson as Jake Gittes and Johnny Depp as Dean Corso in *The Ninth Gate* are once again quintessential loners, men without women. All three have witnessed the death or disappearance of the beautiful woman – Faye Dunaway, Emmanuelle Seigner (twice) – central to their quest, and in whose fate they have been complicit. In both apartment and quest trilogies there is also a clear pattern from *Repulsion* onward, the foregrounding of a central subject in almost every sequence, largely seen from their point-of-view.

William Fraker, cinematographer on *Rosemary's Baby*, notes that Polanski made the switch to the subjective there in a key sequence, a two-minute take where Rosemary's husband (John Cassavetes) prevaricates over her changing doctors; Pawel Edelman who photographed *The Pianist*, notes that Polanski performs a similar switch in that film, establishing Szpilman's family and friends objectively, then focusing exclusively on the experience of his central subject for the duration of the story (Fraker, Edelman 2004: 42). This subjective positioning starts in many other films much earlier. Accordingly, the acting demands that Polanski made of Catherine Deneuve, Jack Nicholson, Harrison Ford, Sydne Rome in *What?* and of himself in *The Tenant* were uncompromising. They are literally almost never out of the picture. Much more than Hitchcock, Polanski developed the potentialities of this subjective camera without ever lapsing into sentimental or melodramatic forms of empathy. We are there, we are with, but we also witness. We are close in, but also on the outside looking in. Long before the age of handheld digital, his moving camera was a following camera that favoured over-the-shoulder shots, but never with the jerky self-consciousness that often marred the work of Dogme95. Though later wary of Steadicam, the movement of Polanski's camera seems limpet-like, almost attached to its subject, always supple and fluid, never excessively conspicuous. It replicates the speed and rhythms of human movement and, unlike the stylistic flourishes of the New Wave, does not draw attention to itself. In Polanski's art of perceiving the technique of the camera is indispensable, yet he is supremely indifferent to the ontological question of its presence.

At the same time his camera is present in subtle and specific ways. Polanski at his best challenges our conventions of perceiving by probing the condition of 'illusion', a word that is at best an imperfect signifier of altered states, of perception slightly off-kilter where our eyes and ears appear to deceive, but are set off-kilter by the perplexing signals they seek to read. He probes in different ways that is, a constant in perception, the endless task of translating the puzzle of what is perceived into conventions of knowing. It is usually one where we overcompensate by imposing our existing conventions of seeing on the new and the strange, and often suffer when they fail to deliver. Moreover, the medium of film itself is only possible on the basis of visual 'illusion' of two kinds: persistence of vision where the eye translates the succession of 24 frames per second into a continuous moving image, bemused by the rapidity of changes in light; and the phi phenomenon, where the swift alternation of flashing lights from two sources is read by the eye as a single light. Human recognition of the moving image that has helped define the culture of the last hundred years would be impossible without either, both signs of the eye's limits. Film is not so much a window opening onto the world as André Bazin suggested, more an uncertainty principle in the realm of sight and sound. Polanski explores this uncertainty in a clear, methodical way. He starts with conventions of seeing that gradually shift and then crack under force of circumstance.

His camera techniques are close to those praised by Bazin but the consequences are totally different. Perception does not naturally reveal a knowable world, a new undiscovered world of poverty or enchantment that we can lock into with a ready-made system of signs. In Polanski when we 'see' something new we are never sure what we see. For the framing of that uncertainty and of the tensions it creates Polanski uses the inspiration of Welles, a Bazin favourite, for staking out a post-mimetic form. Polanski often favours the use of a wide-angle lens with depth of field to encompass action in long takes and at the same time project the detail of the scene that is always, in his way of filming, precise and meticulous. The celebrated triangles, or three-shots, of *Knife in the Water* and *Cul-de-Sac* seem Wellesian in origin, and owe their triadic frame to the famous snow sequence early in *Citizen Kane* (1941), a three-shot where the distant figure of the young Kane outside the window bisects the two adults inside the cabin who are deciding his future. (Such 'triangles' are also to be seen in the court sequences of Olivier's *Hamlet*, where the camera films the distant hero in long shot from behind and between the near-field thrones of king and queen.) Shooting on location, Polanski constantly renews this deep-focus strategy to create a sense of uncertainty and mistrust between his characters. In the yacht sequences of *Knife in the Water* on the Mazurian Lakes his nameless student (Zygmunt Malanowicz) constantly bisects in middle distance the profiles of his bored married couple captured close-in, cueing his status as outsider but also his powers of disruptive intervention. In *Repulsion* just before the first killing, the close-in figures of Carol (Catherine Deneuve) and Colin (John Fraser) are bisected by the distant figure of an elderly neighbour, staring at them from across the landing through the open apartment door. The neighbour knows something is afoot but she knows not what. The visiting Colin is bemused in turn by the non-reacting Carol, who seems to behave as if he is not there. Polanski plays with the tension within the shot of the uncertainty principle as the intimate scene unfurls. Colin moves forward and blocks the neighbour off from the camera, but when he steps back she is still there, her presence betrayed only by her barking dog. Which prompts Carol's hapless suitor to close the door and thus seal his gruesome fate – which neither he nor the audience can see coming.

Cul-de-Sac repeats the visual trope of the bisecting gaze but this time with a sly humour, framing lop-sided competition between wounded gangster Dickie (Lionel Stander) and wimpish captive George (Donald Pleasence) through the observing eyes of the captive's alluring young wife Teresa (Françoise Dorléac), who sympathises with neither. Defiant, quizzical, she recurrently bisects their antagonistic profiles and she is the one who will escape from both of them. The same film shows Polanski at his most ambitious in using deep-focus. A continuous coastline sequence becomes an eight-minute take. While the static three-shot is recessional, this time the movement is mobile and horizontal. As Dickie and George argue drunkenly, Teresa runs out from the castle left of frame, undresses, and runs out into the sea to bathe right of frame. A small plane, low on the horizon repeats Teresa's horizontal movement left to right and finally goes out of shot, dashing Dickie's hopes of being rescued. The camera pans right with both movements then back again to the odd couple on the bank as Teresa returns, and Polanski also uses a lateral track for the left-right, right-left motion. Encompassed in the same virtuoso shot, therefore, is a brilliant spatial illustration of impasse. All three characters have different agendas that never really intersect. More conventional in its framing, fluent deep-focus also plays its part in *Chinatown*'s exteriors, or the fluent panning shot across the dried-up riverbed that starts as a long shot of Hollis Mulwray's distant car, then moves right to catch in close profile the watching eyes of Jake Gittes on the hillside above. Here Polanski had not only embellished Welles: he had literally taken the techniques of *Citizen Kane* out of the

Three-Shot: Leon Niemczyk, Jolanta Umecka, Zygmunt Malanowicz in *Knife in the Water*

Hollywood studio and into the Hollywood desert. As surveillance continues Polanski uses deep focus for a crucial reverse-angle. A point-of-view shot has Jake stalking Mulwray (Darrell Zwerling) from a cliff above the shore as the engineer awaits a run-off from the pipeline. Cut to Hollis turning round, sensing he is being watched: but as the camera pans up towards the cliff, Jake has already disappeared from where we expect him to be. He finds a style of *mise-en-scène* to generate the uncertainty of the watching Gittes about the motive and meaning of Mulwray's actions until a conceptual focus is created. Gittes is secretly trying to figure out the actions of a water-engineer who in turn is secretly trying to figure out the scenario of a man-made drought.

Polanski, however, also departs from Welles and his American inheritors – Stanley Kubrick, Martin Scorsese, Francis Ford Coppola, Oliver Stone and Michael Mann. The baroque dimensions of Wellesian filmmaking, his delirious use of visual labyrinth that was a trademark of *Othello* (1952), *Mr. Arkadin* (1955), *Touch of Evil* (1958) and *The Trial* (1962), is something Polanski shuns in favour of modulated rhythms of daily experience. The true Polish successor to Welles in this respect is Andrzej Zulawski's 1981 film *Possession. Possession*, set eerily in the modernist apartment landscape of West Berlin bordering the Wall, was a fusion of the swift wide-angle tracking shots of *Touch of Evil* and *The Trial* with the claustrophobic feel of Polanski's apartment films. Zulawski's casting of Isabelle Adjani as a deranged housewife is not only a nod in the direction of *Repulsion*, but a giveaway, considering her role as Stella in *The Tenant* five years previously. But Zulawski's Wellesian delirium and his upfront embrace of the supernatural (complete with apartment alien) also highlight his difference from Polanski. The latter has never had recourse to the supernatural, neither in *Rosemary's Baby* nor in *The Ninth Gate*. What does goad him on is the sense that he can produce a supernatural delirium in his spectators, a form of delusion where they perceive action through the genre frame of horror to imagine the supernatural and stir up their wider fascination with extra-sensory perception. Thus some spectators read witches and devils, heaven and hell into his films when it is never clear that they exist (Polanski 1985: 270).

Unlike Welles and Zulawski, Polanski sticks to the human scale; he makes no attempt to outrun it and dazzle us in the process. Welles made space and time uncanny by constantly undermining it; Polanski makes space and time uncanny by establishing its fixity. In the age of relativity, we might say, these are two sides of the same coin. Sometimes our sense of place is so febrile we cannot nail it down; at other times it is so oppressive we cannot get rid of it. Perhaps we rely on our film artists to validate one or other of these contrary impressions. And finally Welles provides specific inspirations. Some suggest that *Knife in the Water* is indebted to René Clement's Highsmith adaptation, *Plein Soleil* (1959), but an earlier source is the more luxurious yacht in *The Lady from Shanghai* (1947) where the bored Bannisters recharge their batteries through the presence of big baby-faced Michael O'Hara. It is after all the same triangle as Polanski's – wealthy older husband, young attractive wife and raw young outsider. Wellesian motifs last far beyond the early works. With regard to look and texture, the variations in darkness forged in the monochrome *Touch of Evil* inspired Polanski and Darius Khondji to create the colourations of *The Ninth Gate* (Pizello 2000: 39). Then there is the passing matter of Welles' version of *The Trial*. Whereas Hitchcock and Fellini with their Catholic backgrounds have traded in different ways on the myth of Original Sin, *The Trial* and *The Tenant* both hinge on something more modern (and cod-Freudian?): the performing of Original Guilt – loud, nervy and paranoid in the respective deliveries of Anthony Perkins as Joseph K. and Polanski as the hapless Trelkovsky. No laughing matter, and yet somehow both are – before darkness falls.

In terms of shock and suspense, many would compare Polanski with Hitchcock. There is, certainly, overlap in their art of perception. Both register the human dimension of things seen, usually keeping the focal length of the shot close to the perspective of the eye, then varying it at key moments, Polanski much more so than the master of the previous generation. Generally, the camera adopts and embraces the speed of human movement, the walk or the run, neither slowing it down nor quickening it excessively. With mishap or madness, though, they consciously stretch the limits of perception. If a character's vision disintegrates, it is duly coded as a metamorphosis of perceiving. Things go awry and the audience bears witness. Hence both directors know well how to create menace or tension within the shot, and to transmit the desperation or dread of their heroes to the audience. The frame of the event is equally important. Both create an enduring sense of place and know the power of a meticulously designed look, even in the realm of the ordinary. Both can be hugely provocative, and transform the creation of shock into an aesthetic value.

Yet there are subtle and telling differences. Polanski pushed things more boldly than the more cautious Hitchcock. In *Repulsion* and *Rosemary's Baby* he charted the mental descent of Carole and Rosemary (Mia Farrow) with increasing resort to wide-angle shots for long takes with a short focal length, keeping the camera uncomfortably close to his heroines and creating minor but telling distortion within the frame. And he was a more spontaneous filmmaker, not given to Hitchcock's storyboard style of preparation. Until very recently he has been a filmmaker of locations not one, like Hitchcock, who added studio compositions to blend artifice and reality. In *The Birds* (1963) Hitchcock used complex mattes and studio back-lots to create the illusion of Bodega Bay as a real seaside town instead of what it was, a collection of jetties with a couple of shops and diners. For *Cul-de-Sac* Polanski, in contrast, filmed the causeway and the island and the castle of Lindisfarne as they were then and as they still very much are today. In effect, we have contrasting coastal visions in films that are only three years apart; two very different ways of seeing.

In narration, there was also a parting of the ways. Hitchcock usually disrupted the ordinary by dramatising the chance encounter, the transaction or exchange that suddenly alters the fate of his protagonists. The kidnapping in *North by North West* (1959) and the shower killing in *Psycho* (1960) come out of nowhere; yet everything is then changed utterly. By contrast, Polanski's vision of perception required slow-burn transformation. Change at first is imperceptible. In retrospect we cannot put our finger on the exact moment that Carol becomes homicidal, that Rosemary fears witchcraft, that Trelkovsky becomes clinically paranoid, that Jake wrongly suspects Evelyn Mulwray: we cannot say precisely when in *Bitter Moon* the fiery liaison of Oscar and Mimi (Peter Coyote and Emmanuelle Seigner) is finally on the rocks. True there are clinching sequences, moments of revelation, explosions of shock and terror where Polanski zaps his unwary audience, but they always follow gradual metamorphosis. *Frantic* is the exception that illustrates the rule, its kidnapping motif a clear echo of Hitchcock's *The Man Who Knew Too Much* (1956), a seismic shift that changes everything. Yet even here Polanski plays on his American doctor's frustration at Parisian bureaucracy, on the slow-burn process of convincing different authorities that his wife's sudden vanishing from their hotel room is indeed a kidnap. In most of his films, the importance of the slow-burn experience for Polanski's audience is clear: they feel the ground has shifted from under their feet without quite realising when or why. Here Polanski taps into a common experience of the frailties of perception in the modern age. To watch him at his best is to feel that unsettling metamorphosis. Indeed Polanski's harsh autocritique of *The Tenant* came from his sense that Trelkovsky's change was too abrupt, that it lost impact because it was not gradual enough (1985: 343). Some of his admirers for whom this has become a cult movie would beg to differ: Trelkovsky's double transformation, from man to woman and from nervy outsider to clinical paranoid, is unsettling for any viewer, and not merely a repeat, as some claim, of Carol's experience in *Repulsion*.

Much of Polanski's cinema thus depends on the art of perceiving and its multiple layering. Within his narrative there is always a key encounter between the strange and the familiar. Outsiders have to figure out for themselves the nature of the ménage into which they intrude, and what it is that 'insiders' really want of them. In *Knife in the Water* the young student hiker has to figure out the relationship between the wealthy couple that invite him onto their yacht. In *Cul-de-Sac* a bizarre wounded gangster on the run has to work out the even more bizarre liaison of the married couple he takes captive. In *What?* a bemused Nancy has to figure out the raison d'être of all the strange slackers in the Neapolitan villa to which she has fled to escape being raped. In *Chinatown* Gittes has to figure out the common thread of murky events that go far beyond his remit as a private eye dealing in 'matrimonial affairs'. During the winter cruise of *Bitter Moon* the bewildered Nigel (Hugh Grant) is forced to ponder the perverse liaison of odious Oscar and desirable Mimi through Oscar's lurid cabin confessions. How truthful are they, and how far are they meant to stir up his lusting after Mimi? How far is Mimi complicit in Oscar's charade? How sure is the fearful Paulina (Sigourney Weaver) in *Death and the Maiden* that friendly Dr Miranda (Ben Kingsley) who has just fixed her husband's car in a storm, is the same man who tortured her in prison fifteen years earlier? Suspicion walks the edge and can go either way – into vindication or self-delusion. Likewise, book dealer Dean Corso embarks on a rare manuscript journey in *The Ninth Gate* at the behest of collector Boris Balkan (Frank Langella) who may or may not be playing deadly games with him. Finding the manuscripts is inseparable from his quest to find out whether not Balkan is deceiving him.

Ambiguities of perception run through Polanski's concept of filmic space. In *Rosemary's Baby* the heroine at one point looks through the open doorway of a room in the neighbouring apartment but cannot see the figures who converse behind the wall that separates her from them. Tantalisingly, faces and gestures are just out of visual reach. Is her quest therefore doomed? In her desperation, does she impose an illusory order upon the meaning of ordinary things by imagining the worst, or has she discovered through her paranoia and persistence, evil in its purest form? We can take sides but we can never be sure. While Aldous Huxley saw experiments with hallucinating drugs as leading us through the 'doors of perception', Polanski's films take Huxley's metaphor in a different direction. The doors are never closed but they are never wide open either; always ajar in different degrees, inviting us in but blocking our vision. In general, there is never a complete picture to which Polanski's protagonists or his audience can finally sign up. But even when there is, it merely throws the moot question of meaning further and further back into an oblique history. The terrifying revelations at the end of *Chinatown* lead not to final comprehension but final incomprehension, stupefaction that what has to come to pass has indeed come to pass, accompanied by total bafflement at its genesis and secret lineage.

Perception and emotion: Repulsion

As Polanski's favourite philosopher of perception Richard Gregory states, the nature of perception is at times inseparable from the question of emotion (1998: 224–5). Emotion colours perception and vice versa. How we feel can influence how we see and how we see sometimes defines how we feel. If *Repulsion* is about perceptual extremes it is also about emotional extremes. In the film the two converge, as it keys in a core emotional spectrum of desire: at one end is the pull of attraction, at the other the push-sensation – the push away – that gives his film its stark, unremitting title. It is not that Carol finds all men repulsive *a priori*, more that she transfers her ambivalence about *one* man, her sister's married lover whom she can hear making love at night through the wall of her bedroom, into unambiguous aversion to all men. The film's pathology lies in this critical transfer, prompted by the messy intersection of rivalry and desire, and not in any original 'state of being'. But it also begs the question: what deeper thing is it that provokes the pathological transfer? Enigmatic to the end, the film does not tell us – even though the final panning shot of the film alights on the family snapshot we have seen before with Carol the excluded young girl lurking at the back of the family circle, semi-detached. The horror of the film lies in the wrong kind of transition, in rites of passage not from innocence to womanhood but from innocence to butchery. Her sister violates a mild social norm of the time – sleeping with a married man – but Carol's fervid imagination transforms it into a moral violation through her stifled desire for the same man, which she then turns into a repulsion that breeds in the smallest of things, like the shaving kit he leaves in her glass on the bathroom shelf. The presence of the shaving brush seems quite harmless, blown up out of all proportion; but as we later see, the razor gleaming beside it proves to be deadly.

The film begins with a double layering technique that enables us to see Carol both from the outside in and from the inside out. As the action moves on, the outside fades and the inside takes over. At first we see her through the eyes of others, sister Hélène (Yvonne Furneaux), her opportunistic lover Michael (Ian Hendry), Carol's vapid young suitor Colin and the various women at the beauty salon where she works. Yet when she is left alone in the flat as Hélène and Michael head off for a holiday in Italy, her perspective alone starts to dominate. At this point she defines the space of the empty flat and it defines her. As madness accelerates, the oppressive space will *expand*, not contract in size. Unlike *Rosemary's Baby* where Rosemary is increasingly paranoid but almost never alone, this is a study of bleak physical solitude later echoed in *The Tenant* but which Polanski does not reprise with such grim detail until the later stages of *The Pianist*, this time with a sane hero surviving human extremes. Yet added in the earlier is something quite unique in Polanski's work: Carol's growing schizophrenia, heard in the magnification of ordinary sounds like the nuns laughing in the convent yard or the kitchen tap dripping and seen dramatically in the varieties of rape hallucination that all but destroy her. Prior to this, those around her do not exactly ignore the onset of Carol's disintegration but feel it pays to underplay it for the sake of their own comfort and well-being. Thus Michael remarks at one point early on 'You should see a doctor', but tries to jolly her along rather than follow up his own suggestion. Either they wilfully misread the signs or in Polanski's view they exemplify 'the lack of awareness of those who live with the mentally disturbed, familiarity having blunted their perception of the abnormal' (1985: 209). All sense something is wrong with her but none can imagine the final consequences. The returning sister and lover witnessing the bloodbath reveal all through their startled eyes – horror, stupefaction, incomprehension: the very attributes that prefigure the ending of *Chinatown*. Briefly, Carol ends up in the arms of an attractive rogue denied her by 'morality' and sibling rivalry and whose pale substitutes, one romantic, one lustful – embodying the spectrum of Michael's own character – she has brutally slain. She smiles, unable to connect the reaction of his disbelieving face to actions performed in his absence.

But then this is a fable of detachment in extremis. It turns a neutral attribute into a pathological disease. Carol is all too close to the surface of things around her yet cannot react to any of them. It is as if inches from her nose, they are not really there. She can only respond to those things that feature in hallucination, or feel in daily life like *its continuation*. The rotting rabbit is truly decomposing before her eyes but does not engage her sense of smell at all; the presence of the street navvy in her bed is pure illusion but the touch of his body seems all-too real. Claustrophobic as her condition is, surely the walls should contract? But she is literally pushing them away, *repelling them*. Polanski's title mirrors its pathology through visual metaphor, the inner world through the outer. While the inside expands, the outside contracts as Carol withdraws. For the discontented outsider London normally conjures a vast labyrinth in which to lose oneself, yet Carol never strays from a cluster of locales within a radius of South Kensington tube station. Though the flat interior was filmed at Twickenham studios, Polanski's camera too never strayed far on location from its compact South Ken habitat (Reeves 2001: 298) and never indulged in the usual cheating of those who start a shot in one London borough and end it in another miles away. Not only does the anti-sexuality of the film run against the grain of Swinging Sixties myth, it also stifles that idiom's hedonistic delusion that the capitol is anybody's oyster. His characters stay put, so much so that the old adage about London being nothing but a set of cosy villages is subtly turned around. In *Repulsion*, South Kensington is the capitol's nightmare village. The viewer's response at the end of this film is to be drained of all will and energy, and yet still want to run like hell.

Chinatown: the disaster of normality

While Carol's distancing is a sign of the abnormal, of an abandonment of life, the distancing poise of *Chinatown*'s private eye is a professional skill, a survival strategy, a sign of seasoned normality. You take people into your confidence for tactical reasons, but resist their attempts to do the same to you. It stems, as many have noted, from the genre Polanski inherited in his takeover of Robert Towne's original screenplay. Raymond Chandler's Philip Marlowe had, after all, become a mythic LA figure in the hard-boiled canon, not taking anything on trust and taking on the unseen territory of the new and the dangerous with few illusions about the human condition. Yet a different comparison seems more appropriate here, J. J. Gittes with L. B. Jeffries of *Rear Window* (1954). In Hitchcock's film, James Stewart as the chair-bound hero turns an implausible scenario into an amazing revelation. In Polanski's film, by contrast, a plausible scenario that fails because it does *not* entertain the idea of the impossible finally undoes Jake. He draws all on his reserves of experience to forge the wrong conclusion about the murder of Hollis Mulwray and only discovers his mistake when it is too late. He plays out the role of smart private eye to the hilt, and loses terribly. Jeffries boldly jumps to conclusions no one would think of and a miracle exonerates him; Gittes makes the mistakes that anyone else would, had they his boldness too. For sure, Gittes has his vanity and his limitations, just as Jeffries has his snooping obsessions. But in *Chinatown* there are no miracles.

Yet because this is Polanski's picture more than it is Towne's, there is a deeper horror, a diabolic tissue of deceit more rooted, more actual, more ubiquitous than anything in *Rosemary's Baby*. The tragic flaw of Jake Gittes, who is effectively Polanski's Hamlet, lays not so much in the realm of inaction as deep in the arena of misperception. He is the victim of a perceptual implant, of irresistible bait to which he rises too readily. He takes the template of the expert on matrimonial affairs way out of its depth into the realm of political skulduggery. What he gains through patience and stealth, working out the reason for Mulwray's resistance to the proposed dam and the detail of Noah Cross's illegal purchase of cheap arid land to incorporate into the city, he loses through his deep misreading of human intimacy. He follows a convention we all would, but more quickly and easily, born out of the practice of paid snooping. The first sequence with Curly the cuckold shows how he plies his trade, capturing on film the flagrant acts of errant spouses. His mind-set is fixed by the second image of (photographic) watching in the lake on Echo Park which the false Mrs Mulwray sets up for him, Hollis in the rowing boat with the teenage blonde (Belinda Palmer) that he wrongly assumes to be the engineer's lover when she is in fact Hollis's stepdaughter, Katherine, the daughterr of the real Mrs Mulwray. His secret photographing of the affectionate couple from a rooftop at the El Macondo apartments, the image that finds its way into the papers as an engineer's love-nest motif, is the icing on the cake. As we find out with Gittes much too late, the 'adulterer' turns out to be the girl's protector and is murdered (partly) for that reason. Too late because like Gittes we have organised images of secret assignation between a middle-aged man and young girl into a convention of desire: perverse, cheating, illicit. Things are not what they seem, but how does Gittes redraw the cognitive map formed out of secret watching when future images feed into it and thus fail to undermine it?

When he meets the real Evelyn he has to admit that he has been set up but he cannot let go of the 'images' of adultery that Evelyn will not contradict for secret reasons of her own. His mind moves forward in its new domain, the political intrigues around the LA water supply. But even here cues are ignored or brushed aside. The images filmed by one associate, of Hollis arguing with Noah Cross (then unknown), are brushed aside in favour of information from another associate about the Echo Park rendezvous. Gittes only assimilates things that fit the paradigm. The new paradigm, of the water conspiracy, has yet to be formed from a new series of stakeouts and violent set-tos that include the slitting of his nostril and only then, piece-by-piece, does Cross come into the picture. Hamlet's knowledge of murderous conspiracy comes from the visitation of his father's ghost; he knows the score but not how to carry out his avenging strategy. As a private eye in a genre movie Gittes has to find out the score for himself and act simultaneously. Like Hamlet, Gittes too makes wrong moves but for different reasons. The pattern of knowing changes with the pattern of events and

Gittes is no Prince of Denmark, just a private investigator scared of losing his licence if he gets in over his head. But that of course is the point. He is out of his depth, socially and politically. His attempts to redeem himself lead to tragedy: he inadvertently promotes further evil through his failure to perceive the reach of existing evil. But that deficiency is something we all share. If anything Gittes is smart enough to be one step ahead of his cinema audience who are privy to what he knows – but still one step behind his nemesis, the ageing patriarch into whose hands he unwittingly plays. The film is powerful because we are taken on a journey of baffling discovery the private eye mediates and made all too aware of our own frailties at the film's end. Gittes's supreme helplessness is also ours.

To say that Gittes is blind to the evidence in front of his eyes is highly misleading. As the naked eye is dazzled by brilliant flickering light and has to readjust so the investigator's brain must adjust and readjust at speed to what confronts him, to rearrange the pattern of words and images and events that appear at times to make no sense but in fact bear the bitter fruit of a tragic yield. Nothing in *Chinatown* is easy to read, nothing obvious to the eye. Needless to say, mistakes will be made and mistakes will be deadly. So convinced is Gittes of Evelyn's guilt over her husband's death (the private eye's mindset locked in the jealousy motif) that he phones the police department to betray her whereabouts; so convinced is he of the need to atone for this terrible mistake once he realises it, he embarks on a chivalrous mission to confront Noah Cross as the true killer only to be forced at gunpoint to lead Cross to daughter and granddaughter waiting in Chinatown to escape to Mexico. He thus leads the police to Evelyn and then Cross to Katherine. The tragic double error, tumbling out of the shooting script that Polanski first wrote (with a resistant Towne) in transforming Towne's third draft screenplay and then again in last-minute scene changes on set (written entirely without Towne), profoundly alters the tone and meaning of the narrative (Benedetto 1999: 52–4).

Polanski's unilateral decision to write in a love-scene between Jake and Evelyn also sparks new levels of ambivalence in his investigator to match those of his heroine, for Jake is still prepared to betray her to the police (and save his own skin) when he wrongfully deduces her guilt from his discovery that Hollis has been drowned in the salt-water pool of their back garden. This betrayal, for sure, is only possible in post-romantic Hollywood. Love does not impel him to believe her innocent against all odds; rather post-coital coolness impels him to believe her guilty when in fact she has been a life-long victim. Following the Shakespearean analogy made earlier we see here echoes of Hamlet's devious spurning of Ophelia, done under the self-defeating guise of strategy. The private eye of hard-boiled fiction, and following this, of classic noir is a regular guy, tough, seasoned and sceptical, taking the rough with the smooth. Polanski wants to push this much further. He wants to take his hero outside of the frame, to make him utterly fallible and capable of tragic error, a man whose judgement is flawed by a crucial breakdown between perceiving and acting. It is perhaps one of the most damning indictments cinema has to offer of someone for whom any audience will come to have a growing sympathy. Yet Polanski's upending of expectation is never capricious: it seems, in fact, to lock into an irreversible fate.

The Ninth Gate: perceiving Heaven and Hell

The Ninth Gate is a millennium film that went unrecognised as such since it was released two years before the mini-apocalypse of Manhattan's 9/11. Appropriately enough the action starts in Manhattan, a back-lot Manhattan that is, of Epinay Studios southwest of Paris. But looking back it is already one of the most disturbing of cinema's end-of-century features; over-long perhaps, and with some leaden touches but always sharp and mordant in its wit, and in the end as sinister as any of Polanski's pictures. What holds the film and our attention is the fanatical eye of its crumpled hero, Dean Corso. Johnny Depp with rimless glasses and goatee beard, downbeat yet demonic, and guaranteed to outlive his Satanic rivals who opt for excess and extravagance, makes the long journey from cultural hustler with no values to True Believer in the Devil's Book, as long as he finds the one authentic copy. Yet all three copies are equally 'authentic'. Corso discovers the demonic secret lies in combining engravings from *all three* where there are key variations with Lucifer's initials – LCF – attached, as opposed to those engravings initialled by its fronting author, a seventeenth-century heretic who had perished in the Inquisition. The reward is entry into the Ninth Gate – of Hell? Polanski is indebted here to his fiction source Arturo Pérez-Reverte's *The Dumas Club*, using one of the book's two plots and discarding the other (about Dumas and the Three Musketeers). The persona of Corso is much as he is in the book, though no longer Spanish for Depp gives him a tigerish New York edge, and so is the enigmatic Girl in White Sneakers (Emmanuelle Seigner), though Polanski makes her even more enigmatic. What Polanski does is to subordinate the novel's postmodern playfulness to a higher design where he ends up playing straight the descent into evil that marks Corso's growing infatuation with the riddle of the Ninth Gate. 'Do you believe in the supernatural?' his shady client Boris Balkan asks Corso early on, to which he replies 'I believe in my percentage.' By the end, however, a satanic nexus has replaced the cash nexus as the 'rare book' detective turns from money cynic into metaphysical monster.

Typically narrative has a double register in the realm of perceiving. As sleazy detective Corso has to figure out the mystery of the Book(s) and the mystery of the murders that dog his footsteps. As audience, we in addition have to figure out his transformation from cynic to fanatic as the addiction of the rare text and its key variations begins to take hold. The novel already contained the engravings the film would adopt. Polanski in fact employed the same graphic artist who had drawn the illustrations for Pérez-Reverte to redesign them for the film. Since film is a visual medium the demonic text is thus made manifest through the engravings, which may possess the clue to the Book's secret. We see the clues through Corso's eyes, and watch the puzzle unfold as he does. Typically Polanski uses short focal length and wide-angle lenses along, atypically, with Steadicam to keep us close to his hired investigator. At the same time the journey also moves us closer in sympathy to this culture-mercenary whose sincerity seems to increase with the risk of his mission. Polanski's project is then to leave us stranded as appearances are undermined. What seemed at first a reverse rite of passage from cynicism to sincerity proves something darker and more sinister. Yet this is pure Polanski – slow-burn transformation making it impossible to detect the moment that Corso has been 'turned'. Here the Girl is a variation on the *femme fatale* of film noir, just as Corso is a variation on its typical fall guy. At one point she calls herself sardonically his 'guardian angel' but she is also his fallen angel, Lucifer's sidekick, who lures him to his true fate. Noir's classic financial conspiracy of passion to murder most foul (always punished) is replaced by metaphysical conspiracy of passion that murders for 'higher' ends and goes unpunished. Goaded on by the Girl, there is something Nietzschean in Corso's Antichrist, a perverse transvaluation of values through the upending of all values. Having perpetually trashed everything of value except money, he embraces the anti-value of Death, prizing it as transcendence.

The ambiguity of the image lies in the journey. Is this a journey where Corso transforms his persona? Or is it a journey of self-realisation? Does he *become* one of Lucifer's fallen angels or does he discover that he already *is* one? We can never really know. Though we see Corso enter the Ninth Gate at dusk in a blinding flash of light, we never know if this is the gate of Hell or a mock inversion of the gates of Paradise. Is this indeed a satanic parody of Christ's Stations of the Cross? There is something at the end that suggests more, an end-of-millennium feel that disturbs profoundly. Polanski has earlier distracted us through the spoof versions of Satanism that he lampoons en route, a brief comic relief. But in the end there is a clear undertow of apocalypse as the deranged Balkan immolates himself in his Cathar castle while calling on the Devil, and Corso, who shoots him dead, is triumphantly seduced by the Girl in the glowing light of the castle's flames. Corso has entered completely into the story the engravings tell, mimicking the illustrations of the demonic text that so fascinate him. It is a life both archaic and apocalyptic that he lives out to the full, at once ancient and contemporary. Contemporary Paris this certainly is with contemporary faces and bars and cars but no faxes, no mobile phones, no computers, no video screens or cameras. Yet Polanski's style of filming *is* part of the digital revolution so conspicuously absent from the screen, full of special effects and computer-generated images that mark a significant break from his previous work but which recur again in the war-ravaged Warsaw of *The Pianist*. *The Ninth Gate* constitutes a complete break with naturalism in its forging of a self-contained world.

The vexed relationship between money and metaphysics is always fascinating. At first the Sacred Text has a price, but then a secret that makes price redundant. The crisp tactile feel of the rare edition out of a dark history is the sound that dominates the film: the serried rows of rare books in dark handsome leather in libraries both private and public, is the look that dominates. In this very *designed* film that benefits from the inspired touch of Dean Tavoularis, the look is oppressive and constricting, even in wide-angle. The camera lenses open up the space but the textual objects that it films close that space off again. Corso goes from bookshop to library to villa to private apartment but the same precious collection of rare editions seems to confront him, shelf after shelf after shelf, and where the dust of ages seems to filter through a perpetual twilight. It is an enclosed world into which reality scarcely seems to intrude. And yet archaic secrets are dependent, irony of ironies, on modern technology. Balkan tries to stay a step ahead of Corso by stealing the engravings of the two books he destroys: but Corso recovers and stays ahead of Balkan by use of the photocopy.

For satanic purposes, in this world of originals, copies are as good as originals, thus inverting the premise of Corso's 'honourable' profession. It is one of the film's few concessions, story-wise, to state-of-the-art technologies. Yet it proves to be vital in allowing the game can be played out to its end and allowing Corso alone to enter the kingdom of hell.

Dark spaces of the world

Polanski is one of the great directors in exploring the dark spaces of the world. They often seem to loom out of nothing, out of the banal, the ordinary, the unthreatening. Hence the gothic is not normally the source of Polanski's horror though often as in *Cu-de-Sac*, *The Fearless Vampire Killers* and *The Ninth Gate* it can be a vital accompaniment, a source of his dark humour and his mockery. But normally horror emerges out the humdrum detail of everyday life. In *The Pianist*, at a time of brutal occupation and war, the eruption is most dramatic. But that is because most of the violent and terrifying incidents in occupied Warsaw are ones filmed with great fidelity from Wladyslaw Szpilman's almost dispassionate memoir. And the horror of each violent act of Nazi terror that Szpilman (Adrien Brody) witnesses – the tossing of a disabled man out of a wheelchair to his death from the balcony of a second floor window or the random execution of comrades in his team of ghetto building workers – are matched by equal concentration on his strategies of survival, of playing piano for a meagre living in a ghetto cafe, or rescuing his brother against all odds, or simply overcoming illness and finding food and refuge. The great contrast between this and Polanski's other pictures lies in the question of madness. Here the madness is collective, not individual: it comes from the invader, from the outside and not from within. Here we can see a key divide: in *Repulsion*, *Rosemary's Baby*, *The Tenant* and *The Ninth Gate* the imagining of the worst can lead to insanity. In *Chinatown* and *The Pianist*, actual experience of the worst leads to a different impulse, that is to retain one's sanity and cling onto life at all costs.

In *The Pianist* the power of Polanski's vision derives from a particular rhythm and sensibility. In truth it is stylistically functional, good as ever in its detail, but largely unadventurous in its *mise-en-scéne*. The screenplay is conventional, at times wooden and often simplifies a complex history. There is too much reverse-angle cutting, excessive use of reaction shots and computer-generated images, and an exaggerated use of invisible narration. In his urge to document such a harrowing memoir, it seems that Polanski, nearing the end of his career, has simply given up on filmic innovation. The film does, however, touch base with his earlier sense of the uncanny in a specific way. It moves progressively from a cauldron of noise and bustle into silence and emptiness. Starting with the brute oppressiveness and sheer physical mass of the occupation, soldiers in the streets, arrests, killings, ghetto construction, relocations and transportations, it reaches at the end a point where Warsaw becomes after the failed Uprising and the German retreat a silent, devastated city. We can see here Polanski's use of the elliptical vantage point of the high window that Szpilman, having escaped the ghetto, occupies in his fugitive hiding-places. Virtually imprisoned, starving, left alone and furtively watching for signs of action in the street below; it all comes back to that template of partial perception that is Polanski's *metier*. The mute horror of his hero's witnessing segues into a lack of knowing. We see on the gaunt and haunted face of the fugitive a fear born out of the fusion of the worst of both worlds – having witnessed atrocity but not knowing if there is worse atrocity elsewhere and yet still more to come. It is that sustained note of uncertainty in the enclosed room that Brody's performance executes with such utter conviction, a perfect match between the frailties of perception and the depth of emotion. Here it exhibits an array of emotions that have become almost inexpressible.

Postscript: the dilemma of exile

The final question we have to pose is one that matches biography to virtual history. It may well be unanswerable, but we must ask it anyway. Did Polanski's flight from California in 1977 to avoid criminal charges seriously damage the rest of his career? The charges may yet be dropped and he may, now in his mid-seventies, be allowed back. But thirty years will have passed in which not only did he not have access to American soil but for legal reasons would not reside in countries such as the UK where the threat of extradition might loom. In short, much of the English-speaking world has been off-limits. For someone whose career has been so nomadic it is a tough price to pay. We can note that his two British pictures shot in exile have both been historical, *Tess* shot in Normandy which doubles for Hardy's Wessex and *Oliver Twist* shot in Prague's Barrandov Studios which double for Dickensian London. Wisely, perhaps, he has not attempted anything contemporary with stand-in European locations and studio sets. But knowing what he achieved with *Repulsion*, *Cul-de-Sac* and *Macbeth* we can only speculate on what his return, at some point, may have achieved.

   We can also see his thriller trilogy with Emmanuelle Seigner his Parisian *femme fatale* – *Frantic*, *Bitter Moon* and *The Ninth Gate* – as a form of proxy noir, a tribute to the American genre he loves, and his dark riff upon the popular Hollywood theme of an American in Paris. True, the trilogy goes wider. *Bitter Moon*, in the present, takes place on a cruise ship bound for India. In *The Ninth Gate* Johnny Depp travels through Portugal and Spain before reaching Paris. But none of these films are conceivable without Hollywood genre, American male leads and Parisian locations. They are all ingenious re-workings of genre; but they also highlight the limits on Polanski's access to the English-speaking world. His reliance on the pre-formed text too is often to his disadvantage. In Szpilman's memoir and the novels of Hardy, Bruckner and Pérez-Reverte he adapts, one feels there is too much there already on the printed page for someone of Polanski's inspired, improvisational powers. It is true even of *Death and the Maiden* where Polanski's claustrophobic *mise-en-scéne*, the remote cliff-top house where Sigourney Weaver claims to be taking revenge on her torturer in a previous political life, is back to the triumphant powers of invention he had shown in the 1960s. The screenplay by Ariel Dorfman from his acclaimed play ends, however, in the bathos of moral melodrama, undermining the fluid ambiguity of motive and memory that Polanski sustained so consistently for three-quarters of the picture.

Exile notwithstanding, the question of style looms large. In his pre-exile period up to and including *The Tenant* Polanski had shown himself to be a master of the mobile long take. His camera became a fluent instrument for the unbroken exploration of rooms and places, and the exploration of subjectivity on film. While this continues with *Tess* where Polanski alternates inventively between formal static long shots and subjective hand-held camera, it gradually begins to change thereafter. It may be that Polanski was simply going the way of all flesh. David Bordwell notes that other long-take specialists on the Hollywood scene – Billy Wilder, Otto Preminger and Mike Nichols – all began in the 1970s to shorten substantially their 'average shot length' (2005: 150). Polanski in exile followed suit. The average shot length in *Rosemary's Baby* and *Chinatown* had a 15- to 16-second rate, but in *The Ninth Gate* this had gone down to 7.8 seconds – roughly half (Bordwell 2006: 260–1). In extended sequences from *Frantic* and *Death and the Maiden* the long take still features in the exploration of claus-trophobic rooms. At the start of *Frantic* the eerie sense of foreboding Polanski creates in the room of the newly-arrived American couple at the elegant Grand Hotel remains one of his greatest achievements. But in both of these films he sharpens suspense through more frequent cutting and in so doing, attunes himself to the wider culture of the time; to the demands of television networks that have shown reluctance to black-band the letterbox frame of widescreen features, and to the film audience expectations of the last twenty years themselves framed by the experience of television.

Thus the technical pressure on Polanski was much the same as others of his gener-ation. The long take specialists of the current age – Theo Angelopoulos, Hou Hsiao-Hsien, Aleksandr Sokurov, Michael Haneke, the Dardenne brothers, Béla Tarr and, recently, Gus Van Sant – are generally outside of the Hollywood orbit, and have to put themselves on the line through their audacity. Thus returning to the Hollywood orbit would not necessarily have resolved the issue of Polanski's changing style. In truth the technical pressure on the art of perceiving that registers in his recent films cannot be attributed to any one source. It is a combination, one suspects, of three things: the pressure for cutting which can vitiate the power of the subjective shot; the preformed text that gives him a ready-made narrative but sometimes limits his visual inspiration; and the fact of unwanted exile which can distance him from his English-speaking audiences, from new narratives and locations that would freshen him up and inspire him. Yet despite this deadly triangle, Polanski has maintained his uncanny knack for rendering the rooms and places of his narratives with a texture and a density that is still much greater than other directors. We feel we are there holed up with Adrien Brody in his Warsaw hiding-place. We are there to witness the deadly game of Sigourney Weaver and Ben Kingsley in the secluded house in the middle of a storm, and which Polanski filmed atmospherically on the coast outside of Boulogne. We are there with Harrison Ford in his Paris hotel room when his wife inexplicably disappears while he is in the bathroom having a shower. And we are there with Fiona (Kristin Scott Thomas) in the cramped cabin of Mimi and Oscar as the final grisly act of their insane passion unfolds. We are close witnesses but never lose the power to judge because at the extremes of human behaviour Polanski never reduces meaning to pure sensation or perception to cheap emotion. And that is crucial to his enduring legacy.

CHAPTER TWO

Polanski's Existential Body – As Somebody, Nobody and Anybody

Helena Goscilo

Peintre de l'angoisse, des tourments, maître incontesté des univers clos oscillant entre réel, cauchemar et fantastique: les films de Polanski arpentent le monde du masque et de la solitude.
  – Séverine Kandelman

Sex is very similar to torture or surgery.
  – Charles Baudelaire

For all his interest in voyeurism, [Polanski] may be the cinema's most visible director.
  – Barbara Leaming

Roman Polanski is a household name: reviews of his films abound, biographies – partly stimulated by his tabloid-rich life – occupy shelves of numerous academic and municipal libraries, and his autobiography, *Roman* (1984), was a bestseller. Given his fame and his international directorial status, the relative paucity of analytical studies devoted to his oeuvre astonishes readers conversant with publications on the cinema of Truffaut, Coppola and sundry lesser talents. Viewed broadly, Polanski's entire output, which spans more than four decades, vividly illustrates Goethe's cherished concept of 'Dauer im Wechsel' ('continuity in change'), even as it charts a qualitative zigzag during the 1970s that subsequently settled into a steady decline (*Pirates, Frantic, Bitter Moon, The Ninth Gate*) until the new millennium's unexpected, Oscar-winning *The Pianist*. Polanski's contentious habit of endlessly re-shooting a single scene manifests itself on a larger scale in his tendency to revisit a given situation or structure from one film to the next, resulting in such imbricated pairs as *Knife in the Water* and *Cul-de-Sac*; *Knife in the Water* and *Death and the Maiden*; *Repulsion* and *The Tenant*; *Rosemary's Baby* and *The Tenant*; *Rosemary's Baby* and *The Ninth Gate*. For audiences benumbed by Hollywood's addiction to happy endings solemnising heterosexual love and the tattered triteness of 'family values', Polanski offers a refreshing if disquieting antidote: virtually all his films end with incertitude, despair, catatonia or death, with the notable, logic-defying exception of *The Pianist*. In collusion with Polish Romantic mythology, which since Adam Mickiewicz (1798–1855) has equated Artist with Nation,[1] *The Pianist* ultimately affirms the imperishability of art in the face of inconceivable inhumanity – the monstrosities of the Second World War and the Holocaust – depicted in an extraordinarily balanced, understated mode for more than two leisurely hours. The film not only celebrates survival, but also spotlights courage, loyalty, friendship and moral steadfastness – a perspective on human nature that in a director who conceives of everyday life as banal horror may mark a *volte face* triggered by advanced age; Polanski, whose earlier cinema combines elements of Surrealism with Hitchcockian devices calculated to unnerve the viewer, turned seventy in August 2003.

Scholarship on Polanski primarily focuses on his obsession with evil, violence, voyeurism and power relations, more briefly registering his purely visual solutions to cinematic issues, his transformation of claustrophobic settings into psychic space (*Knife in the Water, Repulsion, Cul-de-Sac, Bitter Moon, Death and the Maiden*),[2] and of everyday objects and landscape into symbols: for example, the knife in *Knife in the Water, Repulsion* and *Chinatown*; water in *Knife in the Water, Repulsion, Cul-de-Sac, Chinatown, Bitter Moon* and *Death and the Maiden*; mirrors in *Repulsion, The Tenant* and *Frantic*. Inexplicably, criticism has largely ignored Polanski's complex handling of the human body as a marker of identity and alienation – a phenomenon particularly freighted in light of Polanski's childhood traumas of survival in Nazi-occupied Poland; his absorption with physical appearance; his own diminutive size and unprepossessing looks; and his geographical/cultural transplantations from boyhood into middle age. The indivisibility of the moving body and cinema's origins to a certain extent naturalises the centrality of the former in Polanski's oeuvre, even in such extreme instances as *Repulsion*, where the camera rarely leaves the protagonist's body. Yet few directors match Polanski's intricate reliance on the body to articulate his works' dominant preoccupations.

The body exposed, or the defenseless self when I meets eye

The body in Polanski's films is existential, materialising an embattled identity liable to destabilisation and challenge through unremitting interaction between the inner impulses and desires of the subject, on the one hand, and the omnipresent self-consciousness originating in the inescapable awareness of self as object, on the other.[3]

Accordingly, 'self' for Polanski entails self-presentation and is invariably held hostage to others' perceptions. Jean-Paul Sartre's play *No Exit* (*Huis Clos*, 1944), with its three *dramatis personae* at the mercy of one another's relentless gaze (*le regard d'autrui*, whereby everyone finds the self reflected, literally and figuratively, in others' pupils), most precisely delineates the human condition à la Polanski, whose films emphasise eyes, keyholes, glasses, binoculars and mirrors. On the basis of the eroticism he finds in looking, Barbara Leaming's highly readable psychological biography of Polanski ascribes these elements to voyeurism without addressing their more profound implications for the Polanskian gaze (1981: 73, 100, 199).[4] That gaze both defines and possesses, temporarily empowering observers and potentially delaying or suspending their own subsumption by others in the endless chain of subject/object relations that *No Exit* neatly sums up in the maxim, 'Hell is – other people!' Polanskian self-consciousness as object is not social, as in Tolstoy, but existential, Dostoevskian. The process of watching and being watched not only evokes associations with the Eye of God/Heaven and the specifically cinematic relational configurations generated by kino-eye, but captures Polanski's notion of visibly enacting – or, as Judith Butler would put it, performing – a self under pressure ('But don't forget I'm here, and watching. I shan't take my eyes off you' (Sartre 1949: 36)). Andrzej and the young hiker in *Knife in the Water* try to escape objectification through displacement onto the objects to which they are attached. In *The Tenant* Trelkovsky experiences existential despair and ultimately commits suicide because he gradually loses his subjectivity to the point of becoming pure (feminine) object. As Antony Easthope observes, in psychoanalytic terms, the masculine ego within a patriarchal system strives to become 'a mastering subject', and for 'a position of mastery … vision is part of its effect' (1992: 152–3). In a sense, Polanski's films culminate the huge corpus of literary and cinematic narratives exploring the contingent, enigmatic nature of modern identity, exemplified in numerous stories by E.T.A. Hoffmann, Fyodr Dostoevsky's *The Double*,[5] Robert Louis Stevenson's *Dr Jekyll and Mr Hyde*, Vladimir Nabokov's *Eye* and *Despair*, Franz Kafka's *Metamorphosis* and *The Trial*, Robert Musil's *The Man Without Qualities*, Max Frisch's *I'm Not Stiller*; all of Witold Gombrowicz's novels; and in films like Ingmar Bergman's *Persona* (1966), Peter Greenaway's *A Zed and Two Noughts* (1985), Daniel Vigne's *The Return of Martin Guerre* (*Le Retour de Martin Guerre*, 1982) and Giuseppe Tornatore's *A Pure Formality* (*Una Pura formalità*, 1994).

In Polanski's world, scrutiny operates simultaneously on metaphysical, psychological and cinematic levels – which partly explains Polanski's enthusiasm for Michael Powell's *Peeping Tom* (1960), whose chilling protagonist 'possesses' victims by murdering and photographing them in the process; he exercises a dubious omnipotence by 'recreating' people even as he annihilates them. Of all body parts, for Polanski as existential thinker, aggressively insecure individual and dictatorial, control-obsessed director, the eye reigns supreme. It figures prominently in the Buñuel-indebted opening of his Western directorial debut, *Repulsion*, which superimposes his name on the subjective, defining eye in close-up.[6] Likewise, in *Chinatown*, spying and various vision-aids, such as J. J. Gittes's binoculars and camera lens, the murdered Hollis Mulwray's glasses and Noah Cross's bifocals trope the drive for power through control of the visible.

Evelyn Mulwray (Faye Dunaway), significantly, loses her life and her daughter when shot in the eye; Gittes's constitutional myopia regarding people and situations renders him impotent in influencing events and, in fact, leads to his unwitting facilitation of Evelyn Mulwray's death.[7] The flaw (a black spot) in one of Evelyn's eyes is a metonym for her more profound shortcomings – in judgement and perceptions.

Distinctive eyes, cleverly evoked off-screen and eliciting Rosemary's horrified exclamation, mark her demon child, presumably endowed with 'supernatural' abilities, in *Rosemary's Baby*. *The Tenant*'s binoculars, through which the displaced, diffident Trelkovsky peers at fellow lodgers as they use a Parisian apartment house's communal toilet, gradually cede to the mirror that fails to affirm his 'self' and eventually reflects a facsimile of the dead Simone, whose identity replaces his. At the film's end Trelkovsky experiences the existential terror of having performed someone else's self under the vigilant, coercive eyes of the entire apartment house, which, in a realised metaphor, becomes a theatre of spectators. Despite his unquestionable sufferings at the hands of the Nazis, once his family disappears, Wladyslaw Szpilman in *The Pianist* similarly spends much of the war as a shock-filled eye, staring at the Warsaw uprising through a window and, during the last days of the German occupation, through a hole in the broken glass. By analogy with the omnipotent God, who purportedly sees all, power in Polanski's celluloid universe accrues to whoever sees the most and most clearly.

If the vision(ary) eye can penetrate beneath the surface or the camouflage donned for self-projection and self-protection, in Polanski's irredeemably fallen world of universal solitude nakedness tropes defenselessness vis-à-vis others – the bare body signifying a risky, unveiled transparency. Though Lady Macbeth's nudity during the sleepwalking scene in his *Macbeth* – whether on account of *Playboy*'s financial backing or Polanski's notorious attraction to nubile flesh – irritated some critics and viewers as superfluous titillation, Polanski reportedly intended it as a visual sign of vulnerability (Leaming 1981: 136). Shedding garments leaves one without a psychological shield, as illustrated in *Rosemary's Baby*: whereas the protagonist's girlish mini-skirted outfits merely index the immaturity she exhibits in other ways, her nakedness, more significantly, opens her up to possession/impregnation by Evil, which the birth of her demonic offspring will perpetuate. Other films by Polanski multiply the signification of clothes and their absence, depending on the terms of the given scenario. While the repertoire repeats itself, its meanings vary, as Polanski's own sartorial practices on the set of *Two Men and a Wardrobe* (*Dwaj ludzie z szafą*, 1958) confirm: though behind the camera, he reportedly changed outfits 'four times in a single day', presumably striving for different effects with each change (Leaming 1981: 33).

The body as transferable or transient identity

As the visible locus of the self, the body in several of Polanski's films externalises/materialises assumption or appropriation of others' identities. A simple, pragmatically motivated instance occurs early in *Chinatown*, when Ida Sessions, hired for the part, fools the slick but unperceptive Gittes (Jack Nicholson) by successfully posing as Evelyn Mulwray. This fleeting impersonation, apart from advancing plot and generating mystery, establishes the fatuousness of Gittes's short-sighted smugness but little else.

Incomparably more complex from a psychological standpoint are the two films in which cross-dressing enables men to assume women's roles – a metamorphosis signaling not only the slipperiness of gender (one of Polanski's chief convictions) but also, paradoxically, diminishment in light of Polanski's misogynist notions of womanhood as attested in gender disposition within his oeuvre. The bored young Teresa's (Françoise Dorléac) sadistic self-assertion over her older husband George (Donald Pleasence) in the macabre *Cul-de-Sac* involves not only cuckolding him, but 'forcing' him to don a frivolous, semi-transparent nightie and make-up (the first castration), then ridiculing his feminine appearance and manner (the second castration), in a tautological ritual of humiliation. He willingly participates in their mini-act, which casts her as the male trying to pick up the simpering female (George). While the game announces itself as such and therefore suspends 'conventional time', it nonetheless concretises George's bleating submission to his uxorial dominatrix, coding his existential identity as feminine and from the outset conveying his deficiency in typical masculine traits to the wounded gangster Richard (Lionel Stander), who mistakenly labels him a 'little fairy' and treats him accordingly.

George wields the quintessential symbol of masculinity – significantly, the *borrowed* gun with which he shoots Richard, its macho owner – too late, and when Teresa finally abandons him, he reverts not only to the tearful, passive helplessness of 'femininity', but also to infancy, calling for his first wife/mother (Agnes – the presumably lamb-like predecessor of the tigerish Teresa),[8] as he curls up in a foetal position atop a rock amidst the receding water that at this juncture evokes symbiotic fluid. Transgressive garb functions as involuntary self-revelation. George's forced cross-dressing exposes his subordination in a gender reversal emphasised by Richard's treatment of Teresa: whereas George pleads with her, prepares his own meals and allows her freedom with his body, Richard issues commands, slaps her, throws her to the ground, thrashes her with a belt and calls her a bitch and a whore. Quickly realising that he 'outmans' her, Teresa responds with masculine camaraderie, bringing Richard her home-made vodka, which they drink together in classic macho bonding (by contrast, Richard *compels* a reluctant George to consume vodka), voluntarily helping him to dig the grave for his dead partner, and finding a common language with him. Consistently dressed in jeans, a gender-neutral bathrobe, or (briefly) naked, Teresa is the smoking, hard-drinking phallic female, first glimpsed on *top* of a male as in post-coital playfulness she toys with his body, only to reject it later when a more promising prospect arrives on the scene.[9] Transvestism in *Cul-de-Sac*, in other words, makes perceptible George's 'feminine' inclinations and impotence within his doomed marriage, visually emphasised in the scene on the beach, where *on his knees* he confides to Richard how he adores his patently indifferent wife.

At a climactic moment, when George springs to Teresa's defense, Richard knocks him down, breaking the spectacles George wears during our first glimpse of him, in a high-angle subjective shot from the gangster's elevated position, which 'shrinks' George, establishing his reduced stature in their relations. By contrast, Richard uses the ocular prosthesis of the binoculars to survey the landscape – significantly, from the empowering height of the castle's turret, just as in *Chinatown* Gittes spies on Hollis Mulwray in the valley and in the courtyard of a private house from an elevated vantage point.[10] Uneducated and crude, Richard nonetheless accurately 'perceives' George and Teresa, as well as the grounds for their incompatibility. Moreover, he personifies a fully-fledged masculinity that finds direct expression in decisiveness, physical (often brutal) action and untrammeled agency – precisely the qualities George lacks, as hyperbolically implied by the frothy nightgown he wears. The male body in drag affords insight into a 'feminine' identity of pliability, hesitancy, inaction and emotional dependence.

The Tenant perhaps more than any other Polanski film disconcerts viewers through its reliance on cross-dressing to dramatise identity in crisis. Unlike the brief but revealing episode in *Cul-de-Sac*, Trelkovsky's (Roman Polanski) voluntary transvestism culminates a terrifying, progressive loss of self/subject. The twinned phenomena of identity and cessation organise the film's circular structure, which begins with the apartment-seeking Trelkovsky's visit to the hospital to ascertain the former tenant's death so as to rent her vacant rooms. An inert, swathed mummy after her suicidal leap, the ex-tenant Simone Choule expires on a scream from her cavernous, tooth-gapped mouth – the only visible part of her body apart from her bloodied hands and fixed, staring eyes – conventionally dubbed 'the mirror of the soul', and, together with the howling mouth, adverting to the dark abyss of the inner self.[11] At the film's conclusion, Trelkovsky lies in an identical state, his body indistinguishable from Simone's, as the earlier hospital visit is repeated, with the object/mummy/Trelkovsky dissociated from his subject/self. Between those two points the film charts Trelkovsky's steady assimilation into her persona in an ambiguously oppressive atmosphere that intimates paranoia, on the one hand, and abjuration of selfhood, on the other. Anna Lawton has justly remarked that the individual's failure to fully realise his human personality 'causes Polanski's characters to become non-beings, to be squeezed out of existence by the monsters that they themselves produce', their spiritual nullity captured by their 'being cinematically frozen into a lifeless image' (1981: 122). While the conclusion of *Repulsion* substantiates Lawton's insight, nowhere is its accuracy illustrated more palpably than in this, perhaps Polanski's most under-appreciated, film.

The Tenant projects the existential terror of an identity transferred not through reproduction but through gradual self-annihilation and a replication articulated through the body. That process takes the form of mimesis, both external (clothes, wig, make-up) and internal: Trelkovsky starts to drink Simone's favourite hot chocolate instead of his usual coffee and to smoke Marlboros, her brand of cigarettes, instead of his Gauloises; he becomes quasi-sexually involved with her lover Stella, is kissed by the admirer who never revealed his love for Simone, receives her mail, and so forth. His final act of duplication entails the self-defenestration that maims him and leads to his complete Simonisation – death. Unlike the revelation of George's generalised femininity in *Cul-de-Sac*, transvestism here makes visible Trelkovsky's complete metamorphosis into an identical double of a specific, dead woman. Polanski prepares viewers for that horrifying transmutation by implanting early signs of Trelkovsky's timidity, tentativeness and passivity – fabled 'feminine' traits that not only allow his colleagues to impose on him and the disheveled, bisexual Stella to enact the sexual aggressor in their encounters, but also explain his self-identification with the disabled young girl whom the other tenants wish to evict and who in the carnivalesque fantasy scene appears as a jester wearing a mask with Trelkovsky's face. Trelkovsky actually evicts himself – permanently, from both building and his own body – in two lethal jumps spatially foreshadowed by the camera's constant shifts along the vertical axis (from the fourth-story window to the courtyard below, from the street to the underground metro, up and down the staircase, and in the quick succession of high- and low-angle shots). This dominant axis encourages a metaphysical reading, in which insecure tenancy functions as a matrix metaphor for our earthly existence.

The conclusion retrospectively imbues a sequence that initially seems straightforward and potentially expendable with symbolic significance: after the housewarming, at which Trelkovsky's utter alienation from his invited co-workers borders on the grotesque, he descends the staircase to the garbage cans in the courtyard. The camera's intent focus on his protracted stay on the stairs, only his face visible above the two huge garbage bags hiding his body, unavoidably conjures up a parallel between Trelkovsky's sense of self and dispensability, his ego-destructive identification with trash.

Polanski's *The Tenant* poses the question subsequently echoed in Peter Greenaway's *A Zed and Two Noughts* and David Cronenberg's *The Fly* (1986): what is the minimal physical form requisite for human identity? Dramatising the weak ego's incapacity to sustain a recognisable identity indefinitely, Trelkovsky wonders aloud, 'At what moment does the individual stop being who he thinks he is?' – an issue he formulates specifically as the relationship of the self to parts of the body. Hence Trelkovsky's constant desire to have his self confirmed as he uncertainly checks his reflection in mirrors. Polanski ingeniously presents Trelkovsky's loss of subject/identity (prefigured by his 'strangling himself', as though with someone else's hands) as the multiplication of his body as seen object: he becomes the object of his own binocular gaze; to his horror, a bouncing football transforms into his severed head; and, finally, he confronts his own face on the mask of the little girl who speaks in *his* voice while pointing an 'identifying' finger at him. The last episode precipitates his complete, and final, collapse into the feminine and the eliminated, Simone.

The possessed body, or variations on invasion

Whereas Trelkovsky succumbs to the identity of another, unfamiliar body, several of Polanski's films in varying detail treat the fact or the fear of bodily invasion through sexual intimacy or violation. *Chinatown* never fully clarifies whether Noah Cross's (John Huston) incestuous penetration of Evelyn's body constitutes rape (the more likely scenario) or consensual sex (the more interesting alternative), and that act, as well as the strongly implied future repetition of incest with his daughter/granddaughter, never appears on screen, though the child who results from that tabooed 'union' does.[12] *Tess* treats the heroine's (Nastassia Kinski) despoliation by the practiced seducer Alec d'Urberville (Leigh Lawson) with kindred circumspection. In like vein, the repeated violation of Paulina Escobar's (Sigourney Weaver) incarcerated body by the sadistic Dr Robert Miranda (Ben Kingsley) in *Death and the Maiden* remains off-screen, retrospectively described for the benefit of her husband (and the viewer) so as to justify her psychological torture of the perpetrator fifteen years later. While non-visual, these bodily invasions testify to a gendered mode of evil that subscribes to Kant's categorical imperative. *Death and the Maiden* symbolises that mode's universality by the giant waves crashing against the unpopulated cliffs at the film's opening, and a kneeling Miranda on the edge of those cliffs at the film's conclusion, after he has confessed not only to the identity he vehemently denies throughout, but also to the pleasure of asserting power through perverse violence visited upon captive bodies.

Paradoxically, that physical violation, though only retrospectively recounted, has a much darker aura than the Nazis' beating of Szpilman and shooting of numerous Poles/Jews in *The Pianist*, even though Polanski depicts these brutalities on screen. The discrepancy stems from the overarching goals and the atmosphere that define the two films: while *The Pianist* generally favours the zero-style of historical documentary and commemorates human resilience in the face of appalling circumstances, *Death and the Maiden* sustains a mood of sombre volatility, emphasising the destructive, irrational impulses prompting our sadistic degradation of others. Paulina's obsession with exacting revenge and the psychophysical humiliation to which she subjects Miranda reveal her own heart of darkness. Evil, however gradated, is infectious.[13] Or, as Noah Cross of *Chinatown* inimitably puts it, 'Most people don't face the fact that at the right time and the right place they are capable of anything.'

The two supreme on-screen instances of bodily invasion in Polanski's oeuvre unquestionably occur in *Rosemary's Baby* and *Repulsion*, the first shot as a dream sequence, the second as repeated hallucination. Whereas the antic humour pervading *The Fearless Vampire Killers* emotionally defangs (!) Alfred's physical colonisation by the vampire's classic bite on the neck at film's end, the oppressive aura of menace built into both *Rosemary's Baby* and *Repulsion* intensifies the shock of forced bodily entry. In the former, Minnie Castevet (Ruth Gordon) preliminarily trespasses on Rosemary's body with the drug-filled chocolate mousse that facilitates her necrophilic rape by Satan in a fascinating montage sequence teeming with images from what Beverley Houston and Marsha Kinder call 'competing mythologies' merging the demonic, traditional Christianity and the modern myth of power (1968–69: 19). The sequence superimposes these symbols *on* Rosemary's body as Satan penetrates it, leaving on her back the lacerations that mark his possession. Use of Rosemary's womb is the price of her husband Guy's professional success as an actor, whose stand-in for the role of 'spousal' inseminator is Satan. Thus, the supernatural dimension in no way interferes, but colludes, with men's immemorial, prosaic exchange of a female body: as reflector, vessel or incubator, that body serves male purposes. Pregnant women's frequently cited sensation of their bodies having been taken over by an alien power (the baby) here acquires a double meaning, for cosmic Evil (Satan) and its mundane representative (Guy – John Cassavetes) do, in fact, commandeer Rosemary's body for their own ends.

As so frequently happens in Polanski's cinema, revelations late in the film prompt the viewer to pose disconcerting questions or to reassess earlier assumptions: when precisely did Guy arrange to barter his wife's body and to accede to others' murders in exchange for professional advancement?; was Terry, the Castevets' alleged protégée, Satan's first choice of mother and did she commit suicide not out of depression, as rumoured, but to escape that fate? Since the audience experiences the narrative from Rosemary's point of view (McArthur 1968–69: 19), it is forced to share her terrified uncertainties and ultimate helplessness, which are coded as 'feminine'. Agency and knowledge in *Rosemary's Baby* belong to men, from the benign friend Hutch (Maurice Evans) and the well-meaning Dr Hill (Charles Grodin) to the demonic Castevets and Dr Sapirstein (Ralph Bellamy), as well as the demon-converted pragmatist Guy.

Though both *Rosemary's Baby* and *Repulsion* deal with male instrumentalisation of women's bodies, the first forces the viewer to accept the fantastic, while the second presents the viewer with a compelling portrayal of psychotic fantasy. Polanski's impressive achievement in *Repulsion* is the eloquent, persuasive translation of psychological disintegration into physical/physiological terms. Like *The Tenant*, the film mines the conceptual benefits of a circular structure, one that visually illuminates both its perspective and the source of the protagonist's condition. A close-up of Carol Ledoux's (Catherine Deneuve) dilated eye, across which the opening credits 'float', establishes the subjectivity of viewpoint throughout the film (handled deftly enough to have earned reviewers' near-unanimous acclaim for its unusual dramatisation of escalating paranoia 'from within'). At the conclusion, as the camera finally freezes on a family photograph earlier registered twice only in passing during slow pans of the Ledoux sisters' apartment, it focuses on the eyes of a girl (clearly, a much younger Carol) intently fixed in horror on a man presumably her father. While he and the other family members form a harmonious group in the foreground, smiling directly into the camera, Carol stands apart and behind them, oblivious to the camera, her face a picture of alienated revulsion. A crucial clue to the adult Carol's dysfunctional state, the snapshot, unaccountably, has been overlooked by some commentators (DeVore n.d.; Durgnat 1965; Brown 1996–97; Guthmann 1998) and short-sightedly interpreted by others as capturing Carol's familial role of the unloved child (Leaming 1981: 65; Butler 1970b: 141). In fact, the photo, with admirable economy, establishes her schizophrenia as a result of paternal (or avuncular) rape – a theme reprised in *Chinatown*.[14] Polanski's reported claim that the process and not the origins of Carol's psychological unraveling interested him (Leaming 1981: 66) misled many critics and reviewers into ignoring his unobtrusive, purely visual means of conveying those origins without belabouring them.

The trauma of incestuous bodily violation accounts for Carol's obsessive and, ultimately, lethal, panic about its possible repetition, manifested in (i) her hyperbolic reaction to *all* contact with men (her suitor, Colin; her sister's married lover, Michael; the apartment's sleazy, opportunistic landlord; the construction worker on the street), (ii) her spatial connection with two male-free environments that offer pseudo-havens: the nunnery next door, upon which she constantly gazes, whose residents, as 'brides of Christ', maintain physical 'purity' by abrogating all sexual experience, and her workplace – the all-female beauty salon, where comments by customers and personnel repudiate men as primitives in mindless pursuit of sexual gratification. A sequence beyond Carol's perspective that buttresses this image of atavistic masculinity occurs at a local pub, where Colin's 'buddies' engage in scabrous 'male-talk' (of the sort that a decade later in *The Tenant* unites Trelkovsky's crude co-workers in chortling idiocy), capped by the kiss one of them plants on Colin's mouth (again, anticipating the kiss Simone's admirer gives Trelkovsky). This sexually-charged context, which spills from the subjective to the objective sphere, codes men as shallow, hormonal brutes. Together with the photograph, it explains Carol's verbally unarticulated, paralysing terror at ostensibly random phenomena, such as the cut she inadvertently makes on a client's finger during a manicure (defloration) and the cracks in the pavement along which she drifts like a sleepwalker (evoking the anal 'crack'). These subjective, minatory signs of violation expand into the hallucinated fissures that suddenly appear in the apartment walls and are made sexually explicit in Carol's three fantasies of anal rape, as well as in the hands that eerily extrude from the same walls to grab at her breasts.

Since the inability or unwillingness to communicate verbally symptomatises her descent into madness, Carol conveys her state of mind graphically, through the body: while gulping down glasses of water to assuage her panic, she barely eats, as if to ensure her body's 'purity'; in what becomes a disquieting behavioural tic she brushes invisible matter off her nose and upper body to remain uncontaminated; after Colin's hesitant, innocent kiss, she frantically wipes her mouth and brushes her teeth; like Trelkovsky a decade later, she seeks verification of her identity in the mirror and the distorting kettle; her eyes blank, she sleepwalks dreamily but defensively along the street and throughout the increasingly devastated apartment; she huddles fearfully in her virginal single bed and disconnects the telephone by cutting the cord; she uses two 'phallic weapons' – candlestick and knife – to dispatch the two men who 'invade' the apartment; and, as a final retreat from perceived attack, she seeks shelter under the bed. Polanski's inspired cinematic metaphor for Carol's pathological measures to defend her body from sexual invasion metamorphose her immediate environment into a devastated corpse-strewn womb,[15] thereby eloquently rooting her madness in an earlier, 'innocent' phase of her troubled existence, while simultaneously troping her current state as maximum regression.

The demented murders and childhood sexual trauma conjure up Hitchcock (especially *Psycho* (1960) and *Marnie* (1964)), as do the bloodstains Carol finds on her sister Hélène's bed-sheets, which disturb her because of their associations with menstruation and loss of virginity. That blood becomes the blood of vengeance when she kills the clueless, well-meaning Colin and the vulgar, aggressive landlord. All victims, Carol included, resemble the defenseless, bloody rabbit rotting throughout the film, and in Polanski's morbid worldview, their transformation into victimisers merely illustrates a 'law' of human nature.[16] Polanski provokes the viewer's visceral, immediate response to his disturbing case study of insanity by relying on the body as a palpable reflector of mental activity while enlisting sound, gesture and everyday items unexpectedly invested with lethal potential to build a shiveringly eerie atmosphere. If, as Lawton contends, such Polanski films as *The Fearless Vampire Killers* feature doubles who embody the classic body/mind division, *Repulsion* posits a perfect, fatal continuity between the two: a process that originates in the abuse of a child's body eventually ravages her adult mind.

The gendered body

Provisionally setting aside Polanski's media-hyped anomalous relations with women on and off the set, his predilection for teenage girls, the Playboy Club and one-night stands, plus the criminal charges that 27 years later still make him *persona non grata* in the United States, one cannot resist speculating why, *Bitter Moon* aside, the only exposed and invaded bodies in Polanski are female. No one could accuse Polanski of idealising human nature, which his cine-world portrays as weak, egotistical, cruel and devoid of a stable centre. Yet, whatever its common frailties, humanity in Polanski's cinema divides along gender lines as soon as body politics enter the equation. In polemic with a male-authored review of *Chinatown* asserting that through the photographs that capture a couple engaged in anal intercourse Polanski shows how 'in this world everyone takes it in the ass', Barbara Martineau protests the reviewer's glossing over 'the fact that it's a woman taking it in the ass and, as usual, having even her specific oppression denied her by the sexist language that melts her into the everyone she isn't' (1977: 349). Moreover, by the film's end, 'while the male star gets a slit nose, the female star gets shot in the eye' (1977: 351). Martineau has a point. The uncharacteristic *The Pianist* aside, all the rapes and virtually all the violent deaths of women in Polanski's cinema are inflicted by men or by the patriarchal 'system' (as in *Tess*).

Polanski's oeuvre depicts ostensibly empowered women, such as Krystyna (Jolanta Umecka) in *Knife in the Water*, Teresa in *Cul-de-Sac*, Paulina in *Death and the Maiden*, the 'angel' (Emmanuelle Seigner) in *The Ninth Gate* and Fiona (Kristin Scott Thomas) and Mimi (Emmanuelle Seigner) in *Bitter Moon*. Upon closer scrutiny, however, the agency and gender-specific teleology of these characters reveals their entrapment in regressive stereotypes of femininity, above all the automatic (Biblical!) pairing of women with body rather than intellect. Krystyna's sole recourse to power is sexual betrayal, the form of marital humiliation Teresa favours, along with ignoring and belittling her spouse.

Desire and pragmatism likewise motivate women to rely not on their brains, but on their bodies: an hour or so into their acquaintance *The Tenant*'s Stella (Isabelle Adjani) assuming the role of aggressive male, gropes for the 'feminine' Trelkovsky's crotch in the movie theatre and thereafter pursues him sexually, despite his conspicuous asexuality. In *The Ninth Gate* a few minutes after meeting Dean Corso (Johnny Depp), the widowed Liana Telfer (Lena Olin) offers him sexual congress in exchange for the occult book in his possession. If women deploy sexual favors, *faute de mieux*, as barter or weaponry within his films' diegesis, Polanski's camera also commodifies women and projects them as disempowered vis-à-vis the viewer by virtue of their nudity, and not only in the case of Lady Macbeth. Though Paulina emerges as stronger than her ex-political-leader husband, Polanski's cinematically unmotivated shot of her naked body as she changes clothes in the bedroom diminishes her image. Similarly, the camera provides several lateral glimpses of Evelyn's bare breasts during the post-coital sequence in *her* bedroom (women's proper place?), but not Gittes's naked buttocks as he pulls on his trousers, though the discreet shot requires an awkward angle from above and behind Gittes's head. During Corso's two sexual bouts in *The Ninth Gate* the camera displays only his bare chest (and, in the first case, part of his bare legs, with his trousers drooping around his ankles), whereas during the completely gratuitous copulation he enjoys with the 'angel' on the grounds outside the burning castle the shot frontally exposes her nudity and lingers on her breasts, while she looks straight into the camera. The abrupt, diegetically-irrelevant metamorphosis of the angel into a blazing-eyed *succubus (s)ex machina* runs completely counter to her image throughout the film and implies that sexuality demonises women.

Gender imbalance centred in the body reserves aural discretion and visual propriety for men. In *Repulsion*, the only orgasmic moans heard by Carol and the viewer belong to Hélène; Michael is silent. Having undergone unimaginable bodily violations by Miranda, Paulina in *Death and the Maiden* briefly contemplates subjecting him to anal rape with an object, but softens his physical degradation by merely extracting his *unseen* penis from his trousers so that he can urinate with his hands tied behind his back. What these and other Polanski films, such as *Repulsion*, suggest is that (i) the body constitutes the tangible locus of humans' paramount fears and desires; (ii) in the market of human relations, bodies are women's most valuable possessions; (iii) within the universal dynamic of sadomasochism, women use their bodies to torment men psychologically rather than physically, mainly because their anatomical equipment ill equips them for rape; (iv) cinema, like early pornography, 'naturally' taboos male nudity, whereas women's nakedness may, and should, be flaunted. Such notions presuppose a heterosexual male audience unencumbered by maturity and inhere in the immemorial sexist principles embraced by those 'civilised' societies in which Polanski has resided: Poland, America, England and France.

Nonetheless, two radically dissimilar Polanski films mitigate such glaring gender inequity: *Knife in the Water* and *Bitter Moon*. Herbert Eagle contends that Krystyna in Polanski's feature cinematic debut is the sexual object not only of both men's competing egos (so far so good), but also of viewers' and the young hiker's voyeurism (1994: 107). Yet all three protagonists of *Knife in the Water* spend most of the film half-naked (unsurprisingly, given the setting); neither the two men nor the audience directly witnesses the potentially titillating sight of Krystyna removing her wet bikini; and the camera actually devotes more attention to the young hiker's semi-exposed body than to hers. The prolonged focus on his bare torso and overall shape as he 'treads water', watched by the married couple and the viewer, renders him a scopophilic object. Moreover, the dramatic overhead shot of his spread-eagled form on the deck places the audience in the unusual, eroticised position of 'being on top of him'. Repeated juxtaposition of Andrzej's (Leon Niemczyk) somewhat slacker and bulkier middle-aged body with the hiker's (Zygmunt Malanowicz) sinewy, lean build underscores the latter's physical appeal. Finally, *both* Krystyna and the young man wreak revenge on Andrzej through the consensual sex from which, presumably, each derives pleasure. In sum, Polanski's official directorial debut significantly reduces the vast expanses traditionally separating male and female identity and redistributes the exercise of power through the gaze and the body.

In its mirror-reversal structure, Polanski's *Bitter Moon*, paradoxically, showcases increased gender parity, as well as a comparably increased perversity in Polanski's celluloid treatment of bodies. As a lamentable transfer to the screen of Henry Miller's sexual 'philosophy' and persona as deduced from his writings, the film vacillates unproductively between the conventions of porno trash (the end-product) and the rhetoric of an 'existentialist statement' (the pretension). In a sense, the film broadly expands on Noah Cross's unapologetic response to the question of culpability regarding incest: one attains self-knowledge by daring to trespass against all moral taboos – in this specific instance, chiefly sexual prohibitions and norms. Tellingly, *Bitter Moon* is not only Polanski's worst, but also his 'talkiest' film, resorting to long, voiced-over flashbacks and pseudo-philosophical declarations within the *Ich-Erzählung* sections that preponderate and are intended to provide an ideological and psychological rationale for the remarkably fatuous on-screen activities. These encompass voyeurism, exhibitionism, S/M games, water sports and lesbianism, accompanied by the writer-protagonist Oscar's (Peter Coyote) excruciatingly purple-prosed paeans to the alleged self-revelations vouchsafed by the sexual experimentation into which his younger French mistress initiates him. Culminating a series of equally self-conscious exercises in pseudo-eroticism, including Liliana Cavani's *The Night Porter* (*Il Portiere di notte*, 1974), Lina Wertmüller's *Swept Away* (*Travolti da un insolito destino nell'azzurro mare d'agosto*, 1974) and *Seven Beauties* (*Pasqualino Settebellezze*, 1976) and Adrian Lyne's *9½ Weeks* (1986), *Bitter Moon* strives for a major existentialist *profession de foi* and ends up courting ridicule as a disastrously failed attempt to shock while delving into the dark recesses of the psyche.

True to the expectations of viewers familiar with Polanski's repertoire, terminal self-involvement, manipulation, betrayal and callousness are the mainspring to action of the two couples, Oscar and Mimi, Nigel (Hugh Grant) and Fiona. And, once again, the power-obsessed male, Oscar, kills his 'beloved', as well as himself, though much later than the viewer would wish. What distinguishes *Bitter Moon* from all other Polanski films is its exposure of the naked male body (with the sacred genitals safely if clumsily screened) and its physiological humiliation. Rendered impotent and paralysed from the waist down by an accident, the formerly promiscuous, self-assertive Oscar not only observes and listens to his wife's sexual escapades with other lovers, but at one point involuntarily urinates as he sits in his wheelchair, awaiting her return home from a rendezvous. Until Oscar eliminates his garrulous self and the vulgar Mimi with two bullets, the film appears to credit women with agency and a degree of self-sufficiency, intimated by Mimi and Fiona's preference for sex with each other rather than with the ready Nigel – a decision completely understandable to any viewer watching Hugh Grant in the role. The same-sex romp, however, proves to have been orchestrated, and delectated, by Oscar, thereby reducing the women to puppets who cater to his 'perverse' pleasure as voyeur. Perhaps Polanski's awareness of his own diminishing sexual energy (or appeal) at the age of 59 can explain why he undertook such a project. Nothing else can.

Though Polanski himself has authored or collaborated on the scripts for most of his films (*Knife in the Water, Repulsion, Cul-de-Sac, The Fearless Vampire Killers, The Tenant, Pirates, Frantic*), several of them adapt literary works: novels by Ira Levin, Thomas Hardy and Arturo Pérez-Reverte, plays by Shakespeare and Ariel Dorfman, memoirs by Szpilman. One might tenably argue, therefore, that the mélange of violence, relentless sexuality,[17] startling visual and sound effects and the aesthetic of the horror film that defines Polanski's unmistakable signature belong to the sources rather than to Polanski's fertile but unsettling imagination. Yet even when financial pressures and dearth of alternatives limit directors' options, those constraints leave them a measure of choice, and Polanski fairly consistently has chosen to engage precisely those works that resonate with his *idées fixes* and suit his directorial sensibilities. While Shakespeare's *Macbeth* teems with murders, they typically occur off-stage, and the minimalist stage directions for Lady Macbeth's sleepwalking contain no reference to nudity; nor does Shakespeare's Act IV, scene I, call for a subterranean coven of naked witches. Levin's novelistic treatment of Rosemary's rape scene likewise acquires quintessentially Polanskian touches in the transfer to the screen, as does the ending, which eliminates Rosemary's optimistic rationalisations about the child's half-human origins and therefore its possible redemption. Above all, the copulating sequence in Polanski's *The Ninth Gate* has no counterpart in the original text, though an incomparably less melodramatic, indoor coupling takes place earlier between Corso and the decidedly undemonic young woman who acts as his guardian angel throughout Pérez-Reverte's novel. In short, whatever the cinematic effectiveness of Polanski's modifications or additions, they tend toward a sensationalism anchored in the body. One of the most vivid examples is the conclusion of *Chinatown*: the original scenario by Robert Towne, reputedly a master of dialogue but short on purveying visual interest (Leaming 1981: 141), ended with Evelyn's escape. Polanski, who edited and changed huge sections of the script, not only wrote Evelyn's death into the finale, but also insisted on its graphically heart-stopping nature – the bullet in the eye – which conforms to and culminates the violence and symbolism pervading the film. It seems appropriate that Polanski's arguably most disciplined film end not with the disappearance of a body, but its bloody devastation, for throughout Polanski's career the visible body has pulled together the threads of his ruling obsessions.

Notes

1 *The Pianist* proved uncharacteristic in virtually all respects for a director who, in Colin McArthur's astute words, 'never had to accommodate his sensibility to even the outward trappings of socialist realism and the flagellative tradition of Polish romanticism', drawing, instead, upon the Surrealist strain of the avant-garde (McArthur 1968–69: 14).

2 Ivan Butler, for instance, astutely remarks that the contrast between distanced personalities and confined setting results in an 'atmospheric compression that

generates the tension' that Polanski relentlessly builds (1970a: 178).

3   Anna Lawton also has noted this disjuncture, which she formulates as the inability to integrate mental and physical faculties (1981: 126).

4   Leaming's eminently reasonable thesis, that Polanski converts personal problems into cinematic texts, basically disallows the possibility of existential profundity combining with temperamental immaturity – a view with which I categorically disagree. Polanski's repellent behaviour and misogyny in everyday life have not prevented him from making at least one superb film (*Chinatown*) and several excellent ones distinguished by faultless structure and penetrating insight into human psychology (*Knife in the Water, Repulsion* and *The Tenant*).

5   For fundamental ties between Dostoevsky and Polanski, see Lawton's analysis of the *Doppelgänger* theme in both (1981).

6   Polanski's insistence on control, documented in detail by Leaming, doubtless prompts his eagerness to act in those films he directs, for the double function enables him to compose his identity as object (filmed actor) along subjective lines (filming director). Moreover, his notorious, insensitive manipulation of actors and actresses aims to subordinate their performances to his own comprehensive vision, just as his expensive penchant for re-shooting the same scene or sequence even at the risk of the cast's safety and health evidences his conviction that 'it is the director who bestows importance – not the actor' (Leaming 1981: 126) – particularly when the director is Polanski.

7   The 'eye' neatly structures the film, which opens with the on-screen camera 'capturing' illicit coupling and concludes with the eternal 'closure' of Evelyn Mulwray's equally illicit, incestuous eyes.

8   According to Donald Pleasance, he and Françoise Dorléac wished to make Teresa 'more two-dimensional, whereas Roman wanted her to be simply sluttish' (Butler 1970a: 110).

9   Those critics (for example, Leaming 1981: 69) who draw parallels between Teresa and Krystyna, the adulterous wife in *Knife in the Water*, do so irresponsibly, for the only common element between the two is the act of adultery, which in Krystyna's case may be the sole such lapse. Moreover, unlike Teresa, Krystyna listens to her domineering spouse, obeys his orders on the boat, and does not humiliate him on a regular basis. Nor does she leave him at the film's inconclusive end. In short, she does not qualify as the phallic woman.

10 The binoculars here and the camera in the boating scene conceal Gittes' face, in effect turning him into a disembodied 'watching eye' that in the latter instance reflects Mulwray and a young girl during what Gittes assumes is an illicit meeting. That moment offers an ideal example of *le regard d'autrui*, and, as Leaming maintains, 'a perfect emblem for voyeurism, the use of the camera to glimpse the forbidden' (1981: 146). The film teems with sequences of spying, observing and photographing unsuspecting objects of scrutiny.

11 That image recurs at the spine-tingling conclusion of Phil Kaufman's 1978 remake/ semi-sequel to Don Siegel's 1956 classic, *Invasion of the Body Snatchers*. My thanks to Bożenna Goscilo for noting this parallel.

12 *Frantic* is the sole exception to the rather perverse rule in Polanski's films whereby only fateful seduction (*Tess*) and rape (*Chinatown* and *Rosemary's Baby*) yield offspring. The married couples/protagonists in *Knife in the Water*, *Cul-de-Sac*, *Macbeth*, *Tess*, *Bitter Moon*, *Death and the Maiden* and *Ninth Gate* are all childless. McArthur has remarked, 'It is fitting that the only birth in the Polanski canon should bring forth the child of Satan' (1968–69: 17). The only other progeny to have appeared since results from incest. Furthermore, Macduff in *Macbeth* is 'not of woman born', Nigel in *Bitter Moon* explicitly refuses to sire offspring, while the infection occasioned by Mimi's abortion in the same film leaves her barren – a condition that in *Death and the Maiden* likely explains Paulina's childlessness. The single instance of a sizable, close-knit family in Polanski is Szpilman's in *The Pianist*. Otherwise, instead of fulfilling the conventional task of vouchsafing generational continuity, women's impregnation perpetuates the world's evil or perversity.

13 Herbert Eagle accurately describes this phenomenon as the victim turned victimiser (1994: 114).

14 Eagle numbers among the few critics to realise that incest is at the root of Carol's adult dementia (1994: 124).

15 Polanski uses a wide-angle lens to achieve this distorting effect, a fact also noted by Eagle (1994: 123).

16 While Eagle has noted the reversibility of victim/victimiser relations, he, however, does not connect that exchange of roles with the subject/object paradigm, which strikes me as fundamental to Polanski's cheerless view of the human condition.

17 McArthur's early review article discerned a 'strong thematic continuity in his feature films' released before the 1970s: 'All examine aspects of sexuality' (1968–69: 15). I contend that what underlies sexuality in Polanski's films of the 1960s and the majority of subsequent works is the issue of beleaguered identity.

CHAPTER THREE

Power and the Visual Semantics of Polanski's Films

Herbert J. Eagle

One of Roman Polanski's earliest student films, *Murder* (*Morderstwo*, 1957), lasted about a minute and consisted of three shots: seen from within a room, a door handle turns and a door opens, the camera pans to follow a man dressed in black with a cane as he walks to a bed where another man lies sleeping, naked and covered to mid-chest with a blanket; in a second closer shot, the man in black draws a pen-knife from a pocket and, using both hands, presses it between the ribs of the sleeping man and into his heart; finally, from our initial vantage point, we see a thin trickle of blood extending from the naked man's breast and down one arm, while the camera then pans to follow the man in black across the room and out the door, which closes behind him. This very brief exercise exhibits features which were to characterise Polanski's film-making throughout his career: a theme built on an opposition between two characters (or sets of characters) – one aggressive and violent, the other passive and powerless; symmetrical binary structures, both in terms of narrative development and in terms of visual composition and style; and the use of symbolic visual images to embody graphically (and often shockingly in terms of the ways they emerge) the opposed states of power and helplessness.

Power, and the violence used to sustain it, emerged as central elements in Polanski's cinema, both in the more schematic and often absurdist films for which he authored or co-authored the filmscripts, and in the more complex narratives scripted by others. The underlying structure of Polanski's early absurdist films was very simple, but highly effective nonetheless, because the basic dynamic (power/powerlessness) could appeal to the personal experience and perception of virtually every viewer. In his more realistic and narratively dense films (where Polanski was working with literary works, usually adapted by others, or with original filmscripts by other authors), the central opposition is grafted onto a variety of historical circumstances as well as onto specific political and social issues. Narrative structure here is less schematic (governed as it is by a more complicated already determined literary plot), but Polanski's use of highly affective images of power (dominance, violence) and powerlessness (innocence, meekness) provide the films' most compelling moments. The alternation and reversal of images which frequently have both a visceral and a symbolic effect was to remain the unwavering mark of Polanski films.

In *Murder*, the action advances and then recedes in an entirely symmetric way in terms of the movements of the man in black, the door opening and then closing. Opposed images command our attention – on the one hand, nakedness (the sleeper is unprotected, and, by implication, sexually vulnerable as well) and, on the other, the black outfit, the cane and the knife (the former associated conventionally with evil and the latter with violence and with rape, due to the phallic shape of the two objects). Polanski's approach to shooting the scene is matter-of-fact; nothing privileges either character; we have no motivations for the action; there is nothing that arouses partic- ular sympathy for the victim. A dispassionate display of aggression and passivity, of dominance and subjugation, remained a constant feature of Polanski's films as well.

In other short films, Polanski expanded on the basic structure of *Murder*. In *Teethful Smile* (*Uśmiech zębiczny*, 1957), a man descending a stairway pauses to peep into a high window – he sees a young woman standing in front of a sink drying herself, her breasts are fully exposed to his view (and ours). Polanski thus places the spectator in the position of his protagonist, possessing, through voyeurism, sexual power over an innocent and unknowing victim. The man is forced by propriety to move away from the window when another tenant emerges from his apartment, but as soon as he is alone again he goes to the window to continue his scopophilic pleasure (and the male spectator of the film is likely to anticipate further erotic pleasures as well). However, this time what greets the peeping tom's view is a man brushing his teeth who turns towards the voyeur (and us) with a mouth full of toothpaste and seems to direct at us a mocking grin. In *Teethful Smile* we see the same symmetric structure of shots as in *Murder*, only this time the power relationship is reversed in the second half of the film – now it is the peeping tom (and we) who are the victims of the smiler's accusatory aggressive gaze.

Let's Break the Ball (*Rozbijemy zabaw*, 1957) explodes the intimations of violence and rape, as well as the principle of the reversal of power, into a longer narrative exercise. This time the subject is a dance at a private estate (the film was actually set on the grounds of the Łódź Film School); the invited guests were students (played by actual students, who did not know that a gang would crash the party once it had begun). First we see the estate's garden being decorated, then the guests arrive and the dancing begins, with some students dressed rather scantily and a hint of sensuality present in the women's outfits, with their skirts flying as they whirl around. Outside the gates, a group of young toughs seeks admittance (again, these were actual hooligans, acquaintances of Polanski, so that the ensuing events had the character of a directed happening); a man in coattails refuses to let them in without a ticket. They crash the party by climbing over the fence and attack the dancers, the man who refused them admission is beaten, a woman falls to the ground and her skirt is pulled up above her waist in the process (now it is the young hoods who are in possession of her, in this rapacious image). The film ends with shots of the garden after the brawl, the decorations torn and scattered in disarray. Once again Polanski uses symmetrically placed sequences: the party decorations (in opposite states) begin and end the film; smiling faces and dancing legs at the beginning of the dance, beaten faces and flailing legs at the end. The props and images associated with light-hearted mildly erotic pleasure are transformed into tools for assault with intimations of rape. In Polanski's films normalcy often masks the human potential for aggression which can erupt at any moment and turn every meaning into its opposite.

Although it is not the purpose of this chapter to explore Polanski's psychology, some remarks about the personal experiences which might have made him so adept at capturing the abruptness of a transition from peaceful life to horrific violence is certainly in order at this point: his living through the omnipresent, frequently sudden and arbitrary violence of the Nazi occupation of Poland. It was only in his most recent film *The Pianist* that Polanski returned explicitly to the traumatic years of his youth, but it would appear likely that those years provided him with his characteristic view of the world and of the ubiquity of evil. In 1939, when Polanski was only six, his family was forced to move into the Cracow ghetto. He saw Nazi soldiers, upon their whim, delivering beatings and, once, shooting an old woman who could not walk fast enough: 'There was a loud bang, and blood came welling out of her back' (1984: 26). Blood suddenly pouring out of wounds was an image Polanski was to use often in his films. Polanski survived after his parents were deported to the concentration camps because he was taken in by a series of Gentile families, but he could not be seen in public and he was constantly aware of his powerlessness and vulnerability. At any moment he could be discovered and killed.

The crowning achievement of Polanski's student years was his short film *Two Men and a Wardrobe* (*Dwaj ludzie z szafą*), which won the Bronze Medal for Experimental Film at the Brussels Worlds Fair. The film is built upon repeated motifs embodied in actions and props, objective correlatives for the respective states of innocence and aggression, both of which are shown to be ever-present. From beneath waves rolling in on a sandy beach, a very large wardrobe is carried onto the shore by two men, who have also magically emerged from under the waves. As it is carried out of the water, the wardrobe's mirror reflects the waves and sky as in a seascape, and later, as the men dance around it, it reflects their playful pleasure. The two men are also very distinctive in other respects. Their actions and gestures are delicate and somewhat effeminate (they might be a gay couple) and they look Jewish (both of the actors, 'Kuba' Goldberg and Henryk Kluba, were Jewish, and Kluba was asked by Polanski to grow a beard so that he would more obviously look like a Jew). Thus, Polanski alludes to two of the categories of people who were the Holocaust's explicit victims, marking them visually as disempowered. When the two men attempt to board a trolley, carrying their wardrobe, they are cursed and threatened by the angry commuters (Polanski plays one of these; as we shall see, when Polanski takes a role in his own films he plays either a victim or a tormenter). An attempt to take the wardrobe to a restaurant is similarly rebuffed. Then the two men meet a woman whose potential for empathy is suggested by the way she is gazing at a caged bird in a pet store window. But when the two men, gesturing like Chaplinesque clowns, attempt to introduce the wardrobe to her, she runs off.

The friendship and civility of the two men subsequently is countered not only by annoyance and indifference; we see increasing evidence of deception and violence in society. As the men walk along a canal, two younger men, clearly drunk, laugh, with arms thrown over each other's shoulder; but we see from behind that one man is picking a wallet out of the other's back pocket with his free hand. *Two Men and a Wardrobe* continues to present us with an alternating series of images – in one set the wardrobe and the two men demonstrate their positive and humane qualities; in the other, the inhabitants of the town move from indifference and dishonesty to violence and an obsession with order. One particularly striking sequence begins with the image of a fish flying through the sky; the camera pulls back to reveal that it is a dried fish, lying on the wardrobe's mirror which reflects the passing clouds – the two men are using the wardrobe, turned on its side, as a table for their lunch (the wardrobe thus proves itself both useful and capable of creating beauty). Such scenes of innocent and sometimes elegant utility (as when a passerby is able to straighten his tie in the wardrobe's mirror) alternate with images of society's indifference. When the wardrobe moves toward a more engaged effort to prevent evil, society becomes more brutal. As the two men carry the wardrobe past a deserted pavilion, four young toughs are tormenting a cute black kitten, throwing stones at it until they kill it. When they notice a pretty young women approaching, the gang members begin to sneak up on her with the intention of shoving the dead kitten in her face. The wardrobe passes in front of the young woman, positioning itself in such a way as to reveal to her what is about to happen. She is able to escape. In retaliation, the gang beats up the two men instead. As the bearded Kluba comically shadow boxes in mock self-defense, he is brutally smashed in the face; the strongest gang member holds him, while the smallest (again played by Polanski) punches him repeatedly (only 24 at the time, Polanski looks like a scrawny teenager, a weak punk who can only prove his masculinity by attacking those who are weaker and defenseless). Perhaps because of his own experiences as an adolescent, Polanski instinctively understood that sadistic pleasure can be a driving force for those who have been themselves abused. The victim can become the torturer, a reversal which Polanski explores in many later films. The beating is undoubtedly the most disturbing sequence in the film, as Polanski deftly creates out of common place images of innocence (a kitten, a pretty young girl) and cruelty (a sadistic gang) a searing portrait of man's inhumanity to man, with metaphorical allusions to the Holocaust signaled in the choice of key details.

Violence now escalates and another theme, regimentation, accompanies it through the choice of images. The men pass further scenes of impending or actual brutality (a defenseless drunk staggers down the steps toward a river; at the bottom of a ravine, one man has just smashed the head of another with a rock). When the two men attempt to rest in a yard filled with empty barrels, arranged symmetrically, they are beaten by the watchman. They escape to the beach, where they trudge past a boy who is making neat rows of rudimentary sandcastles by inverting his sand-filled pail. He does not even seem to notice them as they walk back into the sea and disappear beneath the waves. These final images suggest to us a society that practices regimentation, order and power, and has no room for beauty, imagination or compassion.

In *Two Men and a Wardrobe*, Polanski advanced the patterns of narrative and imagery which would provide the structural backbone for almost all of his films. The narratives feature an alternation of humane (compassionate, cooperative, peaceful) actions and inhumane (aggressive, selfish, violent) actions, with prominent props used to signal each kind of behaviour. Shifts from kindness to indifference or cruelty are abrupt, and in Polanski's early absurdist films, do not involve any prior psychological motivations. This is quite evident as well in *The Fat and the Lean* (*Le Gros et le maigre*), made in France in 1961, and in *Mammals* (*Ssaki*), made in Poland the following year. Both work with the oppositions of weak and strong, victim and tormentor, master and slave. In the first film, a young slight servant (played by Polanski) provides his fat, middle-aged, greasy master with food, grooming services, entertainment and other services, his labours interrupted only by stolen glances toward the gleaming city of Paris in the distance. His master then bestows upon him a goat, but unfortunately the goat then has to be chained to him to prevent it from escaping. The servant's tasks are now all repeated again with the necessary variations; of course, they end up being much more difficult since the servant has to do them with a goat chained to his leg. The sequence of tasks is repeated a third time when the servant is released from the goat; now he performs his tasks very happily, indeed ecstatically – although his situation has merely reverted to what it was at the beginning of the film. In *Mammals*, the plot is even simpler. One man carries or pulls another across a snowy field in a sleigh. The men alternate roles and their relationship oscillates as each man uses his injuries or infirmities to get the other to serve him. Both films are based on a series of actions which are then repeated with ironic variations.

Although *Knife in the Water* (*Nóż w wodzie*), as Polanski's first feature-length film, had a realistic setting and thus was in a position to refer more substantially to social and historical issues, it remains in many ways similar to his short absurdist films. The film's dialogue (written for the most part by Polanski's co-screenwriter Jerzy Skolimowski), is cleverly constructed out of relatively mundane preoccupations – the differences in standard of living and attitudes between a poor college student (Zygmunt Malanowicz) and a well-off middle-aged sportswriter, Andrzej (Leon Niemczyk), with a much younger wife, Krystyna (Jolanta Umecka). In spite of the references to the social realities of the characters' lives, the real concerns are power, gender and sexuality. The married couple is driving to the Mazurian Lakes for a 24-hour sailing vacation when a student hitchhiker forces them to stop by standing in the middle of the road, refusing to budge as their car approaches at high speed. This determined effort to get a ride succeeds. Andrzej brakes at the last minute and is then furious at the hitchhiker for winning this battle of will (Andrzej's only other option would have been to run over the hitchhiker, a path with clearly more serious consequences for him). Knowing that his wife would have slowed down to pick up the hitchhiker had she been driving, Andrzej politely asks him to join them in their car (after insulting him verbally), as if to spite Krystyna. A desire on the part of both men to continue their verbal battles soon results in an invitation to the hiker to join the couple on their sailboat as well.

The film traces roughly 24 hours in the lives of the three characters with virtually the entire action limited to three confined spaces: the interior of the car, the deck of the sailboat, and its even smaller interior cabin. Polanski later wrote of the film that he wanted it 'to be rigorously cerebral, precisely engineered, almost formalist' (1984: 156). Even more than his absurdist shorts, the film uses the positioning of characters within the spatial composition to signify the shifting power relationships, mirroring the competitions, alliances and oppositions. Particular objects used very pointedly remind us that the central issue is sexual power. A frequent pattern involves one of the characters positioned between the other two. For example, in the opening sequence we are positioned in the back seat of the car, so to speak, as Andrzej and Krystyna in the front seat argue about her driving skills. Suddenly, the small figure of the student hiker appears in the distance between their heads, growing larger as the car speeds towards it. Visually it seems as though the student will split the couple apart, an impression which is later confirmed by events. This pattern is repeated once the student himself takes his place in the back seat of the car; from behind, we still see his head right between theirs.

In other scenes it is the two men who are at the extremes of a diagonal, along the sailboat's deck, for example, with Krystyna between them. For most of the film, it is Andrzej who is giving orders from the stern to the student who is at the front of the boat. Krystyna functions essentially as a sexual object; she lies outstretched on the deck in a bikini. Whenever she emerges from the cabin below deck, the camera peers down at her cleavage, putting the spectator in the role of voyeur (whether or not such a shot is motivated as another character's point of view). Krystyna's body is essential in keeping before us the male erotic drives that determine the action.

Andrzej is associated with the sailboat itself. His knowledge of sailing is his key to power, a symbol of his efficacy and his virility, as the other two characters are at the mercy of his skills. When the student suggests that sailing is not very difficult, Andrzej invites him to try his hand at it, but then subtly manipulates the rudder so that the sail and mast swing around, almost knocking the student into the water. The student's prop is his main tool, his knife, which enables him to survive in the wilderness. In a series of parallel scenes, Andrzej exhibits his knowledge of sailing, while the student demonstrates the usefulness of his knife in solving a series of practical problems, from preparing food to clearing reeds through which the sailboat must pass. The phallic symbolism of both props is quite clearly suggested in the visual compositions which feature them. The boat is seen in long shots, slicing into and through the water, with Andrzej manipulating the rudder, another auxiliary phallic object. When the student pulls out his 'phallus', the knife, it is from a sheath at his belt. When he presses a button, the knife snaps out directly in front of him, springing into an erection, so to speak.

Other elongated objects also play similar roles, particularly Andrzej's various gadgets, one of them a plier-like tool for holding on to the edge of a hot pot. When the student laughs at this middle-class contrivance, suggesting that it is a sign of weakness, Andrzej invites him to try holding the pot without it. The student does this, but it is obvious that he is in great pain, until Krystyna intervenes and knocks the pot out of his hands. The student is left with burns on his palms; other shots also suggest his Christ-like martyrdom (he lies on the deck with a rope coiled beneath his head like a halo in a painting of Christ; he climbs the ship's cross-shaped mast; and he appears to walk on water when he hangs over the edge of the racing sailboat, swinging his legs), but in the end we appreciate the irony of such suggestions. When the student finally does gain the upper hand he is just as cruel and exploitative as Andrzej had been.

Virtually all of the contests between the student and Andrzej involve the two main phallic objects or temporary stand-ins for them. The student plays a game with his knife which involves holding it in his right hand and moving the sharp blade rapidly between the fingers of his left. Andrzej, in order to demonstrate his equanimity in the face of this potentially threatening display of phallic skill, offers his own hand for the game. The student begins to move the blade very rapidly between Andrzej's fingers, but then lifts his head to look Andrzej in the eye while continuing to move the knife in rapid rhythm, clearly flaunting his complete control over Andrzej's fate. In order to reverse the power dynamic, Andrzej suddenly seizes the student's hand and orders him to go below deck and get the first-aid kit so that the burns on his palms can be treated (thus Andrzej, the solicitous conqueror, seeks to remind the student of his earlier defeat). When Andrzej and Krystyna go in for a swim, the student uses his apparent inability to control the sailboat in the wind to make it difficult for Andrzej to get back to the boat; he 'ineptly' steers the boat away from him whenever he gets close. Krystyna, in her role as mediator, eventually positions herself strategically so as to catch the boat.

The games accelerate when the sailboat runs aground in a sudden storm. Below deck, the trio passes the time playing pick-up-sticks (another game with phallic props, one at which Andrzej excels). The punishment for losing is forfeits, and the losing characters (Andrzej never loses) begin to remove articles of clothing as their penalties, so the game also turns into a striptease of Krystyna's alluring body. Finally, the student forfeits his knife, but instead of placing it on the table he hurls it at a cutting board on the cabin's opposite wall. Andrzej retrieves the knife and does even better, hitting the cutting board dead centre. The next morning, Krystyna and the student have arisen early and are talking on the deck; the conversation is innocent, but the setting – two young people alone, early dawn, Krystyna's partially undressed state – make it seem like an erotic encounter. Andrzej awakens below deck and seemingly responds to what we, the spectators, are seeing. He angrily removes the student's knife from the cutting board and pockets it, as if to emasculate the student. Once the ship is set upright, Andrzej begins to order the student around, demonstrating in no uncertain terms his command of the ship. It is at this point that the student notices that he does not have his knife. Andrzej admits that he has it, but when the student demands to have it back, Andrzej throws the knife at the mast, intending to once again impress with his skill. But he misses. The knife falls into the lake. The student orders Andrzej to jump in after it, but, of course, Andrzej refuses. A fight ensues and the student is knocked off the speeding sailboat into the lake; he disappears beneath the waves.

At the film's conclusion, the battles for power and for control over sexuality implied through the play with props become explicit. The student appears to have drowned. Krystyna accuses Andrzej of being a coward for refusing to go for help; to prove his courage and masculinity, Andrzej dives into the water and swims toward shore. The student reappears once Krystyna has removed her wet bathing suit and is wrapped only in a towel. Although she castigates the student with brutal frankness for his cowardice, she makes love to him nonetheless. The ship reaches shore and the student departs, but Krystyna manages to assert her control over her dominating husband by presenting him with the following dilemma as they once again sit in the front seat of their car: either drive to the police station to admit that he has drowned the student by knocking him into the water or believe her story that the student is still alive, so alive that she made love to him. The film ends at this point, with a shot that virtually replicates the couple's position in their car at the beginning of the film. But the dynamic of power within the relationship has been reversed by Krystyna's taking possession of her own sexuality.

It is not possible here to subject all of the films in Polanski's oeuvre to a detailed analysis of the spatial relationships and props which foreground and emphasise each film's power relationships and (usually) their underlying sexual nature. In the more schematic films which Polanski himself authored or co-authored, this structure is very evident and palpable because of the director's tendency to organise his films in a highly structured way, utilising a developing set of binary oppositions. However, in films based on complex literary works or the filmscripts of others, Polanski was obligated to include much more in the way of the story's actions and explicit dialogue, so that the visual semantics are more intermittant and submerged. This is the situation in films like *Macbeth*, *Chinatown* and *Tess*. On the other hand, when Polanski played the major role in creating the story and scripting it, as was the case, for example, in *Repulsion* and in *The Tenant*, the density and importance of visual paradigms is much more evident.

Repulsion (which Polanski wrote together with his frequent collaborator, Gérard Brach) was at times characterised as a film portraying quite realistically a paranoid schizophrenic who descends into catatonia and murderous violence. The film's acclaim, however, testifies to the fact that it deals with a much more universal theme – the sexual exploitation of women. The limited world of the film's main character Carol (played by the then very young Catherine Deneuve) provided Polanski with the logical motivation for using the kind of structure that he had developed in his earlier films: a restricted set of repeated images, leading first to intensifications of the dynamics of power and violence, and then to their reversal. Carol is the principal character (and often the only character) in the film's sequences, most of which are set in the apartment she shares with her older sister, who is away on vacation. The film's early sequences, which seemingly depict Carol's everyday life, subtly detail the sexual objectification which a beautiful young woman is subject to in Western societies; as is typical in Polanski's films, the spectator is made to participate, as voyeur, in the fetishisation of the woman's body. Carol works as a manicurist at a beauty salon and as she walks home, three workmen ogle her body, one seems to lurch at her uttering some profanity under his breath. In the scenes where Carol is walking on the streets, the camera frequently drops down to the level of the pavement, for no other reason than to give us a better view of Carol's legs. A handsome young man named Colin (John Fraser) attempts to pick Carol up, another typical event in the day of a beautiful young woman. She agrees to a dinner date only reluctantly.

In subsequent scenes, the spectator is continually implicated in a pattern of desire which replicates Colin's (although he is not present). In the apartment, we watch as Carol takes off her dress and walks around (in most of the film's scenes) only in a slip. In the bathroom, Carol lifts her bare leg into the sink, hiking her skirt up to the very top of her thigh. She strokes her leg very sensuously as she washes it; the spectator's scopophilic pleasure is the only motivation for such sequences (they do not serve the narrative of actions in any logical way). Sexual intercourse punctuates the film. There are two scenes where Carol cannot sleep because of the moans of her sister, who is reaching orgasm with her lover in the adjoining bedroom (the dramatically intensifying moans are like those subsequently common in soft-core porn films). On the mornings after, Carol reacts pointedly to a spot of blood on her sister's bedsheet, a reaction which sets off another recurring motif: throughout the film, Carol repeatedly brushes her hand across her nose or her blouse, as if she is trying to cleanse herself of some sort of invasive residue. The sister's boyfriend and Carol's co-workers are both sources of sexual stories and innuendoes, which serve to keep Carol's visibly evident sexual desirability constantly in the foreground for the spectator; Carol is either the object of mild sexual advances or we tend to place her in the context of the stories we hear.

Phallic props play a very prominent role in the film's most striking and unusual shots. Several times in the film, Carol removes, with gestures of fear and repulsion, her sister's boyfriend's straight-edged razor and his toothbrush from a glass in the bathroom (she and we first notice them when she is washing her leg in the sink; these objects are thus in close proximity to her thigh, and sexual penetration comes to mind almost immediately). At first, Carol throws these objects away, but the razor seems to continually return; Carol eventually places it on a plate with the film's most striking recurrent prop, a skinned half-rabbit (the sister's boyfriend had earlier referred to Carol as a 'poor bunny'). Carol's sister had intended to prepare the rabbit for dinner, but after she leaves it simply remains on a plate, first in the refrigerator and later on a shelf where Carol places it. The rabbit's naked skinned body is visually suggestive of a nude woman's torso or, alternately, an engorged penis (both the sexually aroused male organ and its object). There are many shots of this rabbit's torso and once it is placed on the shelf, a pool of blood grows around it. When the straight razor is added to the plate, the image's evocation of sexual violence is overdetermined.

Another image of impending sexual violation is the fissure which opens in the apartment wall (in a clinical interpretation of the film, this image would be regarded as Carol's hallucination as she becomes more deranged). On one of her earlier walks, Carol had been transfixed by a crack in the pavement, in a Y-shape suggestive of a woman's crotch. This is precisely the shape of the crack which opens in the apartment wall; it recurs and grows through the film's second half, to the accompaniment of an earthquake-like sound. The same sound effect is present in a series of rape scenes which Carol imagines, but which the spectator experiences as quite real, since they are not cinematographically different from the everyday events. Carol closes the door to her bedroom and, in the mirror, sees a man lurking behind it; when she turns the man is not really there. Later there is an unexplained light under the door of the adjoining room. Finally, there are scenes where a man resembling the one who had accosted her on the street breaks into her room as she sleeps, presses her face into her pillow, and rapes her from behind. We may understand from the narrative that these are only events which Carol is imagining; that, however, does not prevent them from being viscerally horrifying.

Such visual images and props motivate the film's ending. Carol seizes phallic power herself, quite literally, and avenges her 'imagined' rapes. This transformation is prefigured at the beauty salon, where, for no apparent reason, Carol suddenly cuts the finger of an older woman whom she is manicuring; blood spurts out. When the ardent Colin is so presumptuous as to force his way into her apartment when she refuses to answer the phone, she strikes him over the head with a metal candlestick and kills him (blood spurts out again, of course). Finally, when the lecherous landlord, who has come to collect the rent, realises the vulnerability of the scantily-clad Carol and attempts to seduce her, she cuts his throat with the razor. On its more literal level, the film ends predictably with Carol taken off to a mental institution, once her sister and her sister's boyfriend return. However, a more important universal meaning is quite evident. The everyday world is filled with sexual aggression against women and their disempowerment. Polanski suggests that the impulse to reverse this situation is strong in women, that as victims they must naturally want to seize power themselves and become the victimisers. The film also ends with a return to its initial shot, a close-up of Carol's eye. Now the camera pans around the bedroom and settles on an old family photograph showing Carol, perhaps twelve years old, with her sister, her parents and another man, perhaps an uncle. The film ends by zooming in on her catatonic stare in the photo. Did her obsessive fear of men and of sex begin with an incestuous rape, which she has now avenged? As different as the films are in genre, there are pronounced structural resemblances between *Knife in the Water* and *Repulsion* in terms of the reversal of power within an exploitative sexualised relationship.

The relevance of *Repulsion* to Polanski's own biography and personal psychology became apparent in *The Tenant*. Like *Repulsion*, the film focuses on a single character, the Polish émigré Trelkovsky, living in Paris, and is set for the most part in an apartment which he rents at the beginning of the film. The film begins with an image of a woman standing at the apartment window, an image which dissolves into one of Trelkovsky (played by Polanski himself) standing at the same window. We learn, as Trelkovsky does, that the apartment's previous tenant (her furniture and belongings still fill the apartment) had jumped out of the window and is in the hospital, not expected to recover. When Trelkovsky visits the hospital he finds that previous tenant, Simone Choule, with her head completely encased in bandages – only one eye is exposed, and her gaping mouth with one tooth missing (this image might already be suggestive of sexual violation) – when Simone tries to speak only a long blood-curdling scream emerges from her mouth, echoing through the hospital's hallway.

After Trelkovsky occupies the apartment he is steadily and increasingly harassed and tormented by the landlord and his neighbours, in spite of the fact that he is exceptionally polite, soft-spoken and accommodating. There is a subplot that shows us that he is interested in a sexual relationship (with Simone's friend Stella), but insecure and hesitating in his pursuit of it. Like Carol in *Repulsion*, Trelkovsky begins to go mad, the process suggested visually through props – Simone's missing tooth, which Trelkovsky finds in a hole in the wall; mysterious hieroglyphics on the wall of the bathroom; a hallucination of a mummified woman who unwraps herself in that bathroom. Eventually, Trelkovsky begins to dress up in Simone's clothes and to become her (we might note here that *shule* is Yiddish for synagogue, thus evoking Simone's possibly Jewish identity, and, by association, Trelkovsky's). The film concludes with Trelkovsky hurling himself from the window in imitation of Simone's attempted suicide, not once, but twice. After the first attempt, the bloodied Trelkovsky manages to crawl back up the circular staircase, several flights, only to throw himself out of the window again as the amazed residents of the apartment building watch from their windows as from the side balconies of an opera house. The film ends with Trelkovsky in the hospital bed, with one eye exposed and gaping mouth with missing tooth; now *he* screams as he sees himself approach with Stella. His transformation into the victim is complete. Thus, even though violation initially has external sources, the victim is compulsively driven to repeat it. Evil as an endlessly recurring event is an underlying feature in most of Polanski's work.

In *Chinatown*, perhaps Polanski's best and most well-known film, the director was working with an excellent filmscript written by Robert Towne, to which he adhered very closely in terms of characters, plot and dialogue. However, Polanski elaborated and extended key elements of the visual imagery and made several important changes in the script itself. In the tradition of the American film noir, *Chinatown* features a private-eye hero, Jake Gittes (Jack Nicholson), who investigates extra-marital affairs as his *métier* (as he puts it), but is drawn into a much more complex network of crime involving large-scale capitalist interests arrayed against the people of Los Angeles and the small farmers of the nearby Valley, who are coerced and duped so that a dam will be built to make the arch capitalist villain, Noah Cross (John Huston), even wealthier than he already is. There is, however, an incest subplot which emerges as the real motivation for Cross's murder of his former business partner, Hollis Mulwray (Darrell Zwerling), whose wife Evelyn (Faye Dunaway) is the apparent *femme fatale* to whom Gittes is attracted. It is the imagery which is developed around this subplot that is most reminiscent of Polanski's earlier work in its embodiment of disempowerment.

The incest subplot has a clearly oedipal design, suggested by the Biblical character names – Noah, the ultimate patriarch (who, with his sons, literally repopulated the world through incestuous relationships after the Deluge); Jake Gittes (Jacob, the son of a patriarch, who aspires to become one himself); and Evelyn (Eve), destined to be blamed for evil she did not cause. In Towne's screenplay, the mysteries are well hidden, so that the spectator is unlikely to understand the real nature of things any sooner than Gittes himself does. Jake is an admirer of Franklin Roosevelt and sympathetic to the plight of the common man; he quickly suspects that he is up against corrupt power. In his attempts to investigate, he has his nose sliced open by one of Cross's henchman (blood spurts out copiously, and it is Polanski himself who plays the smallish thug who does the slicing!). Thus symbolically castrated, Gittes retains the mark of his disempowerment throughout the rest of the film – first as a very large white bandage on his nose and later as a reddish wound marked by a prominent row of stitches.

Evelyn has been mutilated (disempowered) as well, through her rape by her father Noah. She bears a symbolic mark of this as a black spot in the iris of her eye (a birth defect which might itself be associated with incest, thus seemingly extending Noah's transgression one generation further into the past). In terms of the imagery, Jake and Evelyn seem to bond over their mutual disempowerment – as she caresses his wounded nose with a cotton swab, he notices the flaw in her eye (Polanski elaborated visual aspects of this scene, going beyond the screenplay's directions). In this respect, the film recalls earlier alliances in Polanski's films, for example that between the student and Krystyna in *Knife in the Water*. But Jake persistently fails to read Evelyn's mark as a sign of vulnerability; he sees Evelyn's reluctance to share information about her past with him as evidence of her culpability and her determination to retain superior knowledge and power. Evelyn has hidden the daughter Noah fathered, Catherine, from him, with the help of Hollis, who married her to protect her. Noah is determined to find this daughter, now a young woman of fifteen, and the film's chilling ending makes clear his likely intent, as he engulfs her in a spider-like embrace. We are presented with an image of incest extending indefinitely into the future as Jake and Evelyn are defeated by a powerful patriarch who will rule everything at the film's end.

Polanski evokes visual representations of a broken or wounded eye repeatedly throughout the film, to link the notion of castration (as blinding) with the inability to see things clearly, essentially a deficit of knowledge and power that Jake cannot overcome. Jake is typically arrogant and self-assured, he refuses to trust Evelyn at a key point in the narrative, and he understands the overall situation only partially. His power (knowledge) is insufficient and this causes him, at the end, to facilitate the horrifying and disastrous result he had hoped to avert. The image which Polanski uses is that of two lenses or circles, one whole and one broken, a motif repeated in many ways throughout the film (here, too, Polanski added details not in the original filmscript in order to achieve the effect): as two watches seen alongside one another, one with its face smashed (Gittes had placed it under a tire to mark the time of Hollis's departure); as Jake's sunglasses with one lens smashed after a fight; as the flaw in one of Evelyn's eyes; as one blown-out tire alongside a whole one, one disabled tail-light next to one still lit. When Evelyn is finally killed at the end of the film, one of her eyes is blown out, leaving, very graphically, only a bloody socket next to a whole eye. Thus, the image captures disempowerment as an inability to see, as a symbolic castration, and finally, as rape (a suggested meaning of bloody orifices and wounds in many of Polanski's films). Jake, himself a victim, is inadvertently complicit in Evelyn's destruction.

The analyses presented here can be extended to encompass most of Polanski's films. His ability to capture in such a visceral way the strong emotions accompanying disempowerment and to constantly hold them before our eyes in his visual imagery is arguably the most compelling aspect of his filmmaking. An attempt to reverse the disempowerment is generally at the heart of the films he has written or chosen to realise on the screen. The results are almost always tragic. With only a few exceptions either the protagonist is defeated, returned to a disempowered state, or the protagonist succeeds, only to become the very evil he has struggled against. It is very tempting to speculate about the extent to which the films replay elements of Polanski's own life, but that would be the subject of a rather different kind of study. What is certain is that Polanski, in embodying this dynamic in his films, has touched an aspect of human relationships which is unfortunately widespread, underlying many historical events, social realities and, most prominently, the power dynamics of gender and sexuality.

CHAPTER FOUR

Polanski and the Horror from Within

Tony McKibbin

The horror genre usually creates characters that function as narrative ciphers moving the plot along from one point of tension to the next. Certainly the characters are often plausible enough to carry the plot. But that is just the point – they are subordinated to the non-human elements and the psychology of character is only as realistic as the story demands. Central to this notion, according to Robert Baird, is the startle effect – the way in which filmmakers generate a fairly primitive suspense out of sudden, emotional impact – so that a standard character can react in a standard way to certain situations (2000: 13). Polanski does not eschew such horror effects as the startle, but in his work we see how they are subordinated to character. Hence, instead of narrative ciphers who are plausible, we have characters who, in all their psychological deviations, are vividly realised through plot, but not at the mercy of its exigencies. In this chapter we shall explore why Polanski is one of the great filmmakers of interior horror.

Cinematic startles

Roman Polanski has always been seen as a filmmaker slightly beyond the horror genre, with *Repulsion*, *Rosemary's Baby* and *The Tenant* working off psychology more than terror. Thus can we not say that what makes Polanski so important to the genre is the way he combines useful conventions of horror with the demands of the psychological probe? For often, of course, what the horror film demands is not explication of character but creation of atmosphere, an atmosphere well touched upon by Baird, who writes about the way 'garden variety startles provide an affective punctuation to various folk entertainments such as hide and seek, surprise parties, spook houses' (ibid.). Baird states that many laymen and some philosophers and psychologists have not been satisfied in reducing startles to simple reflexes, but reckons 'that film startles occur only during a particular scene type', alerting us 'that something complicated and odd is occurring' (ibid.).

Baird goes on to give examples from *Cat People* (Jacques Tourneur, 1942), *Wait Until Dark* (Terence Young, 1967) and *Jaws* (Steven Spielberg, 1975). Now taking *Jaws* as an example, we can see that the effect created is based on 'pure' atmosphere, with minimal psychological underpinning. When the scuba-diving Matt Hooper (Richard Dreyfuss) gets startled by a corpse that pops out of the hull of the boat it is the startle of the practical man shocked by the tangible. When Carol (Catherine Deneuve) is startled by the doorbell ringing in *Repulsion*, we could call this the neurotic startle. The startle does not have the 'objective' effect – how many of us would not be started if we were in Hooper's position? – but a 'subjective' effect. Is it not merely the sound of a doorbell? In *Repulsion* we notice the atmosphere, while no less central than the atmosphere in *Jaws*, works much more from inside the character's head.

Obviously we could say even quite straightforward terror films work from inside a character's head. We can see it in the oft-used dream sequence, where a character wakes up after apparently being killed. But the purpose here is usually to generate an atmosphere of terror over the interior necessity of exploring behavioural subjectivity. Even when the horror dream sequence becomes the very subject of a film – as in *A Nightmare on Elm Street* (Wes Craven, 1984) – this is not really about the central character's neurosis, it is about a cinematic conceit. Its purpose is to wonder what might happen if someone were being haunted quite literally by their nightmares – if every time they fell asleep they were in danger of being killed. We could say then that the leading character in *A Nightmare on Elm Street* is merely a cipher to atmosphere; in *Repulsion* Polanski adopts atmosphere to explore the nature of exiled being. Here Carol's a young Belgian woman living an isolated life in London, a life made all the more so when her sister with whom she is sharing the flat goes off on holiday with her lover. Carol works in a beauty salon but connects with nobody and though she potentially has a handsome boyfriend who cares, she is too alienated to register his empathy. What Polanski does here is create enough 'interiority' to minimise traditional shock and startle effects. While Baird talks about 'garden variety startles', Polanski's are of a rarer breed. The startle comes from the way Polanski lays out the milieu, to the extent that the notion of startle itself seems somehow inappropriate. Instead of the startle on the calm nervous system, in Polanski we often have the minor external gesture creating internal anxiety. We see it for example in the jitteriness of Trelkovsky (Roman Polanski) in *The Tenant* when he is confronted by his landlord the morning after a party. Poor Trelkovsky has only had the party under duress – after acquaintances have barged in and taken over his flat – but he nervously apologises as his neurotic state takes another punishment that would have little effect on a more contained nervous system.

This *neurotic state receiving punishment* is the Kafkan side to Polanski. When Kafka says in 'Letter to his Father', 'what I got from you … was a hesitant, stammering mode of speech, and even that was still too much for you, and finally I kept silent, at first perhaps from defiance, and then because I couldn't either think or speak in your presence' (1976: 563), it once again brings to mind Trelkovsky, with his demeanour always retreating out of a situation before he has even got into one. But it also reminds us of Carol in *Repulsion*, who cannot quite enter into communication with the young man who sympathetically wants to become her friend and lover, or Rosemary (Mia Farrow), in *Rosemary's Baby*, whose nervousness means on some occasions she can hardly enter a roomful of people. Sure, when she enters the neighbours' flat at the film's conclusion, she thinks her baby's been given over to the Devil, but Polanski at this stage is still playing off Rosemary's paranoia over our full awareness of the devilish deeds of her husband and neighbours. It is this 'terrible uncertainty of one's inner existence', as Kafka once put it, that is so often central to the haunting aspect of the director's work.

It is maybe even this terrible uncertainty that drew Polanski to adapting *The Pianist*. Certainly on one level it is yet another big-budget English-language appropriation of the Holocaust, and obviously Polanski's working through of his own demons where his mother was exterminated in the camps and his life was endangered by the Nazis. But it is also a very fine example of the increasing uncertainty of a character's inner existence as the external aspects are chipped away. What Polanski wants to do here is suggest not so much a neurotic man's response to his environment (as in *The Tenant*), but much more the process of collapse when many of the external support systems in one's own life have been removed. From the early stages where the Jewish family cannot call their furniture their own any more, to a neighbour being thrown out of a window, through to the extermination of his family, we watch as Wladyslaw Szpilman is internally excavated. The film brings to mind Primo Levi's despairing statement *If This is a Man*, but it is also a Polanski constant: the idea of a human being in a state of ill-ease menaced by something bigger than the moment. When quite late in the film Szpilman is advised to throw himself out of the window rather than face capture, this serves a practical necessity – if he is caught he could be tortured and give away the name of his saviour – but throwing himself out of the window would also kill the nerves of a man who has been living on the edge of them for too long. It would not quite be suicide, but it could be an impulsive leap, the leap that brings to mind the ending of *The Tenant*, where Trelkovsky goes the way of the previous tenant after feeling himself harassed and mentally tortured by the neighbours.

If we see this as the key scene in *The Pianist* (the scene that conjures up so much of Polanski's other work) it is because we sense Szpilman moving beyond the external necessity of surviving, to the internal possibility of ending a life that is running out of meaning and which has been replaced by a life plagued by fear. Szpilman moves from that of a man who is part of an extended family and with a reasonable standard of living, to a man with no family and a life of constant threat. There is the threat of starvation, of capture, of death. How to regain a degree of control over one's existence? Perhaps by throwing oneself out of a window.

When we talk of inverting the startle effect, this is what we mean. It is no longer a case of a definite menace alleviated, but often a possible terror assumed. And it is this accumulation of possible terrors that create the Kafkan uncertainty, an uncertainty that can lead to one's own death, another's murder or to mental collapse. In *Repulsion* Carol kills the very man she could maybe have turned to: the handsome Londoner who shows her love and affection. She has become so involved in her own world, so scared of both an inner and outer existence, that it is no surprise when she kills the man who pops round simply to ask how she is doing.

Eschewing genre boundaries

Now some critics would see Polanski as a serious horror filmmaker because he eschews the explicit aspect central to much horror. For a critic like W. H. Rockett, filmmakers who go in for an Aristotelian notion of closure, and who offer categorical images of evil, lack the sublimity of terror, and this, Christine Gledhill believes, allows for Rockett's value judgement take on the genre, and resembles that old saw about suggestion being better than explication. As Gledhill says, 'Rockett's description … rests on a judgement of value' (1999: 198). But we need not fall into value judgements here. We are more intrigued by Polanski's singularity than his pantheonistic place within horror. So while it is true Polanski is interested in the creation of atmosphere over the notion of explicit realisation, this is not a brownie-point exercise in sublimity of terror. It is the need to explore a certain aspect of neurotic existence to which the horror genre lends itself. This means some of Polanski's films fall easily into horror (*Repulsion* and *Rosemary's Baby*), others touch upon it (*The Tenant*), and some have no obvious link with the genre at all (*Death and the Maiden* and *The Pianist*), but still have much in common with the films that do, and even of the feelings generated by horror cinema.

Let us take *Death and the Maiden*, for example. Here we have another traumatised woman. Paulina (Sigourney Weaver) lives in an isolated house in an unnamed South American country shortly after the fall of a dictatorship. The opening sequence suggests the horror film: Paulina is alone in the house and the camera follows her as she busies herself making dinner and listening to the radio. There is a storm with thunder and lightning, and we see her startle. She checks the phone: it has gone dead. Polanski cuts to a close-up of a kitchen knife. All these details conjure up the atmosphere of the horror film, but instead of Paulina being terrorised by an intruder, it is the intruder who is terrorised by Paulina. It turns out a man her husband has been given a lift home by may well be her former torturer. But of course Paulina's torturing of Dr Miranda (Ben Kingsley) comes out of her own tortured mind. The potential for a 'woman in peril' film – *Halloween* (John Carpenter, 1978), *Friday the 13th* (Sean G. Cunningham, 1980) – is inverted by the fact that the peril is in the past, and her present state is a manifestation of that past peril. Throughout the interrogation, as she tries to find out for sure if Miranda is who she thinks he is, Miranda's presence brings back aspects of her past pains. Any startle here is essentially the shiver of recollection. Even the moment early in the film – as she listens to the radio announcer talking about human rights violations, and she is startled by the thunder and lightning – comes out of that shiver of recollection. Hence we see how Polanski inverts the 'woman in peril' film, how he turns it not into a series of external threats, but a series of internal memory threats. We can see the inversion again when Paulina takes and eats her dinner in a small cupboard. The cupboard in horror is usually the hiding place from the intruder, but here it seems much more a psychological retreat, and maybe the place of curious comfort; the very type of enclosed space she occupied when being tortured. Paulina thus becomes both victim and torturer: her own former discomfort offering a perverse form of comfort in the present.

She is a figure resembling, we could say, Mark Lewis in *Peeping Tom* (Michael Powell, 1960), and thus illustrates Polanski again touching upon the horror genre. According to Carol Clover, this victim/torturer stance is exactly the position Mark occupies in Powell's film where his need to kill women with his spiked camera is not just sadism, but is animated by, and stems from, 'his own historical pain' (1992: 176). What we have in such an approach is horror by other means, and means so abstract that we would struggle to call *Death and the Maiden* ostensibly a horror film at all.

So what we can say is that *Death and the Maiden* falls into Polanski's mini-genre of 'inverted woman in peril' films, alongside *Repulsion* and *Rosemary's Baby* (if we see the peril from within the vague feeling of unease in Rosemary's very womb), just as *The Pianist* falls into Polanski's version of what Paul Schrader once called 'one man and his room' films, which would also include *Repulsion* and *The Tenant*. This does not mean we are looking for clear taxonomies, merely for useful groupings, useful ways into Polanski's idea of horror. When we talk of Polanski's 'inverted woman in peril' films, we are not looking to say anything especially about the horror film, but we are trying to locate something essential in Polanski's work. We are looking to find out what makes Polanski a filmmaker who sometimes seems close to a hack, but on other occasions so close to a major explorer of human nature.

The horror of loneliness

Looking at the 'one man (or woman) and his room' films we might be reminded of Pascal's comment about man's biggest problem stemming from the idea that he cannot spend time in his room alone. What is it, Polanski asks, that makes it so difficult for one to stand one's own company? Polanski might answer that it is not being alone, so much as being invaded by past presences. When Polanski ends *Repulsion* on a picture of Carol with her family, we can read it two ways. Was Carol always a lonely child who never connected with anyone, not even her family, or is the psychosis rooted in that family? And in *The Tenant* is Trelkovsky just a lonely man, or is it more that he has spent so much of his life losing in human encounters that he has never quite expressed himself, never quite revealed what he thinks and feels to other human beings? When he finds himself increasingly obsessed with the previous tenant who, after the suicide attempt, can offer no more than a horrible attempt at communication through a faceful of bandages, is this a metaphor for Trelkovsky's own lack of communicative possibilities? Of course Szpilman in *The Pianist* does not start from a position of neurosis, but as the film progresses, as he loses his family bit by bit, does the idea of spending time alone in a room become too much for him? The idea of jumping from a great height and joining the rest of his family in death must be a constant temptation, but a temptation so much stronger when one is left with nothing but memories and silence and a small room with an open window. Thus we might be tempted to reinterpret loneliness here, and to see it less as being alone than as being in the presence of too many half-presences, imaginary figures who are never quite present or absent.

Polanski's work thus brings to mind Sartre in *The Psychology of the Imagination* (1972) when he talks about how we perceive a friend elsewhere. For Sartre our imagination serves as a way of keeping in mind the many people whom we know, but whose presence is physically absent. Now in each of us this works to different degrees. Some of us need minimal contact with another human being to hold them in our imaginary, others need a constant reaffirmation of that presence. But frequently this absent presence generates neurosis. We can see it in the initial stages of *Death and the Maiden*, where Weaver's character hides out in the cupboard as if once again on some level at the mercy of her torturer. We see it in *Repulsion*, with Carol imagining hands coming out of walls and groping at her body. Loneliness in such instances is not about being alone, but having absent presences invading one's existence.

Again invoking Kafka, there is a great short story that pinpoints this problem of loneliness and the imaginary. In *A Little Woman*, the narrator reckons a woman who is 'an utter stranger' hates him. Hearing she is physically ill, he says

> I feel a certain responsibility laid upon me, if you like to put it that way, for strangers as we are to each other, the little woman and myself, and however true it is that the whole connection between us is the vexation I cause her, or rather the vexation she lets me cause her, I ought not to feel indifferent to the visible physical suffering this induces in her. (Kafka 1988: 318)

What we have is a projected feeling passing for reality, and a projected feeling that in its intensity is actually a reality. Now maybe if the narrator had more 'reality' in his life – more social interaction – this 'imaginary reality' would be diluted by an 'actual reality'. Even when the narrator discusses the issue with an apparently good friend, the friend firmly believes he should keep the 'affair within its present narrow limits which do not yet involve the outside world' (Kafka 1988: 321). This sense of keeping things to oneself is one of the key problems with loneliness the way Polanski approaches it. Loneliness often releases an over-active imaginary. Now sometimes this overactive imaginary has a real history (as in *Death and the Maiden*), a strange almost demonic presence (*The Tenant*) or a pervasive recent past (*The Pianist*). But what is consistent is the danger of creating a pernicious imaginary.

Now in American cinema a character being alone is a rare trait. It is, after all, a cinema of social values, so the examination of isolated characters we find in European filmmakers (in Robert Bresson and Eric Rohmer for example) gives way to the immediacy of social interaction – often of tasks to be performed and situations to be resolved. The presence of a character alone in an American film is often utilised in horror to suggest vulnerability. But usually this is not an emotional vulnerability as in Bresson's *Four Nights of the Dreamer* (*Quatre nuits d'un rêveur*, 1971) or Rohmer's *The Green Ray* (*Le Rayon vert*, 1986), but a physical vulnerability – a trip to the shower, a walk in the woods – resulting in a character's demise. Polanski wants to work off something that is in-between a European aloneness and an American being alone. There is often in Polanski the American cinematic notion of a lonely character being menaced, but the characters are usually menaced by an interior characteristic, an impulse or psychological aspect that is closer to the expectations of art-house film. But by tying a vivid imaginary to the idea of loneliness Polanski asks of the horror film a degree of subtlety and the art-house film a degree of literalisation.

The confines of space

But finally we might ask to what end? The notion of subtle cinema is all very well but it is only useful if we can apply the term not as a relative compliment within the horror genre, but if it usefully addresses more fundamental questions of being. Has Polanski managed to offer us a fresh perspective on being? Has he given us a performative case study in neurosis? When Trelkovsky throws himself out of the window at the end of *The Tenant*, what has Polanski offered us? Let us say it is amongst other things the comprehension of urban living as a space of simultaneous socialisation and isolation. Trelkovsky's problem is not only that he is possessed of a loneliness that leads to an over-active imaginary, it is also that he has never been quite alone enough nor sociable enough to live what Jung would call an 'individuated' life (1964: 160–1). When Jung talks about individuation, he is talking about man's ability to unite himself with himself, to combine social values with internal personal values. Now one way to achieve this sense of self is to escape from the social values for a period of time: the sort of escape present in Jesus' forty days and forty nights in the wilderness, in the retreats of the Naskapi hunter, or teenage aborigines going walkabout.

This type of escape is not offered as an option (except perhaps ironically in *Cul-de-Sac* – where a new confinement of space occurs out of apparent open space, or too late, as in *Death and the Maiden* – where the natural isolation can add to the despair). Generally Polanski wants to turn social pressures into internal despair, not into searches for external flight. Consequently we frequently see Polanski's characters living in the very places from which they should escape. Their inability to live in their room stems, it would seem, from their inability to have found that necessary psycho-geographical space earlier in their lives. With their timid nervous systems, Carol, Trelkovsky and Rosemary live in spaces that are too small not only because they are too small, but maybe because they have never found big enough spaces to live comfortably in at an earlier stage of their lives. There is this air of un-individuation in Polanski that leaves his characters hemmed into literal space and creating out of this claustrophobia an expansive imaginary. If they could have found a way to live a psychically and geographically unified existence, would they be suffering the same problems?

This is Polanski's way of using the horror film for something more challenging. When Baird says atmosphere is absolutely central to the horror film, what he is partly talking about is this idea of space, of the way a filmmaker conjures up threat through momentary disturbance out of carefully laid-out filmic space. Baird gives as an example a scene from *Alien* (Ridley Scott, 1979):

> The *mise-en-scène* is classic dungeon darkness and gothic gloom, the literal bowels of this massive ore-mining ship. Following the readings from her motion-tracker, Ripley stops before a row of squat metal lockers. She whispers to her hunting partners, 'Parker, Brett, it's in this locker.' The three prepare to open the locker door, and Ripley gives a countdown: 'All right, Parker, when I say … right now.' From a low-angle three-shot of the tense crew members, the startle effect is timed to a shock cut of an extreme close-up of Jonesey the cat, mouth agape, scratching and shrieking inside the locker; a reaction shot of the three crew members quickly follows. (2000: 18)

Much of the fear generated out of Alejandro Amenábar's *The Others* (2001), for example, resides in this spatial excess with a hint of the enclosed. As *Time Out* critic Tom Charity points out, this is a house with fifty doors, an endless expanse of rooms (2005: 972). But it can just as easily, as Polanski shows, come out of specifically confined spaces. It is as though in the minimised space the imaginary can expand, while in the expansive space the atmosphere is more external. When Baird says that the core elements of the startle film are '(i) character presence, (ii) an implied off-screen threat, and (iii) a disturbing intrusion into the character's immediate space' (2000: 15) he is pinpointing the externally atmospheric. But the atmospherically external relies chiefly on the off-screen space as a shadowy presence often just out of frame. When Stanley J. Solomon says 'shock all too frequently springs merely from surprise … Sheer sensationalism, the standby ingredient of the genre, is of course merely an avoidance of art and thought' (1976: 112) what he is getting at is the externally presented atmosphere. Obviously he throws around a few value judgements, but that need not invalidate the argument. If horror is so often seen as an insubstantial area of cinema it may lie in the idea that off-screen space is so much more important than, say, off-screen time. By utilising characters who are in a state of nervous exhaustion to begin with (characters like Trelkovsky, Carol and Rosemary), Polanski suggests this off-screen time, and then manipulates minimal off-screen space (how many of Polanski's films could be plays?) to create the necessary horror effects by other means, by more psychological means.

Issues of space and time

We might compare Polanski's approach to David Fincher's semi-horror outing, *Panic Room* (2002). For Fincher, the besieged Jodie Foster and her child must fend off three hoods that break into their apartment. What Fincher looks for here is not human texture but a spatial tension: how does he generate a cat and mouse game of intelligence between the ultra-astute and quick-thinking Foster, and the vicious crims? Though Fincher is working in an enclosed space (more or less Foster's apartment) nevertheless he makes the space as expansive as possible to generate external tension. Certainly there are emotional problems (Foster's husband has left her for a younger woman), but these are not present as aspects of a psychological probe, they are more reasons to set in motion a degree of vulnerability and a degree of distrust. In Polanski it is usually the vulnerability and distrust that makes acting so difficult. Where in Fincher's film we have Foster finding ingenious ways to escape the panic room of the title – a special room in which Foster hides out but that becomes a room in which she is trapped – in Polanski the how question is closer to a why question. The how question asks how can Foster beat the criminals; the why question asks what case history created so much neurosis and despair in the protagonists. This, then, is what we mean by off-screen time – the degree to which actions taken – or not taken – contain internal responses.

Now maybe one reason why we are justifiably suspicious of the surprise endings of many horror films is that they try to create this internalisation but utilise it merely as a shock effect. When a horror film suggests everything is a dream – everything is an internalisation – then we need not dismiss it because it is a cliché. We need to dismiss it because it has not worked hard enough on the internalisation process. It is generally conformed to an external notion of time and space, and then shifted into an internal time and space for the purposes of the shock effect. This is perhaps true even of the more successful 'external' horror films like *A Nightmare on Elm Street* and *Carrie* (Brian De Palma, 1976). True they involve a degree of interior characterisation: the central character in *A Nightmare on Elm Street* is plagued by nightmares that can kill; Carrie has telekinetic powers and a crazy, oppressive mum. But the interiorisations are shallow. In *Carrie* we jump into the mind of Carrie's school colleague, Sue Snell, for the shock ending. In *A Nightmare on Elm Street* the externalised ending turns into a possible dream sequence – a logic that says more about sequel possibilities than narrative consistency.

There is maybe something puerile, then, about the notion of a shock ending. If we compare the ending of *Carrie* with the sober concluding shot in *Repulsion* we can explain this puerility. *Carrie* goes for the immediate shock effect, the startle effect, while *Repulsion* looks for the internally despairing. We could say *Carrie* also looks for a longer lasting impact. Sue cannot get Carrie out of her mind. But the film seems to want a consistent exterior atmosphere over a deeper comprehension. Thus the milky images and creamy soundtrack echo the film's opening, as director De Palma happily moves inside Sue's head not because he wants to explore her psyche, but because he can contain her dream within his own fascination with atmosphere: an atmosphere he has worked on throughout the film – a combination of soft-focus dreaminess and sudden moments of sadistic despair, exemplified in the scene where pig's blood is spilled over Carrie's head at the prom. So for De Palma (and this runs throughout his work) character is subordinated to mood; Polanski is usually much more interested in mood and atmosphere taken from character.

Horror as art and a reflection on life

What we are proposing for horror here is perhaps close to Gabriel García Marquez's comments on the subject of fantasy: 'I believe the imagination is just an instrument for producing reality and that the source of creation is always, in the last instance, reality' (quoted in Mendoza 1988: 31). This does not rule out fantastic possibilities – *Metamorphosis* had a greater impact on the writer than almost any text. It just asks for the fantastic to serve a wider problem of being. When *Carrie* ends on a shock sequence, what does it seem to be serving?

One of Baird's concluding points in his article is that many 'fear startle because it is, to a large degree, patently deterministic, an irrational expression of the mind that cannot be, in the end, reduced to free, conscious agency. Startle slept through the Enlightenment' (2000: 22). But of course one of the things a filmmaker like Polanski is capable of doing is reintroducing startle not so much through the Enlightenment but, rather, to achieve enlightenment, to achieve a better sense of self through aligning shock effects and a wider probe. In that great horror reference book, *The Aurum Film Encyclopedia: Horror* many of the films in the critics' top tens at the back of the book seemed to acknowledge this need for something more from the horror film (Hardy 1985: 397–9). Numerous titles present – *Peeping Tom, Repulsion, Vampyr* (*Vampyr – Der Traum des Allan Grey*, Carl Theodor Dreyer, 1932), *Les Yeux sans Visage* (Georges Franju, 1960), *Don't Look Now* (Nicholas Roeg, 1973), *Shivers* (David Cronenberg, 1975), *Videodrome* (David Cronenberg, 1983) – are as readily 'enlightenment' films as shock films. Shock in itself does not demand enlightenment; it demands a sensory motor reaction at its most immediate. Filmmakers who are willing to use these shock effects to achieve this sense of awareness may not necessarily be great artists – some are, some are not – but they seem part of a wider exploration than the horror genre usually demands. So if Polanski is one of these filmmakers, we could even say our title, Polanski and horror, is a misnomer, if we are led to think we are discussing Polanski and the horror genre: the influences upon him and those he has influenced. But if we think of Polanski in relation to horror, horror as a word reflecting a problem with the world rather than a genre expectation, then we can incorporate almost all of his work within the feeling of horror without worrying too much about genre pedants. It may be absurd to think of films like *Death and the Maiden*, and most especially *The Pianist*, in any generic sense, and yet there are feelings evoked that resemble those extracted by the genre film.

Yet of course Polanski does not really utilise so much as express, with the former suggesting genre convention and the latter indicative of exploring being. When John Huston once said 'motion pictures have a great deal in common with our own physiological and psychological processes' (quoted in Ebert 1997: 474) he was talking specifically about conventional techniques – the way our own blinking is equivalent, he believes, to a cut. But there is a danger that in genre cinema what you get is a petrification of these physiological and psychological responses instead of a constantly evolving phenomenology where you have to interpret the information received. Thus any shock effect should ricochet through the character and audience's being rather than impact on the viewer's immediate consciousness. It should be closer to Antonin Artaud's shock of thought than Baird's startle. From this perspective, then, we are suggesting Polanski is a great filmmaker not of generic horror but existential, even ontological horror. And thus we should look less at the films as complete forms, successfully or unsuccessfully evolved, but as a general, almost uncanny position that makes us realise certain intense states of being we can begin to comprehend because of the director's exploration. From this perspective *The Tenant* is a much 'better' horror film than *Rosemary's Baby*, which conforms to many of the narrative expectations of the horror genre (selling one's soul and the demon child the most obvious). After all, *The Tenant* works much more from Trelkovsky's horror from within. The film then generates from this Kafkan state a series of shocks to the system. And can we not stretch this provocation and say even *Death of the Maiden* is a better horror film than *Rosemary's Baby* if we accept that what is important is the degree to which the horror from within matches the horror from without, the degree to which we move towards comprehending a little of a woman's internal horror? When we talk of the inversion of the 'woman in peril' film, sure Polanski has left out many of the conventions, but he has also arrived in the process at a deeper insight into horror in one's life over horror in the genre.

So to conclude, what we have explored here is horror as an affect expressed in Polanski's films for the purposes of probing being over achieving a mastery of genre. There are others – like Wes Craven and John Carpenter – for example who are superior genre filmmakers, filmmakers who know the genre inside and out, and one might usefully explore how well they use space over time to generate horror. But do they finally compare with Polanski's occasional horrible lucidity, that awful elucidation of the terrible uncertainty of one's inner existence?

CHAPTER FIVE

Knife in the Water: Polanski's Nomadic Discourse Begins

Elżbieta Ostrowska

Interviewed in 1968, Roman Polanski said:

> I am glad I am a nomad. I have always dreamed about leaving [Poland], I have always felt that the significance given by people to borders was ridiculous … Bertrand Russell accurately wrote once that if a human being overestimates his or her own children, family, street, town, country it is because this is a way to overestimate himself or herself. (Polanski 1980: 15)

In 1979 at a press conference at the film festival in Prades he repeated this sentiment:

> I had never imagined my future in Poland. I always wanted to leave for the world, to get to know other countries, new people. I always thought that the Earth belonged to me as much as to other people. (1980: 58)

Leaving in the flesh, he departed from Poland for France in 1963. But, much earlier, Polanski had left Poland in spirit, and this is expressed in his Polish movies. The early shorts and his debut feature can be seen as acts of departure, an abnegation of the Polish mentality, tradition and culture in which he had grown up. Perhaps this was necessary for him in order to pursue his own idea of cinema and not be restrained by the ideological demands to either support or to contest communism. On the other hand this very act of going his own way can be seen as a kind of resistance.

Interviewed in 1966, Polanski expressed his belief in a kind of filmic *genius loci*:

> One cannot film every subject everywhere. Certain subjects are better suited to certain countries than to others. *Repulsion*, for example, is not a Polish subject … It does not correspond to the climate of the country … Maybe the solitude is less great there than elsewhere. (1975: 207)

These words indicate his pervasive preoccupation with specific spaces as a factor influencing people's thinking and behaviour. To put it directly, a particular story happens in a particular place, and identity is shaped and developed in this space. He clearly wants to use the possibilities offered in a fresh exploration of this and, as his later films show, this profoundly influences his ways of seeing the world. Here, however, I would like to look closely at the Polish cultural and cinematic landscape of Polanski's early shorts and, especially his debut film, *Knife in the Water* (*Nóż w wodzie*), in which his nomadic journey into world cinema began.

On entering the film school in Łódź in 1954, Polanski was already somewhat acquainted with cinema due to his minor roles in *Three stories* (*Trzy opowieści*, Konrad Nałęcki, 1953) and *A Generation* (*Pokolenie*, Andrzej Wajda, 1955). The latter work initiated the Polish School marking a break in Polish cinema, distinctly opposed to the schemata of the previously dominant forms of socialist realism. That impersonal model of cinematic propaganda was replaced by films offering an individualised vision of reality, whether in Andrzej Wajda's romanticism and expressionism, Andrzej Munk's grotesquerie and irony or Kazimierz Kutz's realism. However, all of these films dealt with the same theme: the need to revise the experience of the Second World War which had been either suppressed or distorted by socialist realism. According to Polish film historian Tadeusz Lubelski, the films of the Polish School represent 'the strategy of a psychotherapist'. A director using this strategy tries to 'restore his audience to health' by providing self-knowledge which can be gained through an analysis of the recent past. Lubelski claims that Wajda's *Ashes and Diamonds* (*Popiół i diament*, 1958) is the best example of this strategy, as this film managed to re-unite the Polish nation, fractured by the demands of the totalitarian doctrine of communism. This re-unification was made possible through finally being able to represent the suppressed war experience of those who had been members of the Home Army, that is the resistance movement, led by the Polish government in exile and opposed to the Communist take over (2000: 138–44).

When recollecting his role in Wajda's debut, *A Generation*, a story of young people who join the underground communist movement, Polanski said:

> Wajda made the first step – we followed him. He realised *A Generation* – a film that had great significance for us. With this film Polish cinema began. It was something superb and unforgettable. The whole crew including Wajda was very young. We worked days and nights without a break. We all believed in what we were doing. It was something completely new, although the so-called period of Stalinism was not yet over. (1980: 9–10)

Polanski also performed in *Kanal* (*Kanał*, 1957), the second part of Wajda's famous 'war trilogy'. For this reason, it might have been assumed that the young director would have followed his older and admired colleague. Indeed Polanski, with his own ghetto experience and the memory of his mother who had perished in a concentration camp, could have become a follower of this idea of cinema, through which collective and individual traumas of the past might be resolved. However, until making *The Pianist* in 2002, Polanski returned to the past only once, in his short film *When Angels Fall* (*Gdy spadają anioły*), made at the film school in 1959.

The main character of the film is an old, nameless and speechless woman, who works as an attendant in a men's room. Polanski shows her as she spends her whole day there, sitting silently with an expressionless face at her table in the corner of the room. She becomes invisible to the men using the lavatory. Her non-existence in the present is opposed to her eventful life in the past, which is recollected in flashbacks. Polanski contrasts the past and the present in many ways, the use of colour and sound being the most expressive. The images of the present are black and white, and are accompanied by the natural sounds of dripping and gurgling water, whereas the past is pictured as full of sharply contrasted colours with expressive music and the sounds of a soldier's song in the background. However, a closer look at these flashbacks reveals that their content significantly exceeds what can be stored in one's individual memory. They include images from the past that span more than a hundred years (the soldier who seduces the woman when young wears a uniform from the 1800s) and other events in which she did not take part nor could have witnessed (as with the scenes from a battlefield). Interestingly, when Polanski recollected the shooting of this film, the woman who played the main character and whom he had found for his film in an old persons' home in her nineties, displayed exactly the same kind of shattered and incoherent memory:

> Things came back to her, but she no longer understood what they meant. She saw a costume and that said something to her. She spoke then of the Russians who had come in eighteen hundred and something, but what she said had neither beginning nor end. It was just pieces that came back to her. Little pieces of her life that no longer linked together. But that moved me enormously. (1980: 11)

If these flashbacks are incoherent at the level of personal historical accuracy, they recover their cohesion on a different level, that of collective memory transformed into a collective national mythology of the past. All of them are ostentatiously *artificial* in *mise-en-scène*, the style of acting, photography and soundtrack. In fact, they are conspicuous replicas of iconic images from Polish art but to an even greater degree from popular Polish war mythology: a girl looking through a window at passing soldiers; a girl and a soldier on a meadow; a lonely hard-working mother of a son fighting in a war; a mother equipping her son to go to war, and so on.

Interestingly, in the last of these iconic situations, the mother who is saying farewell to her son, Polanski himself appeared dressed up as the old woman. If this device introduces the motif of masquerade, which would recur in his later films, *The Tenant* being the most disquieting example, here it has a specific meaning. In playing the role of the woman as mother he discloses the performative aspect of gender roles. In fact, the woman as presented in the flashbacks is noticeably deprived of any trace of individuality; she performs the roles of a soldier's lover and then the lonely and tragic mother whose son's destiny is to perish on a battlefield. The latter is the role prescribed to Polish women by the national discourse of femininity embodied in the figure of the Polish Mother. Polanski, dressing himself up as the old woman, mockingly re-creates the clichéd image of an iconic and very familiar Polish femininity developed especially in numerous representations in Polish paintings, Artur Grottger's being the most famous. These representations do not reflect the truth of women's life experiences but rather the opposite, their transformation into a collective myth serving a national ideology.

Interviewed by Michael Delahaye and Jean-André Fieschi in 1966, Polanski agreed with their contention that *When Angels Fall* was his 'very' Polish' film and explained that he 'tried to ballast the flashbacks with a range of references, for example to Polish naïve painting, especially that of the nineteenth century artist, Jacek Maichewski [sic – the misspelled name of Malczewski]' (1975: 209). This authorial reference is noted by Virginia W. Wexman who also examines how the old woman's memory merges with the past of Poland as recorded in art: 'The old woman's memories are presented as being, in part, memories of Poland' (1985: 9). Although she aptly notices that 'the woman has embellished her memories by distorting ugly reality to conform to the sentimentalised views of Polish history familiar to her through popular art', eventually she shifts to a somewhat literal reading of the cinematic text claiming that the contrasting of the splendour of past images of Poland with the gloomy coldness of the present brings about a nihilistic message relating to the gradual degeneration of human life and Polish culture (1985: 8–9). Overlooked in this interpretation is the ironic distance of the representation of the past that results from using a pastiche of Polish iconography and elements of grotesque masquerade which reveal Polanski's skepticism rather than what Wexman calls an 'aggressive and self-punitive nihilism' (1985: 9).

If Polanski's film constructs the flashbacks of the old woman as visions distorted by patterns of popular art and imagery, he conspicuously points out that individual memory merges with the collective and that it cannot be separated from the national mythology prescribing certain life roles to be performed by individuals. In other words, it can be said that for Polanski collective memory represses individual memory. Indeed, despite the fact that the viewer has access to the memories of the old woman through the flashbacks, these are contaminated with elements of collective imagination and mythology.

In *When Angels Fall* Polanski expresses his distrust of memory as not capable of re-constructing the past as it is always *re-presented*. Further, an individual in this act of *re-presentation* inevitably uses previously existing representational schemata and conventions. If Wajda (also to some extent Munk in *Passenger* and Tadeusz Konwicki in many of his novels and films) is deeply involved in tracing the past and recovering collective memory as a way to 're-unite' the Polish nation, Polanski uses collective memory with its powerful and deeply rooted iconic images, situations and performed roles as a critique of its dangers. This, of course, highlights the problem of one's individuality and identity, which later becomes the main focus of his films (*The Tenant* being the most disquieting representation). To sum up, Polanski's scepticism toward the possibilities of direct access to memory put him in opposition to the exploring of it, the central task of the Polish cinema of that time. In rejecting, or merely ignoring, the possibility of taking up the role of the 'psychotherapist' of the Polish audience, performed so well by his older colleague, Andrzej Wajda, Polanski decided to take the position of a distant observer, who meticulously examines human reactions 'here and now'. Paradoxically, in abandoning the position of artist as psychotherapist, he himself has been treated as a fit subject for the psychoanalytical approach by Western criticism and has been diagnosed as a mere voyeur (cf. Leaming 1981).

Leaving aside the problem of the appropriateness of this approach to Polanski offered by Barbara Leaming, I would like to stress here that his early departure from the dominant trends of Polish cinema did not mean a total contestation with the traditions of Polish culture. In fact, many specific attributes of Polanski's cinematic imagery which do not fit easily into the conventions of Western cinema come from the Polish tradition of the grotesque, the absurd and irony, epitomised in the works of Witold Gombrowicz (Polanski admits the influence of Gombrowicz's writing in his autobiography while recollecting the time he spent in Cracow's School of Fine Arts (1984–87)) and Sławomir Mrożek who also, and not coincidentally, both emigrated from Poland.

With Gombrowicz, Polanski shares a scepticism and a tragic awareness that individual freedom is inexorably limited through social and cultural conventions which force the acceptance of cultural forms. Inevitably, this vision entails a scepticism toward the possibility of an authenticity in one's life. As Gombrowicz confesses in his *Diary*:

> I … tried this authentic life, full of loyalty to an existence in myself. But it can't be done. It can't be done because that authenticity turned out to be falser than all my previous deceptions, games, and leaps taken together. (1988: 183)

This distrust of the possibility of leading an authentic life led Gombrowicz to a fascination with youth as the closest approach to naked and innocent human nature (this motif takes a literal form in his play *Operetka* in the character of Albertine, a young girl who appears naked in the final scene). However, at the same time, he is deeply convinced that the final destination of youth is to be seduced and corrupted. Polanski shares this bitter consciousness with Gombrowicz, and this realisation prevented him from adopting a naïve belief in innocent youth, as many Westerners did in the 1960s. The motif of corrupted and spoiled youth is undoubtedly one of the most pervasive in his work.

With Sławomir Mrożek, whose first play *The Police* (*Policja*) was performed in 1958, Polanski shares an ability to combine successfully, within a single text, realism and grotesquerie. Moreover, both artists use similar thematic motifs. For example, the action of Mrożek's play *Out at Sea* (*Na pełnym morzu*, 1961) takes place in a setting similar to *Knife in the Water*. Three men are shipwrecked and try to survive on a raft. They play out a complex game of power, using familiar social and political conventions, for example holding debates and voting. These 'civilised methods', so highly valued in democracies, are part of a process of choosing one of them to be eaten by the other two who would thus survive the catastrophe (cf. Esslin 1983: 319). This absurd and grotesque situation purports to reveal the true image of human nature that hides behind the mask of civilised sophistication. Finally, it is animal instinct that enables survival; people in their mutual interactions inexorably adopt a role as either victim or victimiser. The message of Mrożek's play concurs with the diagnosis of human nature in many of Polanski's films. Introduced in his *The Fat and the Lean* (*Le Gros et le maigre*), co-directed with Jean-Pierre Rousseau, the motif of master and slave also appears in his last short film made in Poland, *Mammals* (*Ssaki*) depicting the grotesque situation of two men alternatively pulling one another on a sled. Both use different methods, cheating being the most common, to take advantage of the situation. The pervasiveness of the motif of such power games makes it one of the 'trademarks' of Polanski's cinema.

In the Polish cinema of the 1950s and 1960s Polanski was not the only film director whose films evoked Gombrowicz's and, to some extent, Mrożek's idea that all human relationships inexorably take the form of a game. This is to be seen in a number of films made in that period, although in different variants and with different final conclusions. In characterising the new tendencies in Polish cinema at the beginning of the 1960s, Tadeusz Lubelski claims that a number of directors realised in their films the 'strategy of a play-writer' evident through the significance of the element of 'game'. He writes, 'Firstly, this is the game which takes place within a diegetic world, between the characters. Secondly, it is the game played with the viewer's habits and expectations.' Directors using this strategy claim that 'reality – before being incorporated into the process of communication – needs an injection of artificiality, a reinforced *mise-en-scène* that will prove their professional perfectionism, express the vitality of the period, and finally – agitate the viewer' (2000: 176).

Lubelski names four films representing this strategy: *The Last Day of Summer* (*Ostatni dzień lata*, Tadeusz Konwicki, 1958), *Night Train* (*Pociąg*, Jerzy Kawalerowicz, 1959), *Innocent Sorcerers* (*Niewinni czarodzieje*, Andrzej Wajda, 1960) and Polanski's *Knife in the Water*. All of them have dramatic features in common. Two essential elements are the use of the conventions associated with the theatrical 'three unities' and a fully-rounded and detailed 'naturalist' construction of character. This kind of character allows progress during the fabula, so that they remain 'open' and unfinished at the end. This is compounded by the diminishing importance in these films of the past as an explanation for psychological motivation (2000: 178–83). Therefore, these films might be seen as a symbolic gesture in Polish cinema, a turning away from the war in an effort to engage with the dilemmas of contemporary life or to express 'universal' themes. However, as the later films of Konwicki, Kawalerowicz and Wajda demonstrate, this break from history was merely a transient moment in their work, as all of them soon returned to the exploration of collective as well as individual memory, which for Wajda was probably a big relief. Making *Innocent Sorcerers* was undoubtedly a disconcerting experience for him. In his diary, on 21 June 1959 he wrote: 'I still cannot get a feel for the film. If only I could give it up, it would be a load off my chest...' (1996: 101). The main characters of the film, Bazyli (Tadeusz Łomnicki) and Pelagia (Krystyna Stypułkowska), who engage in a one-night psychological game aimed at hiding their real feelings, were utterly strange to Wajda: 'I had no such friends, I knew no such girls. No wonder I approached the film with a sense of helplessness' (ibid.). Perhaps the 'strangeness' of the young characters to Wajda was because they were partly constructed by Jerzy Skolimowski, Polanski's co-author of the script of *Knife in the Water*, who collaborated with Jerzy Andrzejewski on the script of *Innocent Sorcerers*. This is how Skolimowski recollects this work that started when he was staying in Obory, a 'House of Creative Work', where writers could produce their work with the support of the communist government:

> At the next table Wajda and Andrzejewski made a lot of noise. They were writing something on young people that was supposed to be the script of Wajda's next movie. I was the only representative of the young generation in Obory (the average age there was a hundred). They gave me a sample of this text with a request that I evaluate it. For me cinema did not yet exist at that time; my film taste ... was for example *Fanfan la tulipe* ... I told them that this was flimsy. I said: *these are not real young people; what are you writing about! – young people are playing jazz, boxing.* Wajda then challenged me: *Maybe you, Mr Jerzy, would sketch out how it should be.* So during the night I wrote a draft of dozen or so pages, a story that later became the script of *Innocent Sorcerers*. (1990: 7)

Although it is difficult to assess precisely Skolimowski's input on the script, one can say without much doubt that Bazyli and Pelagia belonged more to his world than Wajda's. Evidently, Wajda did not want to get close to people like Bazyli who is 'fond of nylon socks and quality cigarettes, owns a tape-recorder to record his conversations with girlfriends and has but a single passion – playing percussion in Krzysztof Komeda's jazz-band' (Wajda 1996: 99). Certainly, Wajda would also not want to get close to a middle-aged journalist who owns a fancy car, yacht and has a young, beautiful wife, nor to a young hitchhiker who possesses only a knife but desires all the objects of his older counterpart: the characters Skolimowski created together with Polanski for *Knife in the Water*. Nor would the director of *Ashes and Diamonds* feel any affinity with the main character of Skolimowski's debut *Identification Marks: None* (*Rysopis*, 1965), played by the director himself, who constantly hides behind different masks and questions all the rules of so-called 'common sense', engaging himself instead in absurd undertakings trying to escape the obligations the world attempts to impose on him.

Polanski's and Skolimowski's young men are a radical challenge to the mythologised image of masculine youth developed within Polish ideology to which Wajda adhered from his very first film, *A Generation*, in which Polanski played a supportive role. The dominant Polish discourse on gender originated in the period of Romanticism when a new hegemonic idea of nation was constructed in response to the loss of independence. This engagement with national issues inevitably determined new gender constructs. Analysis of Polish Romanticism's seminal texts such as Adam Mickiewicz's *Forefathers' Eve* corroborates the thesis formulated much later by both George Mosse and Benedict Anderson, that nationalism is conducive to the development of homosocial relationships that usually take the form of fraternity or brotherhood. Moreover, as the authors of the collection of essays *Nationalisms and Sexualities* note: 'Typically represented as a passionate brotherhood, the nation finds itself compelled to distinguish its "proper" homosociality from more explicitly sexualised male/male relations, a compulsion that requires the identification, isolation and containment of male homosexuality' (Parker *et al.* 1992: 6).

Mickiewicz's national Romantic drama introduces a group of young conspirators in a Tsarist prison who address one another as 'brother' and confess their mutual love. This pattern of homosocial male bonds further proliferated in Polish cultural and social life for a long time; in fact, I would claim up until the end of communism. The cultural imperative to co-operate for the sake of the freedom of the Motherland, stifled, in Polish patterns of masculinity, the traditional will to compete with one another. Moreover, the precedence of the national cause over the individual influenced the relationship between generations. In short, the conflict of the generations has not been well articulated for a long time. Jan Prokop describes it in the metaphorical phrase: 'How often the Polish Oedipus, swearing revenge, sharpens over his father's grave the dagger with which he will kill the Tsar-usurper … the Polish oedipal imagination is often haunted by the vision of killing the Tsar, never of killing the father' (1993: 25–6). A similar statement comes from Andrzej Wajda: 'Our generation is a generation of sons who must tell the story of their fathers because the dead cannot speak any more' (2000: 54). Moreover, in his movies, Wajda often presents a pair of male characters modelled on the pattern of father/son with the older man acting as a mentor for the younger.

Polanski breaks with this specifically Polish variant of the homosocial, first by introducing into his films motifs of homosexuality, a taboo within societies organised around the idea of a male brotherhood tasked with defending the nation. To grasp the significance of Polanski's decision to speak of the existence of homosexual desire within Polish society we should remember the permanent silence on this in Polish public discourse. Both the communist state and the Church that opposed each other at almost all levels of public life guarded the purity of a particular model of heterosexuality. Any kind of difference, of Otherness, was erased from the public discourse organised to protect the stability of the Nation and the communist state. Gombrowicz in his *Diary* notices the repression of homosexual desire in Polish culture, although still in somehow veiled form:

> the young man … was destined only for the role and function of the 'virtuous son of Poland'. If carried away … by instinct and temperament, he made his way into the jungle of those forbidden charms, always on his own, without a guide, left to his own unsophisticated, murky instincts. (1988: 227)

Although Polanski has not explicitly focused on the issue, he has undoubtedly admitted the presence of this pattern of desire, even if it was expressed as occurring on the margins of Polish cultural discourse. His short films speak directly to this marginality.

Two Men and a Wardrobe (*Dwaj ludzie z szafą*) might be seen as a metaphor of homosexuality as noted by a few critics (see Eagle 1994: 100). Although such a reading can be easily considered as implausible, it is worth noting here that two men emerging from the sea with a heavy, awkward wardrobe look like the strangest of couples. The people they meet on their way, who express intolerance and hostility towards them, make this clear. Many scenes in the film demonstrate that they do not 'fit' into the world they try to enter – they cannot make it to a trolley and are also rejected from a restaurant. As they walk around the streets the useless wardrobe might be seen as a sign of their 'otherness' as it isolates the two men and obstructs their efforts to engage with other people. Just as homosexuality is conceptualised in Polish culture as useless, due to its inability to allow reproduction, the wardrobe is also useless, making its owners easy to ridicule. Finally, the two men realise that there is no space for them and their impossible burden so they decide to vanish into the immensity of the sea, which can calmly absorb their difference.

In *When Angels Fall*, homosexuality is introduced directly into the narrative. Among men visiting a lavatory there is a gay couple who apparently come from the street not to answer a call of nature but rather to fulfil their sexual desire. Dressed as gays, even if through costume of a culturally elaborated cliché, their sexual orientation is unmistakeable. In opposition to the rest of the men present there they do not use the urinals but they try to lock themselves into a closet hoping to fulfil their desire. Fear thwarts them as the second man, instead, takes the next cabin to the first, preventing them from meeting. What should be stressed here is that these homosexual figures are by no means ridiculed as usually happened in Polish cinema up to the 1970s (although these images were only incidental). Even if these representations have comforting comic elements, they first and primarily signify 'others', and Polanski brings their otherness to the surface, even if in the diegetic world this is an underground lavatory.

In *Knife in the Water* Polanski further destroys the mythologised Polish image of masculinity in which youth and old age support each other prescribed by national ideology. Nor does he respect the ideals of masculine brotherhood proposed by communist ideology. As Barbara Leaming has aptly pointed out, 'Polanski was playing a different game, his own, in isolation from society' (1981: 52), whether understood as Polish nation, or proletarian comradeship. From the very beginning of the film the Student (Zygmunt Malanowicz) and Andrzej (Leon Niemczyk) are presented as rivals who will do anything to impose their own will. Traditional imperatives of mutual support are replaced in *Knife in the Water* by envy and the desire to humiliate. Passion and emotion have to be firmly hidden behind a mask that allows the playing of a game with an adversary in which the prize is to dominate.

When we see Andrzej for the first time in his car, with Krystyna (Jolanta Umecka) his young trophy wife driving, his need to control every situation is revealed through the small gestures of his hands correcting what he sees as her poor steering. When she stops and gives back the driver's seat to Andrzej, he quickly regains his self-confidence, weakened whilst in the passenger seat. However, shortly after, he is again deprived of freely executing his will over the situation. A young man, the Student, appears in the middle of the road and does not move away despite the loud signal given by Andrzej. He has to stop the car. When the silhouette of a young man in his pullover, jeans, canvas shoes, wearing a rucksack on his back, appears on the screen for the first time it strongly contrasts with Andrzej's elegant sports suit, his luxurious car and his arrogant behaviour.

This first encounter of the two men could be seen as a confrontation between free-spirited youth and an adult corrupted by consumerism. However, if we shift our attention away from the Student's dress sense, which serves here as a positive connotation of values ascribed to youth, and toward his actual behaviour, this ideal image of the free spirit becomes less clear. Tellingly, standing in the middle of the road, he decides to trick a driver into giving him a lift. To achieve his goal, he decides to do a mini-performance: he has got the right costume to play the role of a 'young rebel'; he chooses the road as the setting; he casts the driver in the role of his antagonist, and Krystyna as his audience. Polanski's decision to show his figure through the windscreen visually isolates the space of this performance making it have a stage-like artifice. In other words, the Student not only performs the scene but also *directs* it, trying to acquire control over the whole situation. He also provides himself with the privilege of delivering the only line of dialogue in this scene, 'You've got your lights on', that finally drives Andrzej into fury.

Interestingly, the older man quickly responds to the Student's risky performance with his own, when he forcefully 'invites' him to the car with mockingly exaggerated gestures and openly sarcastic words: 'Won't you do us a favour, please? Would you rather sit in front, or in the back? There is a pillow and a blanket, perhaps you could manage a nap; we'll try to not to disturb you. Let me switch the radio off, and we'll keep quiet.' Thus, this scene is *directed*, in turn, by Andrzej in an attempt to allow himself to be in control of the situation. Then, there is a short silent intermission before the performance develops further, again with the two men trying to occupy the position of 'director'. Having a yacht onto which he invites the Student, Andrzej attempts to control how the situation will develop. Apparently, the young man is well aware of this as he says to him just before coming aboard: 'So you want to go on with the game?' A disdainful response is given: 'My Boy, you are no match for me.' Despite this, it is clear that the game has begun.

Polish male solidarity is here negated in a disconcerting image of open conflict that is eventually transformed into a struggle for power. The lesson the older man wants to teach the young one is not aimed at introducing him to the world of adult masculinity, that is, to help him get through the rites of passage, but rather at demonstrating his own superiority. Instead of teaching 'a son' the language of 'the father', to allow him to speak for the father in the future, as Wajda would want, Andrzej excludes the Student from his realm. He ostentatiously uses sailing language that puts him in a superior position to his younger opponent: 'Stow the rope then. In a coil, if you know how to!' When the young man asks him to show him how to do it, he refuses, excusing himself because of the need for him to stay at the rudder. It can be said that Andrzej

The game gets serious: Leon Niemczyk and Zygmunt Malanowicz in *Knife in the Water*

refuses to help the Student to establish the relationship between signifier and signified, the crucial condition for discovering the logic of the world. The sailing language, presently the possession of Andrzej, can be seen as an emanation of a Lacanian 'symbolic order' to which he does not want his younger partner to have access. As Nick Mansfield writes: 'In the symbolic, things appear to make sense, hierarchies of meaning are established, and society functions in a tense but efficient manner' (2000: 45). No wonder that the Student's actions on the boat bring about a disastrous chaos, which the older man attempts to order. Andrzej's efficiency in ruling the boat and his 'crew' demonstrates his knowledge and with it his self-satisfied confidence in seeming to be at one with the logic of the symbolic.

Andrzej's involvement in the symbolic order inevitably entails a sense of lack that needs to be compensated for. This primary desire for the unity of what Lacan calls 'the imaginary' is effortlessly fulfilled by satisfying different types of demand:

> The subject is propelled into and through the world, into its emotional and sexual relationships, its fraught group identities with nation, race and political party, its careerism and material acquisitiveness, all as a result of this insatiable need to fill up the lack at the centre of its being. (Mansfield 2000: 45–6)

Material extensions of Andrzej's figure, the car, the boat with its tourist gadgets, as well as his sexy young wife, reveal the efforts he has put into satisfying different demands with the hope of overcoming any sense of a lack. This primary desire, however, proves to be endlessly impossible to fulfil. Now he directs his desire to the knife, the only possession of the Student, but also a symbol of his young virility and vitality.

The young man in his jeans, canvas shoes, rucksack, and with his knife, initially seems to be living in a harmonious unity, free from the tormenting need to satisfy demands that would alleviate any sense of lack. Although not allowed to enter the language of the symbolic, he is able to communicate with Krystyna in the language of poetry, demonstrated in the scene when they have to buy back forfeits from each other. Symptomatically, when she sings a song and the Student recites a poem, Andrzej wears earphones that exclude him from the act of communication developing above the logic of the language of the symbolic order, where a signifier has to have a precise signified. In preferring to listen to the radio report of a boxing-match, Andrzej declares his attachment to the logic of symbolic language, contested by the language of poetry. This scene, together with the Student's earlier declaration, 'I like walking. Legs are the thing, you know, self-propelling', gives the viewer an impression of his internal harmony, completeness and self-assurance, yet, also that he is a potential victim.

He appears threatened by both the situation and Andrzej, who demonstrates his superiority at the cost of the stranger. His status as a victim is evoked visually in shots presenting him as a Christ-like figure, when he lies on a deck 'crucified' with wide-spread arms or when he 'walks' on water (see Eagle 1994: 109; Wexman 1985: 27). Thus, not only the characters play a game with one another. Polanski also plays with the viewer's expectations and hypotheses for the trajectory of the narrative. For this idealised image of youth is later brutally destroyed, although not simply reversed into its demonic opposite, but rather into a display of banality and shallowness that is probably even more disconcerting for the viewer. As Grażyna Stachówna notices:

> The Boy is finally disgraced in the eyes of the viewer in the fight at the end of the film … instead of fighting back and throwing punches, he scurries after his shirt button, torn off by Andrzej. In this scene Polanski aims his scorn not just at the Boy, but also at the viewers who have grown to like the upstart youth, identifying themselves with his hate. (1996: 165)

Indeed, in this scene Polanski demonstrates his deep sense of irony by means of which he deprives the fight scene of possible pathos and prevents the viewer from having an emotional involvement with the characters. Finally, the now emotionally detached viewer can see that the romantic image of the rebellious youth, apparently idealised in his clothing and his declarations of a love for heroically lonely walks through the forest, turns out to be a disguise for a cynical greed and a readiness to undertake all methods to beat a rival through a more efficient practice in cheating. Stachówna aptly claims that despite the romantic aura surrounding the Student, this mask is finally seen for what is and the viewer can see that the Student is like 'Balzac's Rastignac with his creed, "one needs a knife to get along in life"' (1996: 163).

This revelation about the 'real face' of the Student, here a symbolic representative of Polish youth, can be compared with the publication of a 'Student's Diary' in *Nowa*

Kultura in 1953. This authentic diary, written by a female student of a secondary school, ruthlessly revealed, although unconsciously on her part, the rejection by the young people of the image of them proposed by official communist propaganda. In her confessions, she neither displayed any engagement with the ideas of communism, nor contempt for it. She simply dreams of renting a flat in the centre of a big town, decorating it, 'like a boudoir', growing flowers, possessing a record-player and having a German Alsatian dog and a canary (see Lubelski 2000: 109–11). These aspirations were shocking for 'the architects of the souls' of the Polish society of that time. The protagonists of Wajda's *Innocent Sorcerers* and Polanski's *Knife in the Water* were generalising the singular truth expressed in the anonymous student's diary. If the main character of Wajda's film expresses his relish for American cigarettes and his tape-recorder, it is because he can afford them. The Student from Polanski's film, having no possibility of fulfilling this dream, pretends to be contemptuous of them.

Interestingly, in Polanski's film it is a woman, Krystyna, who knows the truth about the Student for she says to him: 'You're not one bit better than he is, you understand? He used to be the same as you ... And you'd really like to be the way he is now. And you are going to be, as long as your ambition holds out.' Krystyna sees more than both men are able to see or want to admit. She is well aware of her trophy status, the prize of the foolish contest taking place between the two rivals. However, finally, it is she who takes over the position of 'the director' over which the two men have been struggling. Barbara Leaming puts it thus: 'suddenly she reveals herself a true master of the tactic of humiliation' (1981: 53). When she meets her husband at the harbour she possesses knowledge he does not and, therefore, eventually she is in control of the situation.

Krystyna and Andrzej's marriage by no means follows the cultural pattern of male/ female relationships as codified in Polish tradition. There is neither a romantic passion between them, nor do they create a family, as is traditionally imagined in Polish culture as the fortress of those patriotic and moral values endangered by external enemies. Krystyna's character can be located at the opposite pole of the Polish discourse on femininity epitomised in the figure of the Polish Mother, the suffering and sacrificing woman. In opposition to the Polish Mother she is overtly sexualised. Her sexuality is demonstrated from the very beginning and, additionally, she is objectified by her husband, for example in his naming his yacht with the English version of her name, Christine. In the figure of the Polish Mother sexuality was either repressed or sublimated through motherhood, in a process typical of nationalisms: 'This idealisation of motherhood by the virile fraternity would seem to entail the exclusion of all non-reproductively oriented sexualities from the discourses of the nation' (Parker *et al.* 1992: 6). Krystyna, differently from most other women in Polish post-war cinema, is provided with sexuality, which is a trump card to be used in various games to acquire material safety or control over other people. More importantly, this is a non-reproductive sexuality which is ostentatiously emphasised by the childlessness of the couple.

In Polanski's work, the pervasive presence of childlessness, or of a monstrous childhood, is often evident. There are childless couples in *Cul-de-Sac*, *Repulsion* (that is, Carol's sister and her married lover), *Macbeth*, *Bitter Moon* and *Death and the Maiden*.

The figure of the monstrous child appears for the first time in *When Angels Fall* in the character of the woman's son who torments a frog, then returns in *Cul-de-Sac* as the obnoxious figure of the Fairweathers' son, to finally take the shape of a real monster in *Rosemary's Baby*. In *Chinatown*, Evelyn's daughter/sister is also tainted with the monstrosity of an incestuous relationship. Consequently, Evelyn's experience of pregnancy and motherhood is a torment rather than a revelation of the mystery of life. Similarly, Rosemary, Tess and Mimi through their pregnancy enter a realm of madness, solitude and cruelty. Thus, motherhood is not presented as an act of ascending on the path of life but rather of descending into darkness, fear and loneliness. This can also seem to surround a child, as is suggested in the last image of *Repulsion* where Carol as a small girl is visibly detached from the rest of her family. An even more disconcerting image of a child is offered in *The Tenant*, where we see a little girl wearing the cap of Stanczyk, the renowned Polish jester, whose face is hidden behind Trelkovsky's mask. Perhaps Leaming is right when she claims that this is an 'ironic self-portrait – a revelation of the tiny victimised child' (1981: 204). The only image of a 'happy family' in Polanski's films appears in the first scenes of *The Pianist*, only to be brutally destroyed and finally annihilated. In his work, childhood, along with motherhood, never takes the form of a nostalgic space of safety, but rather indicates all the horrors of human life that begins at the moment of conception. Though he deceptively hides behind the mask of irony and histrionic buffoonery, the pervasiveness of these motifs emphasises Polanski's deeply tragic notion of life.

Recently, in Andrzej Wajda's *Revenge* (*Zemsta*, 2003), Polanski delights in self-reflexively adopting the possibilities of the mask, in playing the role of Papkin. Polanski and Wajda brilliantly create him as a tragic buffoon. He appears out of the mist in the long opening shot of the film, trudging through snowy meadows towards a semi-ruined castle. The imagery might suggest a returning tragic Polish hero but Papkin is the reverse of this. It soon becomes clear that this is not an image of an iconically stable and secure 'return to home', but merely another break in a nomadic journey, giving him yet another opportunity to comically amuse those within the fictional world, fragmented Polish families at war among themselves, as well as, once again, entertaining us, the cinema audience. At the close of *Revenge*, when the show is over and the curtain drops, Polanski the entertainer, has to continue his lonely journey.

Thanks to Helena Goscilo, John Orr, and Michael Stevenson for their comments and help in writing this chapter.

CHAPTER SIX

Beauty and the Beast: Desire and its Double in Repulsion

Lucy Fischer

Introduction: Noli Me Tangere

Over the past three decades, literary and film theory has focused relentlessly on the issue of human desire – particularly that of a sexual nature. Here one thinks of such works as *A Future for Astyanax* (1969) by Leo Bersani, *Capitalism and Schizophrenia* (1972) by Gilles Deleuze and Felix Guattari,[1] *Figures of Desire* (1981) by Linda Williams, *The Voice in the Cinema* (1982) by Michel Chion,[2] *Reading for the Plot* (1984) by Peter Brooks, *Alice Doesn't* (1984) by Teresa de Lauretis, *The Death of Desire* (1985) by M. Guy Thompson, *Death and Desire* (1991) by Richard Boothby, *Desire and its Discontents* (1991) by Eugene Goodheart and *Critical Desire* (1995) by Linda Ruth Williams – to name but a few.

The verb *desire*, in its strongest sense, means 'to want' or 'to crave' and, clearly, such a notion assumes the subject's *attraction* to the object or person sought. However, what has received far less scrutiny in contemporary cultural theory is the sentiment's opposite (or, perhaps, its oblique 'double') – the feeling of *repulsion* – a subject's aversion toward an item or individual that proposes itself. This is not to say that no theoretical work has been done on questions of *repressed* desire. Certainly, a text like Mary Ann Doane's *The Desire to Desire* (1987) examines that topic by surveying a series of 1940s American melodramas in which a heroine's erotic wishes are stifled by the weight of convention, tradition and propriety. But *repulsion* (though related to repression) implies something different – that desire is not merely stunted or postponed, but transformed into disgust or abhorrence.

Surely, within the annals of psychoanalytic dogma, both attraction and repulsion have occupied fluid positionalities on the continuum between alleged mental health and infirmity. While heterosexual desire has been traditionally coded as normal, homosexual longing has been viewed as abnormal. However, while it is thought appropriate to feel heterosexual yearning for an individual of no biological relation to oneself, it is deemed perverse in Western culture to direct such an emotion toward a parent or sibling. Similarly, though heterosexual desire is the base line, it is considered depraved for an adult to express this urge toward a child. In these two cases (incest and paedophilia) a feeling of repulsion is considered 'desirable'.

Repulsion, directed and co-authored by Roman Polanski, is a film whose very title suggests that it will serve as a dissertation on the subject of repugnance.[3] It was the artist's second feature film and the first made outside of Poland (specifically in Great Britain). It concerns a pretty young woman who seems disgusted by the prospect of sexual relations with men – many of whom approach her with erotic scenarios in mind. Given what Adrienne Rich has called 'compulsory heterosexuality' within Western society (1986: 23–75), the film's heroine is marked as unbalanced or unnatural for her response and it does not surprise us that the film devolves into an exploration of her insanity. While we expect that such a drama will unearth the spectre of childhood (which in Freudian-tinged communities is seen as the seat of our mental outlook), we do not necessarily anticipate that the entire film's narrative will be overlaid with the aura of fairytale. In focusing on an individual's mental states, and in using experimental cinematic means to do so, *Repulsion* belongs to the European 'art film' movement of the 1950s and 1960s. This ambience conforms to David Bordwell's notion that in the art film, the protagonist experiences a psychic 'boundary situation' and that this sense is augmented 'by compressing duration and restricting space' (1985: 208).

The look of love

Specifically, *Repulsion* tells the story of Carol Ledoux (Catherine Deneuve), a young Belgian woman who works in a London beauty salon and shares an apartment with her older sister, Hélène (Yvonne Furneaux). When Hélène and her lover Michael (Ian Hendry) go away for a vacation and leave Carol alone in the flat, she has a breakdown that seems tied to her aversion to sexual contact with Colin (John Fraser), a handsome and eminently eligible suitor who pursues her. Given that Carol's illness is tied to her loathing of heterosexual contact, certain narrative elements seem important – though in a decidedly contradictory fashion. First of all, Carol is gorgeous, which makes her extraordinarily appealing to men – a drawback given her particular syndrome. Indicative of this, Michael archly refers to her as 'the beautiful younger sister'. Secondly, she works in a beauty salon – a place where women go to make themselves more sexually alluring. Hence this woman – an expert at attraction – would prefer to repel.

Almost immediately in the film (which opens with a sequence in Carol's work place), this disturbance of impulses is registered. One of the first shots shows us a homely old woman lying prone on a metal slab covered by a sheet – her face caked with some substance. At first, we conjecture that we are in a morgue and, only when she speaks, do we realise that she is alive and having a facial applied (rather than a death mask). In another salon sequence, a distracted and depressed Carol gives a woman a manicure and pierces her finger so badly that the setting begins to resemble a hospital emergency room rather than a beauty salon. Hence a scene of potential attraction is transformed into a *mise-en-scène* of revulsion.

There is a further imbalance recorded in the film's discourse on vision and visibility. The movie begins with an oppressively close shot of an anonymous eyeball, which is seen to blink. Only when the camera pulls back does it reveal the face of a young woman who we later learn is Carol. We cannot help but be upset by this image with its clear overtones of *Un Chien Andalou* (Luis Buñuel and Salvador Dali, 1929) in which a woman's eyeball is sliced by a man's razor blade. Moreover, throughout the film, Carol's demeanor seems entirely opaque – especially as she descends into madness. Her affectless stare provides no sense of her eyes as 'windows to her soul' and, given the movie's salon setting, her comely visage remains a 'beauty mask'. Additionally, her vision seems to provide no clue to her desires. Thus what she regards (for example, some nuns and children in a schoolyard across from her apartment window), does not bespeak what she wants. In one scene, she sits in a restaurant staring at her food – apparently devoid of the urge to eat it.[4]

However, male vision in the film (which is decidedly active) stands in direct opposition to the passive spectatorship practiced by Carol. Whereas her gaze is blank and distanced, that of the men she encounters is acquisitive, penetrating and covetous. When we first see Carol walking on the street, she is ogled provocatively by a construction worker. In the next scene, she sits inside a restaurant while Colin peers at her through its picture window. Finally, in one of the more off-putting examples of male voyeurism in the text, her landlord (who is tracking down a late rent payment) drops in on her during her troubled weekend; she greets him in a nightgown and he lecherously contemplates her thighs. Hence, in the scopophilic discourse of the film, both rapacious and disinterested vision seems equally problematic.

Carnal knowledge

However, the most cogent treatise on desire and repulsion in the movie involves Carol's response to her own and to Hélène's admirers. The clearest examples of Carol's sexual repugnance come in relation to Michael, who practically lives at the girls' apartment. Significantly, at one point, Carol resentfully asks Hélène: 'Is he staying here *every* night?' When Carol enters her bathroom to find his toothbrush, shaving kit and razor lying around, she is clearly repulsed and discards them. Furthermore, in one scene, she picks up Michael's dirty T-shirt from the floor, compulsively smells it, retches and jolts to the toilet. Other aversions are encountered on an acoustic (rather than visual, olfactory or tactile) level. On two occasions, as Carol lies in bed at night, she hears sounds from the next room of Hélène in the throes of orgasm. She punches her pillow then clasps it to her ears as though unable to endure such lewd and animalistic noises.

Hearing beyond sight: Catherine Deneuve in *Repulsion*

The next morning she goes into her sister's room and stares at the crumpled bed sheets in disgust.

Her reaction to Colin is somewhat less dramatic but similarly aversive. While Michael seems rather lascivious, Colin is more restrained. Given the actor who plays him, he is a potential 'leading man'. But Carol responds to him as though he were an ogre. He is forever pursuing her – in a restaurant, on the street, on the telephone, at her apartment – despite her refusal to interact with him. As he says sardonically at one point: 'You *really* make me feel wanted.' When she stands him up for a date, he locates her sitting on the street staring transfixed at a crack in the sidewalk, and inquires: 'Are you playing hard to get?' Despite all this, he repeatedly asks her out – continually prompting her to make excuses. When he drives her home one day and steals a kiss, she is wooden – then runs off to her apartment and immediately brushes her teeth. Clearly, she is not simply 'frigid', or sexually unresponsive, she is repelled by his touch.

Certainly (given the assumption in the 1960s of the normalcy of heterosexual relations), we are pressed to find Carol's behaviour pathological and the film proceeds according to this logic. From a contemporary framework however, in which homosexual desire has become more normalised, we might see Carol's repulsion toward men as allowing for her openness to lesbian encounters. There is much in the film that points to Carol's fierce and unconventional feelings toward her sister. She seems inordinately jealous of Michael's intrusion as though she and Hélène were a rival 'couple'. Furthermore, the only moment that her depression lifts is when Bridget, a fellow salon worker, talks of their going to a movie together – but Carol seems disappointed when Bridget immediately turns the conversation to her boyfriend. There are a few oblique references to homosexuality in the film but they are all within a traditional framework that envisions it as a perversion. Colin's pal describes a fight he witnessed between two women and wonders if they are 'lesbians'; furthermore, one of Colin's friends gives him a mock smooch on the lips which he wipes off with the same loathing with which Carol removed his own kiss.

While in terms of heterosexual codes of the 1960s, Colin might seem a normal red-blooded male actively pursuing an attractive woman (in contrast to his more salacious cohorts), upon closer scrutiny, we might well ask: What's wrong with *him*? If Carol seems unresponsive, he seems bewilderingly over-invested in his pursuit of her – given the minimal positive reinforcement he receives. In a sense, Carol's zombie-like demeanor presents him with a *tabula rasa* on which he can project any desirous illusion he requires. As Leo Bersani has remarked, 'The activity of desiring is inseparable from the activity of fantasising. There is no scene of desire which is not an elaboration, a kind of visual interpretation of other scenes' (1984: 10). Beyond that, Colin's wish to pursue a woman who so openly scorns him seems both contentious and masochistic – leaving us unsettled by any expression of sexual desire in the film at all. As Carol's elderly salon client tells her, men 'want to be spanked then given sweets'. But, perhaps, Colin's self-destructive behaviour is not as puzzling as it seems, since many cultural theorists have observed that desire's dynamics frequently assume a lack of fulfillment. As Eugene Goodheart has noted (in discussing Marcel Proust):

> The gap between desire and its object is insurmountable. Indeed it is the very gap that nourishes and sustains desire, because its satisfaction would be its extinction. It may even court rejection, since denial only increases desire. Desire is committed ... to an enduring disappointment as a way of guaranteeing its survival. (1991: 3)

Several critics have noted the manner in which *Repulsion* maintains a tension between its status as a quasi-realistic commercial thriller and an expressionist/modernist film (Leaming 1981: 63; Wexman 1979: 43). Most of its claims to the latter concern its portrayal of Carol's schizophrenic 'break' which occurs when Hélène and Michael leave for a holiday in Italy. The site of this schism is the Ledoux's London flat, where Carol retreats in her illness. As Polanski has insightfully remarked, 'Atmospherically *Repulsion* would stand or fall by the apartment where most of the action took place' (1984: 210). Even before Hélène's departure, Carol has shown signs of mental distress: she bites her nails, chews her hair, brushes away invisible flecks from her clothing or furniture, eats almost nothing, has insomnia, and is mesmerised by a distorted reflection of her face in a chrome tea pot. Her disaffection in the beauty salon leads a client to ask if she is 'asleep'. Similarly, on one occasion, Bridget tells her to 'stop dreaming', and inquires, 'What's the matter?'; another time, she remarks that Carol does not 'look well' and misguidedly asks if she is 'in love'. Furthermore, Hélène calls Carol 'sensitive', and Michael remarks that she is 'a bit strung up' and 'should go see a doctor'. Finally, Colin inquires one day if she is 'all right', and tells her that she looks 'funny'.

But Carol's situation severely worsens when she is left by herself for the week. Sounds seem to be acoustically amplified from her (and our) point of view: a faucet dripping, a telephone ringing, a clock ticking, flies buzzing, a church bell tolling, the elevator running. She becomes progressively unhinged: she draws a bath but lets water run over the tub rim; she forgets to bring the rent cheque to the landlord; she irons without plugging in the appliance; she hums and cries at the same time; she leaves potatoes to sprout roots on the counter; she removes a skinned rabbit from the refrigerator and forgets to return it to the icebox. As the carcass progressively rots and attracts flies, she barely notices – allowing it to stand as an icon of corporeal degeneration – insuring that the audience will be as repelled by it as she is by sexual contact. Beyond this, she begins to hallucinate and the phantasmagoric imagery that she conjures makes a grotesquerie of heterosexual relations. When she opens a mirrored armoire door in Hélène's bedroom, she catches sight of a phantom man (the construction worker who had leered at her earlier). Later, despite the fact that she is alone in the flat, she imagines hearing footsteps and seeing a shadow pass under her door. At another point, as she walks down a corridor, imaginary masculine hands protrude, grab and fondle her. Later, the walls seem to perspire and, when she touches them, her hands leave a clay-like imprint on their surface. Finally, in an orgy of fear and loathing, she thrice envisions the same man breaking into her bedroom to rape her, as she helplessly screams in silence. One such assault is followed by a sequence in which the phone rings and, when Carol answers the call, we hear Colin on the line. By stringing together these scenes an equation is, perhaps, made between him and her ghostly attacker. As a clear objective correlative for her psychological split, the walls of her apartment rupture and separate – imagery that has been anticipated by her earlier obsessive-compulsive fascination with cracks on the street. As the weekend proceeds, she receives a postcard from Hélène that depicts the Leaning Tower of Pisa – seemingly another symbol of Carol's mental imbalance. Like the famous canted building, the spatial proportions of her apartment become progressively distorted. Thus, in one scene, as she lies in her bed, the ceiling seems to bear down on her; in others, her quarters look cavernous. Clearly, Carol's problems are meant to seem erotic in nature and entail an aversion to sex. Strangely, Polanski attempted to impose sexual constraints on his leading lady – a bizarre version of 'method acting'. According to Barbara Leaming, the director prevented Deneuve from returning to Paris during most of the shooting of *Repulsion* to keep her from having intimate relations with her partner – only allowing her to leave when he surmised that she would be menstruating and unlikely to have intercourse (1981: 60–1).

In *Repulsion's* expressionist and surrealist touches (identified with Carol's disturbed unconscious), we are reminded of a more avant-garde work, Maya Deren's *Meshes of the Afternoon* (1943) – a seminal text of the New American Cinema. In that short, experimental film, which proceeds as a kind of trance or dream, a woman (played by Deren) makes repeated forays into a house whose spatial relations are contorted and disjunctive. At one point, she walks up a set of stairs that seem to be askew and, as she moves, she tilts helplessly toward the walls. At another point, she seems to lose her equilibrium and falls backwards. Though in one shot, she is clearly depicted as inside the house, in the next, she re-enters it through a mesh-curtained window. Objects left in one state are later mysteriously found in another: thus, a phone that is on the hook is suddenly found off its cradle.

In the mutable spatial relations of both *Meshes of the Afternoon* and *Repulsion* and in their narratives' focus on repeated incursions into a disquieting home, we find echoes of Goodheart's description of desire as an 'unstable … energy that disintegrates structures of reason … convention [and] all attempts to contain and fix reality' (1991: 2). In both we also see an attempt to represent troubling and ineffable states of mind in terms of the concrete geography of cinematic *mise-en-scène*.

Eros and thanatos

It is no surprise that Carol's decline into madness ends in a *grand guignol* of violence. For as Goodheart has noted, 'The acting out of desire [is often] the courting of suffering and death' (1991: 8). The carnage is initiated when Colin, despairing of being able to contact Carol (since she has not reported for work), appears at her door unannounced. As he rings the bell, we see him (from her perspective) as a contorted face seen through the anamorphic peephole lens – a twisted vision that bespeaks her deranged psychological conception of him. When he pushes his way inside, she batters him with a heavy candlestick that she has grabbed in 'self-defense' – clearly confusing him with her desirous 'dream lover'. As he bleeds from the ear, she drags him to the lavatory and deposits him in the overflowing tub – thus creating a literal 'blood bath'. She obstructs her front door with a plank of wood to prevent another such 'intrusion'.

Her second homicidal episode is prompted by another unexpected ring of the doorbell. This time she sees her landlord (Patrick Wymark) on the other side of the portal – a middle-aged, unattractive man. (Earlier, Hélène had confessed that simply hearing his voice on the telephone made her 'flesh creep'.) Although Carol refuses to let him in, he opens the door with his master key and enters. When he appraises the condition of the apartment (with its drapes drawn, lights out, food rotting, barricaded entrance), he proclaims that it is 'a flaming nut house' – entirely insensitive to the mental state that may have produced this 'decor'. Noticing that Carol is dressed only in a negligée, he inquires lasciviously 'Do you *always* run around like this?' Realising that her sister is away, he suggestively asks if she is 'all alone by the telephone'. He begins to grope her and offers a sexual *quid pro quo* in exchange for rent: 'I could be a good friend to you if you look after me.' As he caresses her, we realise that she has something in her hands behind her back. When she slashes him (an act filmed so that she lunges at the camera), we realise that the deed has been accomplished with Michael's razor (sparking more associations to *Un Chien Andalou*). To hide the body, she topples the sofa upon it and retreats to her bed where she lies perspiring, eyes agape with fear. At the end of the film Hélène returns to the apartment and discovers the catatonic Carol as well as two dead bodies and screams in a hysterical outburst. As Michael transports the stupefied Carol from the apartment, the neighbours look on, rapt in a morbid, voyeuristic thrall.

In *A Future for Astyanax*, Leo Bersani (drawing on Freud's *Beyond the Pleasure Principle*) sees human desire within most societies as necessitating aspects of sublimation. Though I have argued that the notion of *repulsion* is not synonymous with *repression*, clearly the former engages aspects of the latter. For Bersani, it is only through the thwarting of desire that humans produce a coherently 'structured self' (1984: 6). If they entirely unleash desire, they create 'fragmented sel[ves]' that are often consumed with 'suicidal melancholy' (ibid.). Beyond depression, de-sublimated desire involves other kinds of 'murderous'[5] impulses. As Bersani comments:

> Psychic deconstruction … is far from being the kind of peaceful return to the unrepressed pleasures of the body dreamed of by contemporary theoretical pastoralists. It is much more likely to be an enterprise of great violence, a triumph of fantasies of patricide and deocide. (1984: 11)

Certainly, when Carol finally confronts her repulsion with men (a fact she has endeavored to conceal with a distanced, quasi-autistic demeanor), her self becomes hopelessly fragmented and its fracture unleashes her ferocious, aggressive impulses – yet another kind of desire.

In its brutality, *Repulsion* again evokes *Meshes of the Afternoon*. In that film, the oneiric protagonist seems equally trapped in a battle between love and fury – a rift which seems exemplified by the symbols of flower versus knife. In the beginning of the film, the heroine picks up a poppy as she enters her house. And later, after she follows a man up the stairs (significantly played by Deren's husband and collaborator, Alexander Hammid), she lies on a bed with a flower beside her pillow. As Hammid begins to caress her, the bloom suddenly turns into a knife (thanks to a Mélièsian 'substitution trick'). At this point, she throws the weapon at Hammid, and the image of his face (reflected in a mirrored surface) shatters. At other points in the film, she uses the knife against her 'self' by aiming it, in a threatening manner, at her numerous 'doubles'. Clearly, this weapon has parallels to the razor in *Repulsion*. Finally, in both films, the dénouement involves someone discovering dead bodies. In *Meshes of the Afternoon*, Hammid finds the apparently deceased Deren sitting in a chair with mirror shards at her feet, blood dripping from her mouth. While in *Repulsion*, Hélène and Michael find the remains of two men.

There are other elements of *Meshes of the Afternoon* that spark associations to *Repulsion*. Keys (highly resonant objects) play an important role in each work – since both dramas entail repeated entrances into a home. The telephone is also a central prop in each film. In *Meshes of the Afternoon*, it is a disturbing article that moves inexplicably from room to room, whose handset shifts from on to off the cradle. In *Repulsion*, its jarring ring is a brutal reminder to Carol of the outside world and its 'encroachment' on her hermetic psychosis. In each work, nun-like figures appear (as did a priest in *Un Chien Andalou*). In *Meshes of the Afternoon*, the heroine repeatedly (and unaccountably) chases a black-robed character with a mirrored face (played androgynously by Hammid). In *Repulsion*, Carol observes nuns in the courtyard of a church school across the way – ostensibly reminding her of her own early Belgian education. Finally, given the multiple Derens who populate *Meshes of the Afternoon*, its imagery of smashed mirrors seems to invoke the same theme of the splintered self that is enunciated in *Repulsion*.

What the parallels between the films ultimately reveal is a certain shared visual (and even cinematic) 'vocabulary' for screen portrayals of the disturbed self – a codex that links *Un Chien Andalou, Meshes of the Afternoon* and *Repulsion*. All script scenes in which the expression of sexual desire is marred by violence. All include some reference to religion as an advocate of repression. All involve the use of blades to mutilate the body and signal the potential cleavage of the self. Finally, all take place in perturbing malleable spaces that can only be traversed in the mind.

Down the rabbit hole

As we have noted, it is a rabbit that decomposes in Carol's kitchen and stands as an emblem of bodily decay commensurate to her mental disintegration. Similarly, Bridget's discovery of a rabbit's head in Carol's pocketbook seals both her view and ours that the young woman is deranged. Significantly, in the first scene of Colin and Carol together he asks what she is having for dinner and, when he learns that it is rabbit, he calls the animal a 'poor bunny'. This diminutive term also reminds us that this is a creature favored by youth and one that populates many children's stories – like *Alice in Wonderland* (1865) or *The Tale of Peter Rabbit* (1901).[6] Thus, perhaps (to reference the former work), Carol Ledoux's slide into madness approximates (in a more tragic fashion), Lewis Carroll's vision of a bizarre fall through the earth.

Clearly, Carol's mental illness involves regression – a move from psychological adulthood to a stance associated with youth, and there are many hints of this inversion in the film. First of all, it is emphasised that she is a *younger* (or as Michael deems her a *little*) sister, and rather than seeming like her sibling, Hélène acts more like Carol's mother – hence Carol's panic when Hélène announces that she will leave her 'home alone'. And when Hélène eventually returns home, Carol is found crouching under her bed. Like a young girl when her mother is out, Carol rifles through Hélène's closet and holds her dresses up to the mirror. Furthermore, when Carol is upset by the sounds of Hélène and Michael making love, it seems that she is re-experiencing some 'primal scene' of *parental* sexuality. Moreover, her landlord refers to her as a 'poor little girl' and she is forever gazing out the window at the school children who play across the street – as though she were still one of them. The sounds of a youngster practicing the piano waft through the apartment house walls, and Carol speaks in a high, adolescent voice. Finally, she rearranges toy-like animal figurines on her mantel and the final shot of the film tracks into her girlish image within a family portrait from the distant past.

Given the film's theme of reversion (as well as its reference to Lewis Carroll's famous story), it is not surprising that it also mines associations to fairy tales. In the late 1950s, there was a cartoon series for American television entitled *Fractured Fairy Tales*, released by J. Ward Productions. If *Repulsion* constitutes a 'fractured' version of any such tale it would be one belonging to the 'Animal-Groom Cycle' (Bettelheim 1977: 277–310). As though to conjure the framework of fairy tales, Michael once refers to Carol as 'Cinderella', and one of Colin's pals deems her 'Little Miss Muffet'. The basic paradigm for the Animal-Groom Cycle entails its focus upon a heroine for whom a hideous animal suitor declares his love. He is often understood to be under some inexplicable spell. Furthermore, the heroine is urged to wed him by her father, despite her repulsion for this improbable paramour. Eventually, the spell is lifted and the animal groom becomes an attractive and adored mate.

In *The Uses of Enchantment*, a psychoanalytic reading of fairy tales, Bruno Bettelheim sees such narratives as didactic forms through which children enact, rehearse and conquer their fears of growing up. As he states: 'Each fairy tale is a magic mirror which reflects some aspects of our inner world and … the steps required by our evolution from immaturity to maturity' (1977: 309). The kinds of lessons that such stories teach address such problems as how to separate from our parents, how to achieve happiness and how to love (1977: 278, 309).

Clearly, the latter process also involves coming to terms with one's sexuality and it is no accident that many fairy tales trace the dynamics of courtship (as in 'Cinderella', 'Rapunzel', and 'Snow White'). For Bettelheim, their precepts often involve instructing children how to 'undo societal repression' as symbolised, for instance, in Sleeping Beauty's awakening to her prince (1977: 279). It is this kind of knowledge that one particular Animal-Groom tale – 'Beauty and the Beast' – offers. Specifically, Bettelheim sees the narrative as portraying a young girl's initial repulsion to adult heterosexual relations (as represented in her revulsion at her animal-groom). The fact that her beau is eventually transformed into a handsome man signifies that, as the girl matures, she discovers her own attraction to men and learns to respond to their promise of erotic pleasure. As Bettelheim notes, 'what [the child] had experienced as dangerous, loathsome, something to be shunned must change its appearance so that it is experienced as truly beautiful' (ibid.). Bettelheim assumes that such tales have emerged from traditional, patriarchal cultures in which girls are often 'protected' from sexual knowledge, since such societies place a high degree of value upon female virginity at marriage. Hence, he notes, these stories 'convey that it is mainly the female who needs to change her attitude about sex from rejecting to embracing it' (1977: 286). On the other hand, her outlook affects male behaviour as well. As Bettelheim continues: 'As long as sex appears to [the girl] as ugly and animal-like, it remains animalistic to the male' (ibid.). Significantly, the particular creature in which the male admirer is incarnated is frequently a repulsive one (like a frog or toad) whose 'tacky, clammy' skin is reminiscent of the sex organs and whose ability to puff up is suggestive of the engorged penis (1977: 290).[7] While revolting, however, an animal like a frog is not fearsome, indicating that it can eventually win the trust and affection of the heroine.

There are other paradigmatic aspects of these tales. Sometimes, in her initial rejection of her mate, the girl responds with violence. As Bettelheim remarks, in 'The Frog King' the heroine hurls the animal groom out of bed and throws him against the wall, thus demonstrating that 'the awakening to sex is not free of disgust or of anxiety, even anger' (1977: 287–8). Moreover, Bettelheim regards it as crucial that, in many of these fables, the girl weds the groom at the instruction of her father and that it is a maternal figure who has cast the spell on her suitor. Here, he sees the narratives as teaching girls that, to reach adult sexuality, they must leave their parents. Though superficially frightening, Bettelheim sees such fairy tales as ultimately comforting. As he notes:

> Stories about the animal husband assure children that their fear of sex as something dangerous and beastly is by no means unique to them … But as the story characters discover that despite such anxiety their sexual partner is not an ugly creature but a lovely person, so will the child. (1977: 297–8)

Bettelheim views other tales as related to this cycle, despite their lack of a literal animal-groom character because they too tie disgust or terror to a sexual liaison. One such story is 'Bluebeard' which concerns a homely but wealthy man who has been married numerous times and whose wives have all mysteriously disappeared.[8] When he courts another young woman, she rejects him. In order to convince her family of his eligibility, he invites mother and daughter to spend a week at his lavish country estate wining and dining them, whereupon the marriage is arranged. After the ceremony, Bluebeard announces that he must go on a journey and leaves his wife back home with the keys to most of the rooms and cabinets in his house. However, he forbids her to open one particular closet. When he departs, she becomes curious about this space and undoes its lock, whereupon she discovers the bodies of his murdered wives. When he returns and learns of her treachery, he makes plans to kill her, but she is saved by her brothers. For Bettelheim, the narrative

> is a story about the dangerous propensities of sex, about its strange secrets and close connection with violent and destructive emotions, in short, about those dark aspects of sex which might well be kept hidden behind a permanently locked door, securely controlled. (1977: 303)

The relationship between 'Bluebeard' and 'Beauty and the Beast' has to do with the tension between aggression and affection. As he comments: 'One might say that the former presents those primitive, aggressive and selfishly destructive aspects of sex which must be overcome if love is to bloom; while the latter tale depicts what true love is all about' (1977: 306).

For Bettelheim, a final group of related fairy tales are those involving 'one who [goes] forth to learn fear' (1977: 280–2). Rather than focus on a heroine, these concentrate on a hero who realises that he must learn how to 'shudder' before he weds. Though he undertakes numerous hair-raising adventures, he does not experience fear until his wedding night when, in his marital bed, his wife shocks him by pouring cold water (replete with wiggling minnows) on his body. He responds: 'Oh, now I shudder dear wife. Yes, now I know what it is to shudder!' (1977: 281). For Bettelheim, the story articulates the fact that humans experience erotic anxiety before becoming full sexual beings. As he continues, the tale also demonstrates 'that marital happiness requires that [such] feelings must become accessible to a person which up to the time of marriage were not available to him' (1977: 282).

Arrested development

But what have such fairy tales to do with a contemporary thriller like Polanski's *Repulsion*? On one level, the film's narrative evinces strong parallels with 'Beauty and the Beast'. Clearly, Carol is a Beauty. In fact, given the way that the drama unfolds, we might say that she is 'drop-dead gorgeous'. According to Leaming, 'Polanski wanted someone who was at once externally icy and internally demonic – "an angelic-looking girl with a slightly soiled halo"' (1981: 60).

Though ostensibly an adult, Carol's revulsion to male sexuality might well be compared to that of the pre-pubescent girl who cannot yet envision consummating a sexual act. Within this framework, Colin becomes a form of the animal groom. Though, ostensibly repugnant to Carol, for the viewer he already wears the handsome face that he would normally bear only at end of the fairy tale narrative – with its promise of 'happily ever after'. The fact that a rotting rabbit forms one of the iconic images of the film and that Carol rearranges animal figurines on a shelf only secures the link to the Animal-Groom Cycle. That the skinned bunny also resembles a foetus and is 'clammy' like a sexual organ, makes it clear that the narrative rehearses issues concerning sexuality (Wexman 1979: 49). That Carol kills Colin with a candlestick seems significant when one realises that, in certain fairy tales, 'it is the light of a candle which shows the wife that her husband is not [an animal] … but a beautiful prince' – though in *Repulsion*, no such illumination takes place (Bettelheim 1977: 296). That Carol's rapist-lover (whom she both fears and desires) is conjured only at night echoes the fact that, in the Animal-Groom Cycle, the creature appears during nocturnal hours, but not in the day. As Bettelheim explains: 'What seemed lovely at night looks different by day, particularly when the world with its critical attitude toward sexual enjoyment … reasserts itself' (1977: 297). Additionally, there are a few more references to animals in the film that are made by a repulsive suitor, the landlord. When he sees the state of Carol's apartment, he calls it a 'pig sty', and when he notices how dark she keeps the room he retorts, 'I'm not a bloody owl'.

Though Polanski is wise to keep the broader drama of the Ledoux's background a mere outline, as Leaming points out, he leaves 'clues leading to Carol's childhood' (1981: 66). They come through the inclusion of a family photo in the film (which depicts two adult couples and two girls). We assume that at least one set of grown-ups are the Ledoux parents and that the youngsters are the sisters. Here, we are urged to see the young Carol as, perhaps, a troubled child who now continues to exist in a state of arrested development. As Virginia W. Wexman notes, speculatively filling in the psychological and autobiographical 'blanks' in the drama:

> The photograph of Carol's family … shows her alone and detached while her sister … rests her arm on the knee of a man possibly their father. Part of Carol, we may assume, wishes to be her sister, which means embracing sexuality and the love of a man; another part, however, recoils from this desire … for to acknowledge it would mean inviting rejection both by the man, who in childhood preferred her sister, and by [her sister] herself. (1979: 48–9)

Here, we are reminded that Bettelheim sees the child's early disgust with sex as functioning to protect against incestuous impulses. Only after one has become psychologically separated from one's parents is erotic attraction ignited (1977: 308). Clearly, for Carol, this stage has never been reached and its murderous consequences are tinged with Bersani's notion of desire bespeaking patricide.

Significantly, the first moment at which attention is drawn to the photograph is when the landlord (who is a 'dirty old man') picks it up from a shelf and asks Carol about it. 'Your family?' he inquires. 'Very nice.' It is shortly after this reminder of the past that she kills him. The next time that our attention is drawn to the photograph is at the very end of the film, after Carol has been removed from the apartment in which she has slain two men. The camera then tracks past a series of objects in the Ledoux living room (a photo of a matronly woman who could be their mother, animal figurines, the postcard from Pisa) and lands on the photo, moving into the figure of a young Carol – settling upon her eye (the image which opened the film). This shot-sequence has a similar effect as the last moments of *Citizen Kane* (Orson Welles, 1941), in which the camera surveys a series of items, ultimately landing upon the sled. As 'Rosebud' hints at answering the psychological enigma of Kane, so a 'family romance' tentatively suggests an answer to the mystery of Carol's illness.

But, though it is Carol who proves demented and bloodthirsty, Polanski does not leave the men in the story 'off the hook'. If, as Bettelheim would have it, girls within conventional culture must struggle toward sexual maturity, then men should understand this and not behave like animal grooms. This message escapes the male population of the film. Michael jokes about having a 'wild party' with the schoolgirls across the way and tells Carol not to 'do anything he wouldn't' while he is in Italy; furthermore, in the postscript he writes to the card Hélène sends from Italy, he jokes about Carol 'mak[ing] too much Dolce Vita' while he is away. The lecherous construction worker calls her 'darling', and the lascivious landlord forces himself upon her, despite remarking how she is 'white as a sheet'. Colin's crude pals envision a *ménage à trois* with her and call her a virginal 'teaser'. Even Colin repeatedly forces himself on her, though it is apparent that she is an unwilling partner. As one of Carol's matronly salon client's tells her: 'There's only one thing [men] want and I'll never know why they make such a fuss about it.' Furthermore, Bridget is ready to 'cut' herself due to the behavior of her beau. She asks Carol 'Why are [men] are so filthy?' and promises to reveal to her all 'the sordid details' of her latest relationship. Interestingly, moments before Colin's demise, he apologises to Carol for breaking and entering, then muses, 'It's all so sordid.' Thus, for Wexman, *Repulsion* presents a society 'caught up in a pattern of male exploitation and female victimisation' (1979: 53). Colin might also be seen as to blame for pressuring Carol into a sexual encounter for which she is unready. As Bettelheim notes, while a few fairy tales involve a bride's quick recognition that her animal groom is a prince, in most, the process takes time. Thus, the stories imply that 'trying to rush things in sex and love ... can have disastrous consequences' (1977: 291).

Repulsion also invokes the 'Bluebeard' tale – though, in Polanski's film, the male villain's role is taken up by Carol, who proves that sexual aggression is no prerogative of the masculine gender.[9] Clearly, her apartment becomes a chamber comparable to Bluebeard's closet – filled with the corpses of her failed heterosexual liaisons. She tries to keep it locked, as did Bluebeard, but when someone penetrates her barricade, he is punished by death. From the male perspective, *Repulsion* also echoes the tale about a hero needing to acquire fear, except that, in this case, our male protagonists never learn the lesson. While Carol's psychotic deportment *should* have filled Colin and the landlord with dread and terror, it did not – leading to their mutual demise. If Carol is over-endowed with sexual anxiety, these men are, by contrast, under-supplied.

In my book, *Cinematernity*, I have noted that the occult and horrific scenario of Polanski's *Rosemary's Baby* ironically and slyly voices some of the real, pedestrian 'truths' of pregnancy as seen from a woman's perspective: her feelings of illness, her dependency on husband and doctor, her isolation and paranoia, her sense that an 'alien' grows within her body (Fisher 1996: 73–91). It is precisely these verities that the reassuring and unsullied language of child preparation treatises fails to grasp. On a similar level, we might argue that, in *Repulsion*, Polanski exposes the disturbing side of the human sexual response – the aversion and aggression that often precedes or accompanies erotic feelings, sentiments that contemporary culture generally disallows in its discourse of untrammeled desire. Here, we might borrow for Polanski's disturbing thriller, Bettelheim's 'justification' for disquieting fairy tales which he finds preferable to the antiseptic, uplifting discourse of sex education. As Bettelheim notes, such an approach tries to teach the young 'that sex is normal, enjoyable, even beautiful ... But since it does not start from an understanding that the child may find sex disgusting ... modern sex education fails to carry conviction for him' (1977: 309). Thus, honesty is only possible when one simultaneously confronts the good, the bad, and the ugly of the human condition.

Significantly, the first scenario for *Repulsion* was entitled *Lovely Hatred* (Leaming 1981: 58)[10] – a seeming non-sequitur that manifests Polanski's canny insight into the conjunction of converse human drives: desire and disgust, attraction and repulsion, tenderness and violence, fear and trust. Thus, it seems significant that the nail polish that one of Carol's clients chooses for her manicure is called 'Fire and Ice', a moniker which is reminiscent of the extremes of passion and frigidity that circulate in the drama. Furthermore, it reminds us of the title of a famous Robert Frost poem that situates desire between the poles of love and hate. As it reads:

> Some say the world will end in fire,
> Some say in ice.
> From what I've tasted of desire
> I hold with those who favor fire.
> But if it had to perish twice,
> I think I know enough of hate
> To say that for destruction ice
> Is also great
> And would suffice.
> (1930: 268)

Interestingly, when the world ends for the Ledoux sisters (with Hélène's return home to find Carol catatonic and her apartment befouled by carnage), she emits a series of groans in her icy terror that, ironically, are indistinguishable from her earlier moans of fiery, sexual rapture.

My thanks go to Elżbieta Ostrowska for inviting me to write a chapter for this volume and to E. Ann Kaplan who gave me an opportunity to present this paper at Stony Brook University in October 2004.

Notes

1   This was originally published as *Capitalisme et schizophrénie*. It was later translated into English as *Anti-Oedipus: Capitalism and Schizophrenia* in 1977 (see Bibliography).
2   This was originally published as *Voix au cinéma*. It was later translated into English as *The Voice in Cinema* in 1999.
3   He collaborated on the screenplay with Gérard Brach, who also worked with him on *Cul-de-Sac*. However the original treatment for the film was written by Gene Gutowski (Leaming 1981: 58).
4   Virginia W. Wexman sees Carol as having a more active sense of vision than I (1979: 56), as does Barbara Leaming (1981: 65) who uses the term 'voyeur' in relation to her.
5   Bersani entitles the Introduction to his book 'Murderous Lovers'.
6   *Alice's Adventures in Wonderland* was originally published as *Alice's Adventures Under Ground*. *The Tale of Peter Rabbit* was written by Beatrix Potter.
7   A frog appears in 'The Frog King' and a toad in 'The Three Feathers' (see Bettel-

heim 1977: 286, 289).

8   Bettelheim notes that 'Bluebeard' is not technically a fairy tale but a story invented by Perrault (Bettelheim 1977: 299). Nonetheless, there are fairy tales that involve secret rooms in which previously murdered women are found.

9   Wexman discusses this role reversal not in terms of a fairy tale but in relation to the classic Gothic novel in which the heroine is usually a passive subject of male violence (rather than vice versa – as in *Repulsion*) (1979: 52).

10 This treatment was co-authored with Gene Gutowski.

CHAPTER SEVEN

Cul-de-Sac in Context: Absurd Authorship and Sexuality

Paul Coates

Polanski and his double

There may well be two Polanskis, each an auteur, but in two different senses of that disputed word. On the one hand, there is Polanski as 'auteur' in the most common usage of the term: a director – usually a writer-director – whose works lie outside the mainstream and are crafted to express an often idiosyncratic worldview; an auteur in the sense of what is usually called 'art cinema' and sometimes called 'modernism'. The other Polanski, however, may be termed an auteur in the sense of the original, often forgotten auteur theory, rather than that of its later reworking into the banal elevation of the director into superstar: in other words, he may be a director whose strong authorship is quite compatible with the execution of a series of projects on behalf of others (in the case of the first versions of auteur theory, the studio system). If truth to 'himself' has been preserved by both Polanskis, and not just the first, it is because both always had the same aim: to hold at arm's length his appalling wartime experiences as a Jewish child in wartime occupied Poland. Thus works that at first sight might seem to be little more than professional assignments, crafted by a director who prided himself on his professionalism, could be analysed in terms of the symbolic concealments and displacements of trauma theory, though such an analysis (considering, for instance, the way the horror movies transpose the experience of being hunted into another key) will not be conducted here. This second Polanski embraced professionalism, even apparent classicism at times, as a way of both placing at one remove the indiscretions of autobiography and managing searing experiences by turning them into stories that seem no longer to apply to him.

Thus if auteurism – in its original sense, as formulated in relation to such directors as Douglas Sirk or Otto Preminger – is a theory of split and hidden selfhood, of the career as dream, with one directorial personality the manifest company man and another the latent artist, in Polanski's case the doubling takes a different form: that of two different types of auteur. In each case, though, the films have a power compounded of a claustrophobic personal style, repeated motifs (of which more later), and the menace generated by the wary suspicion that experience may be either round the next corner or close on one's heels, possibly – inescapably – both before and behind one. When Polanski himself enters *Chinatown* to rip open Jack Nicholson's nose, he does so as the imp of the perverse, a representative of the hidden autobiographical material that could tear apart the movie of his double, Roman Polanski the (Hollywood) professional. That appearance is a necessary, and necessarily momentary, opening of a safety valve that drips blood. This second, art cinema Polanski was the one who intended initially to cast himself and Basia Kwiatkowska, his former wife, as George and Teresa in *Cul-de-Sac*, or who planned to play the Hiker in *Knife in the Water* (*Nóż w wodzie*) – until Film Unit head Jerzy Bossak vetoed this. It could be argued that Bossak knew something also known – as Barbara Leaming points out – by *Macbeth*'s producer, Michael Klinger: namely, that 'Polanski ... worked best with the pressure of something monitoring him' (1981: 120). Leaming concludes therefore that the closer the fit between the films' scenarios and Polanski's own fantasies, the worse the film. In other words, for Leaming the 'art cinema' Polanski would be not only monetarily but also aesthetically less successful than the professionalised one. *Cul-de-Sac* – the most personal of Polanski's 1960s features – assumes particular interest therefore as a possible test of this argument, as it represents his first attempt to preserve the jokey idiosyncrasy and relative freedom of his early shorts within the differently constrained – because larger budget – production situation of the feature. At the same time, though, as part of its balancing act, it also attempts to professionalise art cinema. As we will see, for all the absurdism that allies it to art cinema, *Cul-de-Sac* has the controlled – even wearisome – imagistic cohesion that characterises the *pièce bien faite,* the classical work of the professional, achieved here through the extensive reconjugations of the idea of the chicken and the egg that must be pursued at length to be believed (and so will be here). This overelaboration of a motif may be described as an absurd, and even absurdist, 'overachievement' of the classical film's economy that may be intended as a virtuoso *tour de force*, or may be meant to work it to death. As so often, Polanski is both 'inside' and 'outside' the genre system of which such classicism was so characteristic, with even 'the absurd' becoming a genre for him – albeit the one closest to his heart.

This may well be why the Polanski of the early 1960s believed himself not so much condemned to alternate between personality-types and roles as capable of fusing them. After all, did they not co-exist within the image of Alfred Hitchcock projected both by the director himself and the Nouvelle Vague devotees who arguably prompted his self-reinvention as much more than 'the master of suspense'? The split between the two Polanskis, however, indicates the precariousness that nevertheless had begun to afflict the Hitchcockian fusion of auteur and entertainer in the 1960s, and which placed Polanski's own work upon similarly fractured foundations. Such cinematic modernisms as those of Jean-Luc Godard and Michelangelo Antonioni had driven a wedge between the two notions. Polanski's 'contentist' modernism (to borrow an adjective from Michael Rutschky (Elsaesser 1989: 56–60)) – a modernism of shock, solitude and suffering, rather than 'formalist' excess – suggests the possibility of their reunification, but the films clearly fall to one side or the other of a gap (with arguably only *Chinatown* fully bridging it). Not surprisingly, the attempted duplication of Hitchcock's feat by another director – François Truffaut – had been compromised by his own constitution's dual reaction against the attempt: its periodic abandonment, on the one hand, and, on the other, an excessive submissiveness towards the vampirically draining phantom of the master, which ultimately drained the authority of the would-be disciple. The effort to fuse the two personae was clearly a futile one to catch and freeze a chimera of historical possibility.

The precariousness that now bedevilled this project echoes into Polanski's willingness or need to place himself before the camera for far longer than had Hitchcock himself, whose near-invisible cameos had functioned as a trademark. Polanski's frequent abandonment of the position behind the camera is overdetermined by his desire both to exploit the acting skill that captivated many watchers in his youth and to achieve a Hitchcockian celebrity and visibility. He could not achieve both ends simultaneously, however. Hitchcock's screen appearances, after all, had been brief, their momentariness simply emphasising the informing louring of his controlling presence all the rest of the time: as if he could not trust anyone else to hold the camera for more than a moment, like the passer-by the tourist asks to snap him. But the humiliation endured by many of the characters Polanski himself plays – which *Cul-de-Sac*, as originally projected, would have exemplified almost as thoroughly as the later *The Tenant* – suggests that the persona of Polanski the controlling director is that of a sadist contractually linked to a masochistic Polanski-actor, whose glee in self-exhibition is also a self-alienating self-exposure; or alternatively, that the director seeks relief from the demands of control in the childlike irresponsibility that pretends someone else (Gérard Brach perhaps?; what *is* the psychological significance of dual-scripting?) wrote the script. In any case, the dialectic of Polanski-director and Polanski-actor is a distorting mirror in the basement of the upper-level split between the art cinema Polanski and the professional one. The fissures may ramify into an extensive, zig-zag network, reflecting the complexity of the fault-lines within what only seems to be a unitary 'Polanski'. (After all, Catherine Deneuve deemed him a different – infinitely more attractive – person once off the set of *Repulsion*.)

Paradoxically, given its prevailing focus on Hollywood, the first version of auteur theory was a theory of modernism: one of the non-communicative director with a 'secret signature', a Jamesian 'figure in the carpet'. Polanski, of course, was unlikely to be so reticent – so thoroughly masked by professionalism – as those Hollywood directors, and so one ought to speak instead of a set of interlocking images explicitly flagged up in the title of his very first feature. Polanski's work, like that of the directors elevated by the auteurists, is open to analysis in terms of multivalent motifs suggesting a hidden, pulsing, often distant centre; in particular, the complex associated with knives and water. One may not always find both elements present simultaneously (*Cul-de-Sac* has water but no knives), but the themes associated with the complex are always intertwined; and the absence of one or the other may itself signify (the presence of water and absence of the knife in this film may indicate a near-total burial of the male power associated with it). The prominence of the complex in Polanski's early shorts is significant, as if the features would simply spin a yarn around these central images to tie them together: the knife that stabs a victim in his student short *Murder* (*Morderstwo*); or the flow of blood and water in one scene in *Two Men and a Wardrobe* (*Dwaj ludzie z szafą*). His 1960s work, up to and including *Chinatown*, is unified by the interplay of these two images, which combined most closely in *Knife in the Water*, *Repulsion*, *Macbeth* and *Chinatown*. The battle of knife and water is the ever-uneven one of *The Fat and the Lean* (*Le Gros et le maigre*), large and small, the one brandished almost as impotently as a Canutian sceptre before an inexorable ocean. In sexual terms, the difference inserts the 'phallic knife' into a scenario as masochistic as it is sadistic. Polanski's basic imagistic set – the combination of knife and water – fuses into a dialectical image, containing the roles of both victim and victimiser: the mingling of blood and water in a recurrent dream of Polanski the victim, hit on a head with a brick in an abandoned German bunker in Cracow just after the war (Leaming 1981: 20, 33, 66); while the knife reasserts control in a violent situation. Entire films might even function as 'knives': the echoes of René Clément's *Plein Soleil* (1960) in *Knife in the Water*, pointed out by Barbara Leaming (1981: 54), bespeak a mimetically desiring appropriation of the power of the older Western director, whose car he had envied and whose time spent with Kwiatkowska he surely disliked. After the 1960s, the concentration of this imagery is dispersed, perhaps because it had come to a head in *Chinatown*.

Thus Polanski's true exile may have been less the one from Poland (for even *Knife in the Water* could be defined in terms of the 'first auteurism', based on minor Hollywood, as a 'professional project', being after all as much a Skolimowski film as a Polanski one) than that from Hollywood, where his ideally self-denying, self-concealing, chameleon mode of working had long been naturalised among earlier waves of exiles such as himself. It is of course also possible that Polanski would have been an exile in Hollywood itself once the late 1960s and early 1970s had passed, along with the mainstream's tolerance for the dark eroticism of films like *Rosemary's Baby* or *Chinatown* (the 'Polanski' of popular imagination as a darker, more genuinely absurd double of his real mod counterpart than Mr Evil is of Austin Powers…). Thereafter, Polanski might no longer have been able to hide in the mainstream: its waters, like those of *Chinatown*, would have been diverted. His homeland may well have been more a brief period in time than a country, and its passage seemed to leave him slightly disoriented.

Cul-de-Sac had a complicated passage to production. Interviewed in 1963, Polanski answered the question of his intentions after *Knife in the Water* as follows:

> I know what I would *like* to do. It's a story of a married couple, he is approximately 46 or 48, and she is 22 or 23. They live in a seaside house which is falling apart. He is very rich but she is ruining him slowly by her extravagance; she is crazy, but he's in love with her. A wounded gangster falls into the house where he finds shelter… (Weinberg 1963–64: 33)

Co-written in Paris by Polanski and Gérard Brach shortly after Polanski's departure from Poland, it was initially titled *Riri* (which Polanski translates as 'Dickie'), before temporary rebaptism as *If Katelbach comes* (a title eventually used by some of its European distributors). Dickie was based on Polanski's friend Andrzej Katelbach, and Polanski and Brach envisaged making the film in France. Producer Pierre Roustang, however, turned it down, citing its lack of 'shock sequences' and Polanski's 'Middle European' sense of humour (Polanski 1984: 165). Several years passed before its acceptance, in England, by the Compton Group, for which it was Polanski's second project: having commissioned a horror movie, the Group may have been surprised to get *Repulsion*, but that film's financial success rendered *Cul-de-Sac* feasible. In Polanski's own words: 'Making *Repulsion* had been a means to an end: *Cul-de-Sac*' (Polanski 1984: 196). Indeed, *Cul-de-Sac* is probably the most artistically ambitious of Polanski's 1960s features, as it steers the absurdist power-games of his shorts closer to their more textured prototypes, Samuel Beckett's *Waiting for Godot* and *Endgame*, demonstrating the possibility of transferring key elements of the low-budget works to the more expensive, expansive canvas. Where the shorts had only one couple, *Cul-de-Sac* – like Beckett's plays – has two, though Polanski's prioritisation of the male/female one is consistent both with his interests and the habits of cinema. Whereas sexual and power rivalry reinforce one another in *Knife in the Water*, in *Cul-de-Sac* they develop separately, as there is no prospect of the woman pairing off with the intruder. Power rivalry drives the main plot, sexual alliance the subplots that interweave it.

Polanski's autobiographical account allows one to imagine a *Cul-de-Sac* shot in Yugoslavia and/or with Alexandra Stewart in the lead role, though it stresses Yugoslavia's lack of necessary tide and the way the wholesomeness of Stewart jarred with 'the offbeat, slightly kooky role of Teresa' (Polanski 1984: 198). The shoot suffered almost as many curses as had bedevilled *Knife in the Water*, including poor weather, Holy Island's Spartan amenities, Lionel Stander's heart ailment – which almost caused the insurance underwriters' withdrawal – and Polanski's altercations with cast and crew. Producer Gene Gutowski described the result as 'worth every minute of the problems it caused', but its relatively cool critical reception and its breaking of its budget briefly frustrated the Gutowski-Polanski plan to set up a major Hollywood deal. More conventional – though still distinctively Polanskian – horror projects would be needed to reestablish a bankability secured in spectacular fashion with *Rosemary's Baby*.

Cul-de-Sac: Plot summary

Following a failed heist that has left both of them wounded, two gangsters approach Lindisfarne, one pushing and one inside a stolen car. When it slides off the road and hits a post, the less severely wounded one, Dickie (Lionel Stander), leaves his companion Albie (Jack MacGowran) in it and goes for help. He arrives at an eleventh-century castle bought by a recently-retired businessman, George (Donald Pleasence), who lives there with his unfaithful wife of ten months, Teresa (Françoise Dorléac). The castle is deserted, but Dickie quickly hides as Teresa returns. Waking up after a sleep in the hen-house, Dickie makes his way to the kitchen in the night, helps himself to food and tries to phone his boss, Katelbach, to explain and get instructions. When George and Teresa arrive to challenge him, he mocks them and forces them to join in retrieving Albie and the car – which he is stunned to find surrounded by the rising tide. Dickie locks George and Teresa in the bedroom, but when Albie dies of his wounds, Teresa – who slips out through the window during the night – helps him to bury him. Dickie awaits the arrival of Katelbach. The only arrivals, though, are old friends of George, Philip and Marion Fairweather (Robert Dorning and Marie Kean), accompanied by their obnoxious child Horace (Trevor Delaney), and a younger couple, Cecil and Jacqueline (William Franklyn and Jacqueline Bisset). In order to conceal the true state of affairs, Dickie functions as an unusually insubordinate butler throughout their visit. Tense and increasingly irritated by their presence, George falls out with his friends, and when Marion calls Teresa a tart he throws them out. As the men snooze on the terrace, Teresa lights some strips of paper she has placed between Dickie's toes, and he avenges himself by whipping her with his belt. Going to phone Katelbach again, Dickie removes his jacket, which enables Teresa to slip the gun from its pocket and pass it to George. Told that he is on his own, Dickie prepares to leave, but decides to lock up George and Teresa before doing so. Possessing a gun now, and prompted by Teresa, George shoots Dickie, and the scene ends with Dickie dead and George's Jaguar in flames. Teresa tries to persuade George to leave before Katelbach can arrive. The car that drives up, and which George confronts, is only that of Cecil, returning to retrieve his gun. Teresa flees with him as George refuses to leave. Instead, he rampages through the studio full of his paintings of Teresa, runs through the rising tide and ends perched on a rock above it, alone, utterly bereft, and sobbing his first wife's name, as a plane flies overhead.

An open air theatre of the absurd

Cul-de-Sac can be situated in the Polish and European absurdist tradition, to which it is arguably the most closely related of all Polanski's features, with the possible exception of *The Tenant*. Len Masterman may deem surrealism the film's governing principle, quoting Polanski's statement of primary commitment to it in an epigraph, but his argument that Polanski pursues a surrealist exaltation of the criminal is forced and it is telling that Masterman closes by comparing him to Beckett, implicitly reframing the work in terms of absurdism (1970: 44–60). If it exalts anything, it is less the crim-

The meeting of the odd couples: Lionel Stander, Françoise Dorléac, Jack MacGowan and Donald Pleasance in *Cul-de-Sac*

inal than a principle of the perverse that is no longer individualised, as in surrealism, but universal and impersonal. The surrealism of the work is only incidental and arguably residual, a matter of the quasi-Buñuelian recurrence of fetishised chickens, or of the way the veil hanging from George's head as Albie looks up at him, mistaking him for his wife Doris, recalls the wedding-veiled beggar in the anarchic banquet sequence of *Viridiana* (1961). The shift from surrealism, a formation whose heyday had been in the 1920s and 1930s, to the absurdism that dominated the late 1950s corresponds not only to Polanski's situation at a particular historical conjuncture but to the irretrievability of a surrealist moment whose hopes of social liberation through the unfettered individual unconscious had proven utopian in the face of the night-marishness of fascism's malign liberation of a collective unconscious. It also indicates his awareness of the difficulty of reconciling the explosiveness of a movement necessarily specialising in shorts with the feature-length filmmaking to which he aspired: something achieved in absurdist theatre through the development of a unified narrative event that represented both a myth and an extended poetic metaphor (Esslin 1969: 186–8) – though Polanski's chicken, egg and flight imagery is a pale, because subordinate, echo of a device the absurdists would foreground. Absurdism restates the surrealist case for the necessity of revolution by documenting a societal encasement in deadening clichés, but in its post-war Adornian 'administered world' their chains are far harder to shake off, as they shackle vast tracts of the individual's inner landscape. Moreover, that landscape is more lunar than volcanic: the dead place of boredom that breeds fantasies of (and then actual) torture as relief. Thus it is hardly surprising that Polanski should have voiced a desire to film *Waiting for Godot* or the plays of Sławomir Mrożek.

To mention Mrożek, of course, is to signal Polanski's simultaneous indebtedness to a Polish absurdism that was not just a post-1956 thaw implicit declaration of a preference for Western traditions over the failed Soviet graft of socialist realism (though it was that too): it also picked up the dropped thread of the inter-war theatre of Witkacy and Witold Gombrowicz. Particularly pertinent among the works of Gombrowicz are *Ferdydurke* and *Operetka*, as has been stressed by Mariola Jankun-Dopartowa (2000: 28–33), though in claiming primacy for Gombrowicz she overstates her case. Dickie's appearance as a parodistic incarnation of the American gangster breathes an absurdist sense of life's suffocation under dead languages, which he appropriates mockingly to render George the mirroring cliché that reinforces him by inversion: that of the affected, effete Englishman. It takes a cliché not only to catch a cliché but also to generate its counterpart. The consequence is that George's every word faces the possible indignity of derisive quotation as a sign of Englishness, wealth, class and presumed snobbishness and effeminacy. Thus Dickie mocks George's use of 'one' by stating that 'one does not choose the time one gets into trouble', or counters his complaints of the cold by instructing Teresa to 'fetch him his mink'. No longer expressive of his individuality, George's language writhes in the impotence of simply strengthening Dickie's position – a bind which does indeed recall Gombrowicz.

At the same time, though, Dickie's stereotypicality also parallels the time-shifting of characters from an outdated genre in a Mrożek play like *The Turkey* (*Indyk*), where Rudolph and Laura – exiles from an inter-war melodrama – seek desperately to inject a bygone optimism into the comically terminal disillusionment of the Poet. Equally relevant would be Tadeusz Różewicz, particularly the preoccupation with brutalisation and violence in *The Witnesses, or Our Little Stabilisation* (*Świadkowie albo Nasza mała stabilizacja*), where a man impassively describes an initially apparently idyllic encounter between a boy and a kitten that ends in its brutal murder (which recalls the attack on the kitten in *Two Men and a Wardrobe*). Nor can one avoid mention of Harold Pinter, whose work bristles with menacing intruders, as if Polanski's attunement to a British influence while in Britain reflected a chameleon actor-exile's partly playful trying on of a new, local identity and set of preoccupations (the almost comically all-pervasive British concern with class): after all, the film seems to splice together a more Beckettian first half and a more Pinteresque second one. It may even be a test case of the recipe for transforming the one into the other (simply add more characters and throw in a tense silence or two between them?). Polanski may be one of a triumvirate of non-French but French-linked absurdists – the other two being Beckett and Eugene Ionesco – the reality of whose exile underwrites and arguably validates the absurdist sense of alienation, preserving it from its own ironic degeneration into what Raymond Williams skewered at the time as 'the most recent and most bourgeois of platitudes' (1966: 153). After his brief flirtation with surrealism in his first short, *Two Men and a Wardrobe*, absurdism is the form of modernism that marks Polanski's work: not the formal modernism of the Nouvelle Vague, with its radicalisation of narrative modes, but one that problematises spectator/text relations – to say nothing of 'identification'

– through the unease of black comedy and unpredictably shifting gender roles and power-plays. Polanski's is the urgently 'contentist' (because East Central European?) modernism of shock, solitude, paranoia and trauma, not the formalist (and largely French) one of narrative play.

Polanski's presentation of sexuality can be linked to the comparison with Beckett, particularly *Endgame*: the fact that there is less tenderness between Teresa and George than between the gangsters (particularly on the side of Dickie, who has a pet-name for Albie) echoes the *Endgame* set-up, in which Hamm and Clov are inseparable while the married couple are in the dustbin. What is foregrounded here is less what Williams calls the tramps' 'way of compassion in degradation' in *Waiting for Godot* than Lucky and Pozzo's 'way of domination and dependence: relationships which can only be reversed' (1966: 154). This inversion indicates *Cul-de-Sac*'s greater proximity to *Endgame*, which itself musically reverses the emphases of *Waiting for Godot* by foregrounding the dominance/dependence relationship. At the same time, though, the non-arrival of Katelbach is of course reminiscent of *Waiting for Godot*, and when Dickie and Albie discuss his anger in short, repetitive sentences, calling him only 'he', this is uncannily like the dialogues of Vladimir and Estragon, particularly when Albie concludes 'he doesn't love us any more'. As for the question of dominance, the camera's frequent proximity to Dickie establishes identification with his point of view (when the camera gives his view of George and his guests through a crack in a door, the resultant image is like a Polanskian parody of early 1960s widescreen), while his solitary occupation of the image in the film's early stages allows him to bulk large in it and control it.

As noted above, Polanski's absurdist modernism unsettles text/spectator relationships. His very first shot catches us off guard. A wide open space, telegraph poles, a long straight road: the imagery suggests an American road movie. But then the title comes up – *Cul-de-Sac* – denying that the road goes anywhere. So much for the suggestion of wide open spaces; the destination – the Holy Island castle inhabited by George and Teresa – will indeed be the narrowest of cul-de-sacs for the two arrivals, the place of their death. This too will be unexpected, as the gangsters are meant to destroy the guests. A car then comes up this road and sputters to a halt. Here too we are misled: shot from the front, it is not apparent from a distance that it is being pushed. Confusingly, in the context of the opening image's play with and against classic Hollywood imagery, an American is pushing it and a Briton is seated within it, so the sense of place is suspended. There is a Beckettian extremity of character polarisation that suggests the interdependence, inseparability and mutual reinforcement of stereotypes, as well – of course – as grotesque comedy (the grotesque being for Bakhtin the co-presence of two bodies within one (1984: 26)): one large and American, one diminutive and English; one burly and insensitive, the other bespectacled and fastidious. When the latter says 'here we are' (even though they are in the middle of nowhere) it has the gnomically *ex cathedra* air of one of Hamm's pronouncements in *Endgame*. The little man is just as immobile as Hamm, while the contrast with the American's mobility also resembles the Hamm/Clov relationship, though later, when Dickie literally becomes a servant – the butler – the film's mode will shift as his imperious grasp of an etiquette he then throttles point by point recalls the Losey-Pinter *The Servant* (1963). As the car moves forwards we start at what sounds like a gunshot. Again, our expectations are deflated, as it turns out to be the car hitting the roadside post that immobilises it definitively.

Polanski's later play with expectations and the non-sequitur does not always involve such instant reorientations (we may assume that the couple Dickie sees on the beach as he arrives are who he will menace, not yet knowing the man to be Christopher (Iain Quarrier), the lethargic, handsome blond neighbour with whom Teresa has been amusing herself, and who makes himself scarce; and we may later be as surprised as Dickie to see water rising around the car). Nevertheless, the speed with which interpretive frames have to be tried and discarded in this overture has engendered a lingering edginess. As in comedy, one expects the unexpected. (The first comic moments are black ones, involving the car lurching up and down and the wounded, doll-like Albie wincing as Dickie thoughtlessly, unceremoniously and repeatedly plumps down upon its back seat.) However, the impossibility of establishing even an approximate knowledge of when the unexpected is likely to come renders it not so much funny as an insistent source of anxiety. As in Beckett, both the humour and the blackness derive from a suspicion that the worst (metaphorically represented by the failed, unseen heist) has already happened somewhere else. The unease is due to not knowing quite when the reverberations of this event – like Katelbach – will reach one: when the work's pervasive chickens will come home to roost. Like a creature hunting prey, *Cul-de-Sac* secures the apparently extra-absurdist reality into which we think we escape when Dickie leaves the car and draws it back down a slope and into the hole of its absurdist starting point: it documents the last days of a humanity that may be in the process of becoming an insect but which (unlike Gregor Samsa) has not yet woken up to the fact. (The idea of escape from enclosure is undermined systematically.) The closest to such transformation is surely George. In the presence of Dickie, his baldness renders his frequently un-coordinated, rubbery writhings – his combination of pipsqueak ex-military self-assertion and subsequent spineless grovelling – a stage in his metamorphosis into a rubber-man indeed. The closest to losing the name of human, this central figure is the locus of identification in our worst, most masochistic dreams.

The abyss of sexuality

Throughout Polanski's work, the scene of postponed, ever-imminent menace yields occasional blatantly masochistic fantasies that hope and pretend that the worst has already happened elsewhere, has been confronted already (after all, knowledge of its existence ought to allow one to see it as past). But in fantasies like those of *The Tenant* or *The Fearless Vampire Killers*, the slightly hysterical air (the nervousness and absurdism of a laughter surely linked to castration anxiety, 'black comedy' being the euphemism for the unfunniness of anxiety) betrays the fact that they have not seen off the menace, only identified with a lesser aggressor in the hope of appeasing a larger one, as if cutting off a finger in a token, smaller sacrifice meant magically to preserve one's life. The males who suffer degradation and even literal feminisation in these films are deprived of the phallus: of the knife that always exists in proximity to water (the most obvious examples being of course *Knife in the Water* itself, *Chinatown* and

Macbeth), the site both of its loss and of its cleansing. The knife is the phallus as object of contention, which can pass from hand to hand: in *Repulsion,* Carol wields the slasher's razor. If Polanski is surely, among other things, registering decade-specific male fears of the implications of an imminent Women's Liberation, the terror of helplessness may well be augmented by his own uncannily hidden wartime experiences. Linked to the knife, and guided by an exploratory libertinism, sexuality takes a nightmarish wrong turning: the knife penetrates the wrong part of the body, or seeks penetration where none is possible, and violence becomes the bloody underside of sexuality as triumph of the will. Another way of saying this is to state that the knife is not just – in what would otherwise be a tedious sub-psychoanalytic cliché – 'phallic', but that it is a phallus that needs to be particularly penetrative, and yield blood: in other words, one capable of rupturing a hymen (the significance of young girls in a 'Polanski' imaginary that is, unfortunately, and notoriously, partly correlated with the biographical in the popular imagination). Its bloodiness makes it also the sign of a historic violence that feminises the victim. The greatest danger the knife confronts is embodied in a water that becomes a projection of a femininity the male can never satisfy (its gendering as such being of course a cultural reflex of the sea's linkage to the periodicity of a moon that in its turn echoes that of the menstrual cycle): it represents the abyss of feminisation the knife can open up, into which the male may fall, but which also offers the best disguise after the violent deed, that of the cross-dressing protagonists of *Cul-de-Sac* and *The Tenant* in particular. When the period in hiding is over, the knife-wielding Polanski of *Chinatown* doubles as a Macduff who rips open his mother's womb to escape its seeling, suffocating night, the claustrophobia that runs through so many of his works, by releasing the waters.

In its final form (with Pleasence and Dorléac rather than Polanski himself and Kwiatkowska), *Cul-de-Sac* suggests a form of defense against these fears that attributes it to an older man who is in a sense already emasculated. Its projection onto an older man indicates its irrelevance, and hence the possibility of its comic treatment. (The initial plan would have exorcised it with a direct representation that had the double force of magic and exhibitionism, and been more like *The Tenant*.) The helplessness is no longer that of the women and children who – as Judith Doneson has shown (1978: 11–13, 18) – are so often linked metaphorically to Jews, and can therefore substitute for them (and so for Polanski himself) in an associative chain.

If George is presented as already emasculated, near-hysterical, kept firmly in his place by Dickie (at one point he and Teresa are held in the frame of a distant door, as if cages, while Dickie warns against hysteria), the habitual way in which Teresa's body appears before him is also worth considering. Its repeated shooting from behind as she moves or runs away from the camera creates a bitterly masochistic sense of Teresa turning away from her hapless worshipper, who is unworthy of her. As so often, the turned back raises questions of power: the woman's over the man, the man's over the woman. The sense of George's emasculation is apparent in his making up and dressing in drag by Teresa, the long beach sequence in which he fawns over Dickie, Dickie's reference to him as a fairy and Albie's description of him as queer and delirious mistaking of him for his wife Doris, or Teresa's general mockery of him.

To what extent, though, may the emasculation be the work of Teresa herself? And – in a related question – how typical is she of Polanski's women?

Polanski's women: an attempt at an identikit

Polanski's women are often presented as also in a sense children. Jankun-Dopartowa speaks of both Tess and Michelle (in *Frantic*) in these terms, evoking 'a terrified child in the body of an attractive young woman' (2000: 120); *Repulsion* concludes with a close-up of the photograph of Carol as a child; in *Bitter Moon*, Oscar defines Mimi as child-like; in *Cul-de-Sac* Teresa is described as a naughty child; and in *Chinatown*, mother and daughter are also mother and sister, so the older woman is almost doubly a child. This is not just a matter of the inevitability that links beauty and youth, or of Polanski's 1960s concern with youth culture and the possibilities of exposure of silken skin (and with extreme isolation in a highly sexualised world whose liberation also means collapsed norms, of those who are not part of it, as in Philippe Harel's *Extension du domaine de la lutte* (1999)). Nor is it – as so many journalists would have it – Humbert Humbert's obsession with Lolita, the lure of rejuvenation through young starlet or trophy wife. What interests Polanski seems rather to be the child's simultaneous vulnerability, intensity and vengeful capacity for cruelty. Moreover, beauty and cruelty go together, as beauty licenses cruelty and is itself cruel, of limited availability, justifying aggression in the scramble to secure it. The interest in the grotesque Grażyna Stachówna ascribes to the young in general may also play a role (1988b: 20), as may Polanski's own perennially youthful looks and stature and consequent willingness to identify with the youngest figure – who, in cinema, is of course usually a woman (see *The Tenant* in particular). Polanski's delineation of a figure both vulnerable and potentially cruel is most developed in *Bitter Moon*, which may be taken as his fullest exposition of a tragic woman's story that figures only fragmentarily in the other films. If children are vulnerable, female children are particularly so, and Herbert Eagle has suggested that in *Repulsion* the final photograph of Carol among older men may hint at the cause of her psychosis (1994: 123–4). If this is so, then *Chinatown* may be the writing large of a nightmarish prequel to that nightmare. The intensity of the child's reaction to suffering can then render it monstrously cruel in return: here again *Bitter Moon* gives the fullest image of how an older man renders a woman monstrous through his own monstrous behaviour. (In the end, with her off-the-shoulder dress and long hair, Mimi may seem an almost grotesquely bloated fusion of Gilda and Fellini's Anita Ekberg, ripe for death because of her glassy-eyed absorption by a myth.)

   Cul-de-Sac, by way of contrast, gives the most fragmentary, least systematic, version of this itinerary, with no explanation of why Teresa is as she is. Teresa's cruelty is cheery, almost debonair, and simply a given. It could be that the only explanation it requires is the appearance of George himself. This, in turn, though, may prompt questions regarding what may have united them in the first place – questions a more thoroughgoing absurdism would leave hanging, but which the greater commitment to realism in Polanski (and in most cinema?) than anything found in Beckett or Gombrowicz allows to resurface. If George's wealth is the obvious magnet, Teresa would be

close kin to the 'aspirational' protagonists of *Knife in the Water*. There is no suggestion here though that the victimiser was herself once a victim, and it would be wholly
illegitimate to attribute any such motives to her. She is just a snapshot in Polanski's
multi-part film about women. Nevertheless, her cruelty may even have the same root
as Oscar's in *Bitter Moon*: disdain for the person who adores you, as George so clearly
does. (In a very disguised sense, of which Polanski himself may or may not be aware,
George himself is a filmmaker, part of this filmmaker's worst, least consciously admissible nightmare about himself: the assembled multiple portraits of Teresa are like the
frozen frames of a film.) Although her boots and trousers may have been widespread
mid-1960s chic(k) attire, they also belong with the imagery of sadism (a sadism
absurdly reduced here to no more than an image, a 'quotable gesture'?): Nancy Sinatra
boots that were made to walk all over you. If Teresa is also akin to Lady Macbeth,
who also reproaches her husband with not being a man – her frustrated-child griz-
zling making Macbeth vulnerable to her urging – she is her transposition into a major
key. Teresa's frequent placement in the frame's centre, behind and between the men,
suggests the status of apple of discord, as in *Knife in the Water*. Unlike *Knife in the
Water*, though, here neither man is bothering to contend for her. *Cul-de-Sac* stages the
Oedipal triangle of the earlier film as an absurd non-event. The suggestions made by
the image are stalemated by the actualities of the narrative.

Chickens and eggs: The Bird-Man of Lindisfarne

Chickens and eggs are central to *Cul-de-Sac*, present even when absent, as – for
instance – in the final image, whose birds and plane overflying the bald egg-head
of George reconjugate elements of the chicken/egg opposition. Donald Pleasence's
decision to shave his head may not have been approved by Polanski, but it shows
his grasp of the work's metaphorical centre. Its elements function in a poetic way
that invites a complex, multi-levelled response, though the dense symbolic network is
surely also of a piece with the strain of classicism in Polanski that prides itself on the
polish and professionalism of the *pièce bien faite*. (It was this Polanski who said that
no one had come out of the Nouvelle Vague unscathed.) That classicising strain, with
its one-upmanship vis-à-vis the modern French and its ostentatious performance of
the control that matters so deeply to Polanski, can be subverted momentarily by the
absurd, however, as when the recurrence of crabs at the beginning (Dickie pulling his
foot back before one, Teresa dropping one on Christopher's bare skin) suggests that
this may be a leitmotif. The puckish, prankish side of Polanski would surely be happy
to describe the crabs as red herrings, for the chickens soon take over, and the extent of
their use does indeed represent a classicist impulse to maximise the use of a resource.
Chickens, of course, do not fly, and so on one level George may be identified with
them, as if he is but one of the many men gathered around a Circe Teresa, tending her
chickens. At the same time, though, chickens and eggs are incompatible here, as Teresa
cares for the chickens but not for George. The fact that chickens and eggs ought to
go together only deepens the absurd irony of the opposition. If George resembles the
chickens, unable to fly – an inability underlined at moments by his wing-like flapping

of his arms, and his passion for kites – perhaps that is why he is unable to go far from the castle in the end. (The kite caught on the telegraph wires at the beginning would thus be a metaphorical forecast of the end.) Earth-bound, the chickens are always getting underfoot, being trodden on and fluttering up with abrupt, long-suffering squawks: images of a life irritatingly strewn with obstacles, of being out of place, and also of what befalls George again and again. Dickie almost treads on one as he approaches the castle, and it clatters up with a shock-effect that may well be a joke recollection of the cockatoo in *Citizen Kane* (Orson Welles, 1941) (itself a horror film reference to a scene in *Mad Love* (Karl Freund, 1935)). A rhythm of irritable tension when nothing is happening, and shock when it does, typifies the film, and the chickens are essential to it, their wandering around the castle evoking a slow-motion settling of the dust of the chaos created by Dickie's demolition of the henhouse – which, like the kite at the beginning, classically foretells something, in this case the destruction of George's household arrangements. But it is a chaos underfoot, through which one wades – not a major threat. The fridge's stuffing with eggs emphasises the castle's isolation, as the only food it contains is from Teresa's chickens. The grotesque image economically underlines the vulnerability of the couple's attempted autarky. After all, a relationship that depends upon isolating one's partner from the world is similarly vulnerable in a society that does not know purdah. George's baldness does not make him an egg-head, however – for all the cultivation of his accent and speech rhythms – but rather underlines his difference from other men, particularly the younger ones who may threaten his marriage. Devoted to paintings that will never be exhibited, he has lost one role – that of businessman – but not found another.

Language, exile and cliché

In *Cul-de-Sac*, the play with chickens and eggs is not only thematic, however, but also involves a Kafkaesque and dream-like literalisation of cliché such as generates *Metamorphosis*, where Gregor Samsa's transformation into an insect pictures a nightmarish enactment of what others may have said about him. Polanski's play with this motif is more comically absurd than menacing, though, as it arguably becomes a slightly tiresome running joke. In one example of such play, George accuses Teresa of 'egging him on', of wanting to see blood, as she condemns his failure to protect her or the chickens. She might indeed have expected more of a former military man, especially since a misunderstanding had caused her to think he had been in the cavalry. (Either she or Dickie might well have called him 'chicken', though Polanski displays an uncharacteristic reluctance to milk the image by declining to have either say this.) 'You're not a man', she complains. Is this because he is a bird-man (remember those waving arms)? Surprisingly, Teresa herself can be identified with the chickens, Dickie saying he does not dig chicks like her as she visits him at night (instead, in a further pun, he is digging something else: a hole in which to bury Albie). (The puns are probably ultimately less Kafkaesque than exhibitionistic examples of the foreigner's mastery of English.) Similarly, George's paintings of Teresa include one of a chicken, as if Polanski is supplementing his earlier joke about widescreen perception – and the kind of film (American?) that this is not? – with one about the Eisensteinian montage that breaks up the framed images of humans by inserting animals as their metaphorical equivalents.

Another example of such play with concretised cliché is detected by Jankun-Dopartowa, who deems George's shooting of the plaster dog a 'visual equivalent' of the phrase 'zabić, jak psa' ('to shoot down like a dog') (2000: 47) – which would of course also be Kafkaesque, recalling Joseph K.'s death in *The Trial*. If all the eggs are in the fridge, this may also sum up the state of relations between George and Teresa: there is no hint of a wish for a child, a non-issue raised by the ten months of their marriage echoing the expiry of a term of pregnancy and by the appallingness of Horace, the child nobody would want. The occasional glimpses of pigeons and planes, meanwhile, suggest that the earth-bound chickens are the patron birds of the cul-de-sac: like George's marriage, going nowhere. The tide rises around him at the end as if demanding his evolution into a creature capable of flight, his incapacity underlined by the insouciant passage of the regular airplane above.

Polanski's Kafkaesque alienation of language infuses it with the absurdist perspective of the exile. All disturbances of reality arguably echo a prior, exilic disturbance in the encounter with language that may also be linked to the polymorphous-perverse refusal of Language that results from its undialectical conception in Lacanian/Kristevan terms, as the Symbolic and the Law-of-the-Father. The sheer range of different forms of that disturbance across Polanski's work can be measured by comparing *Cul-de-Sac* with *Chinatown*. In *Chinatown*, key words are knotted with others to create a hallucinatory oscillation of clues to hidden trauma: the impossibility for Evelyn Mulwray (Faye Dunaway) of saying 'daughter' without finding that word collapse into 'sister', as the words are the two sides of the vertiginously endless-spinning, ungraspable coin of her incestuous experience; while the confusion of 'grass' and 'glass' is the echoing presence of the idea of Chinatown between the film's prehistory and its concluding cataclysm. In *Cul-de-Sac*, however, linguistic disturbance is more pervasive and casual and both less obvious and less telling. The multiple meanings of 'chick' and 'egg' are not a fulcrum of plot development and traumatic climax, and so can pass almost unseen and feel like embroidery, or self-indulgent dissolving stitches in a verbal suturing. At the same time, though, all the characters' idiolects clash, the most spectacular example being that between Dickie's parodic gangster slang and Teresa's heavily-accented English. If these two foreigners are best placed to dominate it is because their awareness of the likelihood of being mocked themselves prompts them to get their retaliation in first and mock the natives, as they do most cogently with George whose Englishness blinds him to his own dislocation. The money that has bought him an out from his business has bought him out of reality too. His ignorance of his true position renders him patsy and cuckold. For if 'the outlandish' is comedy's name for the foreign, Lindisfarne looks like its native home: the isolation of this spit of land renders everything foreign. Undecidability becomes the key feature of the place that is part of the mainland one moment, cut off from it by the tide the next. The consequent lack of an indigenous community becomes apparent in the difficulty of determining just how a dwelling located there should be described. Slightly uneasily, aware of the stiltedness of the expression, George himself calls it a fortress at one point, though it is also a former monastery, a place of literary composition and – in Dickie's eyes – a prospectively fine site for orgies (the Sadean 'secret place'). As if parodying the locution that deems the Englishman's home his castle, the film shows a castle as a very unhomely home, an uncomfortable cross between home and heritage site that has not yet been resolved in a partial administration by the National Trust. No wonder it is abandoned eventually, the image of a culture without a rightful owner, the absurdist home one cannot have. It perches upon a rock as ridiculously as George himself at the end, as if he himself were its reflection in miniature – or a gargoyle blasted away by the explosion of the castle.

CHAPTER EIGHT

Chinatown: Politics as Perspective, Perspective as Politics

Dana Polan

Central to a number of the films of Roman Polanski is a meditation on, or investigation, of the space. In particular, these films examine the consequences for personal surety, security and sanctity when one takes up a place within this or that particular space. This is a meditation or investigation represented not only in the plots that are narrated (for example, the story of Rosemary exploring the space of her home in *Rosemary's Baby*) but also in the *mise-en-scène* that embodies this narration (for example, the female-Gothic inspired tracks that accompany Rosemary on her process of discovery). Many of Polanski's films hone obsessively on characters who move into spaces only to discover that environment is not neutral but is a force that needs to be examined and interrogated.

There are among Polanski's films works centrally devoted to the exploration of domestic space as site of uncanny menace: *Rosemary's Baby* and *Repulsion*. There are also ones that take place in uncommon spaces outside habitual everyday reality: the boat at sea in *Knife in the Water* (*Nóż w wodzie*), the wasteland terrain of the aptly named *Cul-de-Sac*, the village away from the mainstream of civilisation in *The Fearless Vampire Killers*. The former films move paranoia into the privatised space of the domestic realm (and beyond that into the recesses of feminine psychology) and the latter move it into the imaginary realm of fantasy (the films of the latter category are either generically unclassifiable works that seem 'weird' and unsettling, or quirky genre films, such as *The Fearless Vampire Killers* or *Pirates*, set away from everyday life in a realm of otherness – for example, the swashbuckler narrative as an adventure out of the ordinary).

Quite different from these are the several films that Polanski devotes to investigations of *the city*. Here, there is a displacement into the large-scale fabric of urban life of both the fear that the domestic paranoid films had confined to inner space *and* the strangeness that the fantasy films had situated in imaginary spaces apart from an everyday realm. For the city-films, I am thinking here of works like *Frantic* or *The Pianist*, where the central characters try to make their way through the menacing space of the city overall, and especially of *Chinatown* where the protagonist's investigation of local (originally, sexual) infelicities within the city becomes a political path to deeper discovery of a corruption seemingly inherent to the social space of the urban as such.

Of course, the distinctions of types of story and their narration are not so perfect and inviolate. For example, as its very title implies, *The Tenant* is directly about a personage who, through a social contract, takes up residence – this case, in the space of the city – and so one might want to connect it to other works of urban exploration (like, say, *Chinatown*, the Polanski film that immediately precedes it). But *The Tenant* plays out much of its paranoid drama in a very circumscribed space: at most, one tightly-knit neighbourhood and then, for much of its story, one single building with the protagonist endlessly forced back into his domestic space by horrific encounters with the other. *The Tenant* turns quickly from investigation of the space of the social environment of the urban into an extended personal nightmare. Not coincidentally does the title character cross-dress for a long piece of the story: for all its emphasis on social interaction, and despite its coming after the expansive urban exploration of *Chinatown*, *The Tenant* harkens back to the gendered paranoid narratives of *Repulsion* or *Rosemary's Baby*. It is a highly internalised film that associates victimisation and feminisation.

Many of Polanski's films dramatise the processes of investigation of space through a virtually obsessive concentration on one character who is seeking to elucidate meanings in the space he/she inhabits. The camera and the narrative stay intensely and incessantly close to this central character, and it is easy for Polanski films thereby to become explorations of the personal realm above all. Even when they try to reach out to an understanding of a larger social world, the films seem primarily to function as intense depictions of subjectivity. Even the exploration of the space of the city can turn into private *agon* in which increasingly the larger geography turns into mere backdrop, a veritable screen of projection for the protagonist's own fears. The city films may hint at the ways in which perspective becomes political. That is, they flirt with the idea that one's own particular place within the space of the social can serve as leverage in which individual point of view opens up to larger political awareness. But the city films also enable a collapse of political consciousness back into mere subjectivity – into an individualising point of view that cannot lift itself up beyond its own limited perspective to understand the world at large.

Thus, while *The Pianist*, for instance, could be seen in terms of its representation of space as a city-film, with a very precise sense of an urban geography beyond any one person's individual orbit, it is also very much like the films of domestic paranoia in the ways it endlessly shows its title character endlessly shuffling – or shuttled by others – from one circumscribed and even claustrophobic space to another. *The Pianist* is often about the small rooms, the tight interior spaces – little more than meagre boxes – that the protagonist is forced to hide in. From such enclosures, he can become little more than a voyeur onto the rest of the city – peeking out, for example, as the Warsaw ghetto uprising seeks to make its mark in history.

In contrast, by its borrowing of its overall narrative structure from the tradition of the hard-boiled detective story, *Chinatown* appears to gain an expansiveness that is unavailable to Polanski's other films of personal investigation. This expansiveness is first of all, geographic: the modern detective, often in his car, traverses the city, moving across social classes, linking up disparate and often seemingly incommensurate sites and uncovering the links – of power, of money, of politics – that connect them. Investigative mobility is a central legacy of the hard-boiled form. That the modern detective is a latter-day picaro who adventures out in the city to map its meaning, is especially clear in the novels of Raymond Chandler and his self-appointed protégé Ross MacDonald. *Chinatown* comes very clearly from this tradition, the moment in which Jake Gittes (Jack Nicholson) finds the mangled body of Ida Sessions (Diane Ladd) in a bungalow seeming a direct troping off similar scenes in both Chandler and MacDonald. The hard-boiled detective is a cartographer, who finds that the spaces of the city are not random but are traversed by networks of class, power and privilege. In more recent works like Walter Mosley's *Devil in a Blue Dress* and the film made of it (Carl Franklin, 1995), race is added to class, and here the detective's journey is also a crossing of racial boundaries. In this respect, *Chinatown* can still seem rooted in the political stereotypes of an earlier period with its jokes about Chinamen and its plot twists revolving around such things as a Japanese gardener whose pronunciation of 'glass' is confused with that of 'grass'. *Chinatown* crosses some frontiers, but not around issues of race and ethnicity. Indeed, it renders ethnic space – here figured in the name 'Chinatown' which Gittes and his associates virtually shudder at each mention of – as something so other and alien to the main patterns of the city that it seems part of another, ineffable geography. To enter into Chinatown is to leave the space of bearable rationality and personal security.

In *Chinatown*, Jake Gittes moves through the various byways of the city from the small bungalows of the working stiffs to the rich mansions, from the municipal halls to the private clubs, and on and on. At each stage of his trajectory, as befits the detective genre the film derives from, the information he has already gained synthesises with new things he learns to create one overall narrative from the diverse spaces he has visited. Here, again, we might contrast what ensues by means of the detective's cognitive synthesis of geography with the more fragmentary experience of space in a film like *The Pianist*. *The Pianist* has its protagonist move from site to site only to become fixed in places (often for long periods) where he spies on the iniquities of the world. On the one hand, the pianist has little mobility; on the other, his stasis turns the individual sites he stays in into isolated sights that add up to no larger meaning. Each sight the pianist witnesses thus becomes a sort of singular tableau that is at best representative of the greater violence of the Holocaust and war on the home-front (as, for example, when he sees a woman shot dead into a frozen kneeling position) but that never adds up to a story about that violence. Everywhere the pianist goes, he gets another terrifying vision of the horror of his modernity but there is no synthesis of these sights into an overall narrative explanation. The brute, virtually unnameable horror simply is out there to be witnessed.

In contrast, in *Chinatown*, Gittes' movement across the city is an additive process in which each new sight builds on the previous ones to give him more knowledge, more understanding of the vast webs of conspiracy that are the meaningful connections behind the seemingly disparate spaces he has traversed. *Chinatown* is directly narrative in a way that does not seem the case for, say, *The Tenant, Repulsion* or *The Pianist* where the horrific sights and events that come into the protagonist's orbit can seem random, arbitrary and disconnected. In contrast to them, *Chinatown* is directly about a piecing together of bits of knowledge into an explanatory whole (although, it must be said, even after multiple viewings, the exact nature of the conspiracy and how it unfolded is not necessarily apparent).

For much of the film, Gittes looks out onto various realities and fits their individual meanings together into a larger logic: as he does so, the camera frequently takes up a position just alongside him (or just over his shoulder) as if to filter the knowledge Gittes is receiving and deliver it to the spectator at the same time. Paradigmatic of the film's marrying of the detective's perspective with that of the spectator is the first shot that follows when Gittes decides to take on the assignment of following (the fake) Mrs Mulwray's husband and goes out into the field. The shot begins with a focus on Mulwray (Darrell Zwerling) out in the dry beds of Los Angeles and then the camera pulls back to reveal Gittes spying on him and settles on a position just behind Gittes's shoulder as if it were his partner in the uncovering of knowledge. Not for nothing is this shot also the opening of the original trailer for the film: it sums up the extent to which the film has to do with the interaction between events and one man's viewing of them for the purpose of creating a meaningful narrative logic.

In such a shot, the viewer participates along with the detective in the additive process by which knowledge builds up, by application of inductive reasoning, into an ever more convincing and globalising narrative. At the same time, however, it should be noted that this kind of recurrent shot – in which the spectator sees both Gittes looking *and* the reality he is looking at – also sets up the possibility of a disjunction between Gittes' perspective and the spectator's: as much as the reality he studies, Gittes becomes an object for study. This becomes significant for a narrative that is not only about what Gittes understands but also about what is beyond his understanding. The spectator is both with Gittes and beyond him.

To indicate the additive nature of knowledge for both spectator and protagonist in *Chinatown* (even if there is a gap between them) is to say that the expansiveness of *Chinatown* is temporal and even historical as well as spatial. As Gittes circulates through the space of the city, he not only moves forward but backwards – into history: the political history of corruption that is endemic to Los Angeles. Here, we see the specific advantage of the detective genre as probing into historical time. As a number of scholars have pointed out, there are two narratives in the detective story: there is

Suspecting the victim: Jack Nicholson and Faye Dunaway in *Chinatown*

the present story of the detective's forward-moving investigation but there is also the story of the crime that has already been committed in the past (even if, in some cases, a quite recent past) and which can have consequences in the present. Through his investigation, the detective uncovers a logic and sweep of time larger than his own life's temporality: he discovers that his own narrative is relative to a broader span of history.

In one strand of detective narrative – say, the armchair story best represented by the aristocratic British tale – the detective discovers all this from the safe distance of pure cognition: he learns about the crimes of the past but they do not impinge on, do not unhinge, his present in any consequent way. But in the hard-boiled noir tradition, the story from the past – the story of crimes already committed – interferes, interweaves with the story in and of the present, the story of the investigation and the labour of the detective in the here and now. The past reaches out to engulf the detective, to entangle him in its spell. Gittes, for instance, is endlessly finding himself implicated in the story he is investigating rather than remaining cognitively above it: from the start, he is played by the conspirators as a necessary piece in their plot (rather than his being in control as the superior investigator of that plot); he allows sentiment to entangle him in the world of his inquiry (thus, he becomes emotionally involved with Mrs Mulwray (Faye Dunaway)); he is even put bodily on the line (for example, he is beaten and shot at, and his nose is sliced by the knife of a henchman – the bandage on his nose then remaining for most of the rest of the film as a mark of his own bodily involvement in the tale).

Not merely is history something the detective investigates; it is a force that expands into the present and that implicates and threatens contagiously to overwhelm the investigator. This perhaps was one of the important insights of that cycle of paranoid conspiracy films of the early-to-mid-1970s that we can perhaps inscribe *Chinatown* within: you, the individual subject, are not apart from history; indeed, you are one of its subjects, potentially one of its pawns. (The most extreme rendition of this paranoid sense of the inescapability of the larger system's control over the self is *The Parallax View* (Alan Pakula, 1974), where the investigative journalist is made to be the patsy for the very conspiracy he is setting out to get a grip on.)

But the detective genre insists on historical time in a way that is not always explored in other types of paranoid conspiracy films. The detective story is *per se* an investigation of 'what once happened' (even if, as *Chinatown* suggests, what once happened is continuing to happen and can only get worse as when Noah Cross (John Huston) indicates that his goal is to buy up the future: the increasing voraciousness of Capital has no limits). But in many of the paranoid conspiracy films the emphasis is on 'what is happening now' without any impulsion to search for the roots of that menace in a prior cause. What is cannot be explained by what once was. It makes little sense to ask, for instance, where the Parallax conspiracy came from: the only importance is that it exists in the present (and is preparing plots for the future) and that is what needs to be probed. Likewise, in paranoid films by Polanski such as *Repulsion* or *The Tenant*, terrible things are happening in the here and now, and part of the tone of creepiness comes from the sense that they have no explanation, there is no logic, such as the temporal one, that might explain them away. There is no past that explains the uncanniness.

Even *The Pianist*, it must be said, has a tendency toward a present-fixated sense of the horrors its characters are undergoing. This may seem paradoxical since the Holocaust would appear to be the ultimate *historical* event. But this event is often one treated as so much the ultimate horror – the evil beyond belief – that it becomes an event that transcends historical understanding, that corresponds to no logical sense of the things humans do and can have done to them. In popular representation, the Holocaust is often presented as that which is outside of ordinary time and works according to another logic or, even perhaps, illogic. (Hence, one source of the outcry when phrases like Hannah Arendt's 'the Banality of Evil' (1963) or when books like Daniel Goldhagen's *Hitler's Willing Executioners: Ordinary Germans and the Holocaust* (1997) appear: by attempting to find some explanation in everyday behaviour and in historical cause, these ventures are seen as reducing the ultimate horror down to ordinariness. The Holocaust, cliché would have it, moves out of understandable historical time into a realm of the incomprehensible and the irrational). In the case of *The Pianist*, it is noteworthy that the one person who aspires to an explicitly political position on the events that are transpiring, Wladyslaw Szpilman's brother, is presented as a shrill figure without emotional sensitivity, and in any case, he soon disappears from the story so that it can obsessively tunnel into the perceptions of Szpilman who sees but often without comprehending. In *The Pianist*, the Holocaust is not an event of and in history but one that disrupts history and creates a non-temporality of overwhelming and incessant horror. *The Pianist* begins, significantly, *in media res* with the Nazis having already invaded, and to the extent that there is any sense of temporality in the film it tends to be little more than the understanding that the terrors the Nazis are perpetrating will only ever increase inevitably in intensity and degree of horror. (There is another vague level of temporal consciousness in the film. That Szpilman's father continues to dress up for dinner in early scenes is one sign of a will-to-the-past on the part of these middle-class Jews. They cling to tradition and try to find resilience in that. But this does not grant them – or the film – any special consciousness of the historical changes they are being caught up in. Quite the contrary, it is suggested that the Jewish victims are thereby made more vulnerable to the onslaught of horror.)

In *The Pianist*, the Holocaust becomes a symbol of the ineffable mystery of the human capacity for evil. But it must be said that, for all the ways in which its generic inscription in the detective genre gives *Chinatown* a greater potential for temporal comprehension, this film too has its own tendency to slide from historical and political awareness into notions of the ineffable, of terrible horrors beyond comprehension, of realms of human practice that lie beyond reason.

First, there is the very status of 'Chinatown' in the film. Despite the fact that this part of the real geography of Los Angeles gives its name to the film, there is, as already noted in passing, something jarring about the way Chinatown comes into the story to serve as the backdrop for its final set piece. Even as earlier sections of *Chinatown* moved across layers of social class, the film tended to stay within a space of Los Angeles whiteness with little more than hints of another ethnicised world in the figure of the Asian servants and gardener who work for the Mulwrays. With its city hall hearings, its bureau of records, its orange groves tended desperately by down-and-out farmers, its bungalows lived in by small-time operators, and so on, *Chinatown* offers a sharp, even sociological, sense of the consequences of power for the powerless in the urban context. But ultimately the film trades for sociology an exoticism that assumes there is no final understanding – that at the back of everyday things lurks a dark space of irrational malevolence: 'Forget it, Jake – it's Chinatown.'

The move from a sociologically specified and historically rooted Los Angeles to a Chinatown imagined as the space beyond reason goes hand-in-hand with another displacement of the political project of *Chinatown* into the realm of ineffable mystery. This has to do with its image of the capitalist, Noah Cross. The very incarnation of the political conspiracy in a single figure of voracious will is already a move in the direction of the pathologising of capital as a depravity. By imagining the capitalist as an excessive force that has no reason for its will to power than the sheer fact of that will to power, the film posits power itself as beyond understanding. This is in keeping with John Huston's extravagant performance in the film; not for nothing did Huston also play the figure at the centre of the conspiracy in another key paranoia film of the 1970s, *Winter Kills* (William Richert, 1979). Huston's over-the-top energetics render capitalist venture as crazed adventure – a pure force of nature that has to ever expand its reach and that is beholden to no human laws, including those of rational explanation. Capitalism turns from a set of trans-subjective historical processes into a bestial horror, a monstrosity.

Missing the perpetrator: John Huston and Jack Nicholson in *Chinatown*

And in this respect, it is appropriate to the film's ultimate detouring from the ideological analysis of the plays of power that it displaces politics into sexuality (rather than understand sexual power dynamics as themselves a form of politics). Following from a veritably Victorian cliché in which it is imagined that capitalism is a form of decadence or perversion, *Chinatown* makes its capitalist guilty of incest and makes the revelation of that immorality the ultimate consequential act of the film. Depravity in the private realm is deemed to be the most profound form of evil. The assumption that capitalist accumulation is a mere surface feature of a deeper and fundamentally depraved malevolence turns capitalism from object of potential rational analysis – of the sort the detective is committed to professionally – into an irrational horror that can only be looked on with dismay.

Significantly, Gittes solves most of the political crime early on, and he is able to explain with great clarity just what is being done to Los Angeles by the machinations of the rich. The ease with which he makes sense of the murder of Mulwray is almost like that in the classic British detective story where pure ratiocination is rendered as an all-powerful capability. But in the case of the hard-boiled tradition, there are often plots more perverse, mysteries much deeper, sins more pervasive, than the simple commission of crimes in the ordinary sense. For instance, in Hammett's classic hard-boiled work, *Red Harvest*, the murder that brings the detective to the aptly-named Poisonville is solved within a few pages, but he soon discovers that the poisons that permeate the town are far more malodorous, far more malevolent, far more indicative of a basic corruption at the heart of everyday life than the single act of crime committed by one person against another. This narrative in which a local infraction opens up onto a larger dispersal of criminality through all walks of life is a source of those existentialist resonances that French critics found in the hard-boiled tradition: the crime here is no longer sociological but revelatory of a fundamental evil within the human condition. It is significant, then, that Gittes's solving of the crime brings no solution to the problem: he has understood what is being done to Los Angeles, he has even gotten Noah Cross to confess to that crime, but he is unable to make his knowledge make a difference. Ironically, Gittes can explain the conspiracy very clearly but he has trouble getting his explanation heard. For example, at the end, in Chinatown, Jake tries to tell the police detective, Lou, about Cross's perfidy but his explanation is drowned out by others and he is shouted down.

The more conspiracy is rendered as ineffable evil, the more there will be an awareness that the detective's rational comprehension of events is ultimately irrelevant: the detective may piece together the clues that explain that the conspiracy exists but the sheer fact of this existence is a truth so unbearable that it passes beyond comprehension. Against such evil, nothing is to be done. As in some other paranoid conspiracy films of the 1970s – for example, Francis Ford Coppola's *The Conversation* (1974) or Arthur Penn's *Night Moves* (1975) – *Chinatown* ends with the transformation of the investigator from adventuring hero who actively investigates into a figure of passivity, defeated and given nothing to do but stare at the evil around him with benumbed blankness.

Earlier, we noted how the hard-boiled tradition that *Chinatown* in large part derives from involves the detective becoming caught up bodily in the story he is investigating. This means that the detective must boldly move into city space: no longer an armchair 'thinking machine' (to borrow the name of one of the earlier egg-head detectives from the classic pre-hard-boiled tradition), the detective ventures out into the world and seeks to master it. Hence, the stylistic fascination in *Chinatown* with movements of the camera – forward tracks, especially – that mimic Gittes's own penetration of new spaces. Camera movement and the framing of scenes as sights for the penetrating look of the detective become embodiments of consciousness – the detective's, the spectator's – that is coming ever more to understand the reality in which it is immersed.

But just as there can be understanding that helps, there can be understanding that hurts. Much of the trajectory of *Chinatown* is about – to paraphrase Hitchcock – a man who knew too much, and in this case wisdom is not always better than ignorance. If Gittes's forward penetration of space comes with a certain degree of confidence and even bluster – and part of the moral ambiguity of the film comes from the ways Nicholson's performance of masculine cockiness, as in Stanley Kubrick's *The Shining* (1980), makes him charming at the same time that he is repellent in his machismo – there is always the potential for this cocky and aggressive projection of the detective into space to backfire: the world being investigated can snap back at the detective, can resist his attempt to master it. Hence, all the ways in which Gittes is assaulted, is put bodily on the line. And he will even discover the possibility that the world around him can willfully exploit what he assumes is his own initiative and that this world can write him into its story: thus, Gittes is played for a sucker, used by a conspiracy that knows him as much as he will come to know it. If the detective is the figure who provides a narrative to explain mysterious events, Gittes comes to understand that he has been engulfed in a narrative constructed by others.

There are virtually no scenes in *Chinatown* in which Gittes does not take part. This again is in keeping with the hard-boiled literary tradition that *Chinatown* is indebted to and which has so much to do with one man's discovery of generalised corruption in the urban context. To be sure, there are individual shots that are not directly from Gittes's point of view. For example, early in the film, when Jake is trailing Mr Mulwray, there is a shot of Mulwray looking up to where he has heard a noise that Gittes has made; near to Mulwray, the camera pivots up toward the area he is looking at but Gittes has managed to hide himself and Mulwray sees nothing suspicious. Likewise, the very opening of the film offers point of view shots of photographs being examined by one of Gittes' clients and only a cut shows Gittes looking at him looking. In neither case is the optical point of view Gittes's. In other words, *Chinatown* is not like *Lady in the Lake* (1947), Robert Montgomery's film noir experiment in which first-person camera substitutes for on-screen presence of the detective. To be sure, shots like the ones just mentioned could easily be translated into a first-person discourse from Gittes's perspective (one could imagine, for instance, a hard-boiled narration that might say something like 'I watched Curly as he looked at the pictures of his wife' or 'Mulwray looked up to where I was hiding but I pulled back and he didn't notice me'). First-person narration is not necessarily identical to first-person optical point of view, since the narrator can often fill in knowledge about things he or she has not directly seen.

But the potential gap between optical and intellectual point of views can lead to a disturbance at the very heart of the knowledge one hopes to possess. Omnipresence in a narrative is not the same as omnipotence over it. On the one hand, the narrator may make mistakes about things he or she has not seen; on the other – and even more troubling – one can also be mistaken about the meanings of the things that one sees directly. In fact, *Chinatown* suggests that seeing – that is, having an optical point of view – is not necessarily the same as understanding – that is, having a narrative comprehension that goes beyond mere visual perception. Mulwray may not see the essential thing when he looks up and misses the fact that he is being tailed, but the film shows that even if one does see what is before one's eyes, one does not necessarily get the point. If the film begins with evidence of the visual (namely, the photos that prove to one of Gittes' clients that his wife is unfaithful), many of the things that Gittes himself sees – and that we see along with him – he misinterprets. A woman who looks like she could be Mrs Mulwray is not. An interaction between Mr Mulwray and a young woman that looks like a sexual dalliance is not. And so on. Control in the realm of sight is often no better than lack of sight. In part, the film constitutes vision as misleading insofar as it divorces sight from the confirmation that might come from the other senses. Thus, at a number of points in the film, characters who see do so from a distance in which they do not hear and this leads them to false or incomplete surmises: for example, Gittes seeing but not hearing a conversation between Mulwray and a Mexican boy on horseback; Gittes' operative overhearing an argument between Mulwray and Noah Cross but catching only one word; Gittes peeking through a window at an inaudible conversation between Mrs Mulwray and a young woman he has mistakenly identified as the mistress of Mr Mulwray.

But it is not just that sight is lacking its sensory complements that can make its meanings unclear; *Chinatown* suggests that understanding is a deeper process than mere sensory perception. The impressions of the world can easily be pieced together to make narratives that are coherent and yet are false. Thus, Gittes sees and then gives meaning to what he sees, but his interpretations often turn out to be wrong. *Chinatown* opens with optical point of view shots of images that wound a man emotionally; it closes with a woman's eye exploded by a bullet and her lover thrown into virtually unseeing catatonia by this horrendous tragedy. From start to finish, the film plays on the instability of vision and exploits the image of the detective as the ultimate figure of an ostensibly perfect vision that turns out to be fundamentally and fatally flawed. Where a dominant tradition in film study – the one we can associate with the afterlife of Laura Mulvey's influential 1975 essay 'Visual Pleasure and Narrative Cinema' – would have it that the act of seeing with one's own eyes is always already to be invested with a certain power, *Chinatown* suggests that seeing can be a process of fragility, of vulnerability, of weakness: one can see wrongly, one can see in self-damaging ways, one can see but not know, one can act wrongly on one's sights. Not for nothing do motifs of a wounding or blinding of sight run as motif and metaphor through the film: the specks that form a 'flaw' in Mrs Mulwray's eyes; the glasses that have been torn from Mr Mulwray's face when he was murdered; the light that Gittes smashes on Mrs Mulwray's car so as to follow her in the night, and so on.

Perception and mis-perception are caught in a complicated dialectical dance in *Chinatown*. One typical scene in this respect is an early one in which Gittes is telling a racist/sexist joke to his associates, not knowing that Mrs Mulwray is behind him. Gittes is often a character of smugness in the film, but this scene is one in fact in which his control of events is deeply in doubt and in which his cocky machismo directly gets him in trouble. Gittes sees certain aspects of the situation but does not see what is essential: his operatives try to signal to him that Mrs Mulwray is just behind him but he does not get the hint. Gittes' hold on vision is doubly limited: there are things outside of his range of vision (the woman behind him) and there are ambiguities in the things he can see (the pained look on his operatives' faces which he reads as simple impatience).

Earlier, we noted that there is virtually no scene in *Chinatown* in which Gittes is absent. When he is not present in a shot and even when a shot is not from his optical point of view – as in the moments when Curly looks at photos of his wife or when Mulwray looks up ignorantly to Gittes's vantage point – Gittes is still the consciousness through whom the scene passes. But there are in fact two moments that are directly beyond Gittes's point of view and both of these involve the woman, Mrs Mulwray. The first transpires after Gittes, having had his nose cut by one of Noah Cross's henchmen, meets Mrs Mulwray at a bar to tell her that he has been angered so much that he is going to follow his inquiry through to the end. He asks her to come along with him in his car to accompany him on his investigation but she refuses. Gittes goes off-screen to his car and the camera stays fixed on Mrs Mulwray, who remains screen-right in the frame. He then comes back into frame driving past her. As Gittes drives off into the background, Mrs Mulwray stutters out his name, almost as a desperate call for help, but he does not hear her and continues on his way. The second instance of a focus on Mrs Mulwray in full independence of Gittes's point of view occurs as he confronts her after they have slept together and she has snuck out into the night to meet the young woman Gittes believes was Mr Mulwray's mistress. Gittes is again angry and indicates he is going home. In what is virtually a plea for his companionship, Mrs Mulwray asks him if he will come home with her but Gittes refuses and goes off (and out of frame). The camera remains on Mrs Mulwray wracked by emotions.

Here, in each case, something happens for a fleeting instance – something which Gittes is fully ignorant of: the woman hesitantly reaches out to him but he misses her call to him. If the hard-boiled detective genre is often about the omnipresence of the investigating male consciousness in virtually every scene, here for an instant, another voice, another consciousness, emerges. Here, a woman starts hesitantly to voice her own interests but the man holds no awareness of her attempt. Her call out to him floats in the ether and then vanishes. If in one way, *Chinatown* is about men who are wounded by what they see as the conspiracy of the world – from Curly with his photos to Gittes lost in the morass of city politics – another side of *Chinatown* has to do with a vulnerability and voicelessness of women, a fragility that is also a lack of full agency. From Curly's wife at the film's beginning – reduced to mere images that render her a figure of adulterous perfidy – to the young sister/daughter, Catherine Cross, who says but one word in the entire film, to Evelyn Mulwray, her eye shot through at the film's end, women are given little role other than as mysterious figures to be wondered about and/or victims to be manipulated and even destroyed. And we might note that Gittes' inability to be there for Mrs Mulwray is already little more than a repetition of the past: he tells her that Chinatown represents for him the memory of his inability to help another woman who needed his aid there. Gittes is a man condemned to repeat the failures of his history and these failures rebound on women who suffer the consequences.

Similar to that first famous detective, Oedipus, who likewise investigated a social crime that was also the familial crime of incest, Gittes comes to discover a horrific truth: but although, like Oedipus with his cut tendon, Gittes bears the battle scars of horrendous discovery (his cut nose), it is not he who is blinded at the film's end. Evelyn Mulwray dies, her eye blasted out by a policeman's bullet. As in Hitchcock's *Vertigo* (1958), where the detective also discovers that he has been played for a sucker by a conspiracy, *Chinatown* deals with a man who is wounded emotionally by an excessive knowledge, but it is ultimately the woman he loves who dies for this knowledge.

Certainly, we would want to find *Chinatown* significant as an early work in what became by the 1980s and 1990s a full-blown cinematic investigation of a crisis of masculinity: *Chinatown* uses the detective genre to deconstruct masculine cockiness and to show the limits of confident male possession of knowledge and effective vision. But the film's challenging of secure and smug masculinity is not accompanied by a consistent rethinking of femininity away from clichés of helplessness, voicelessness, mystery and ineffability. We might paraphrase the last line: 'Forget it, Jake. It's femininity.' Only for fleeting moments does the film move away from a male point of view that it has glued itself to obsessively, even if for purposes of self-critique: in the evanescent moments in which Evelyn tries to voice her perspective, *Chinatown* gives glimpses of another narrative, but it is one that the film does not and, perhaps ideologically cannot, pursue. Politics localised on one figure's perspective is also then in this case about the exclusions of other perspectives. Ethnicity, sexuality, history itself: these, the film says, are mysteries that will ever remain in the dark; they are forces that both reason and vision can never do more than fall short of.

CHAPTER NINE

Into the Mouth of Madness: The Tenant

Maximilian Le Cain

Roman Polanski not only co-wrote and directed *The Tenant* (1976) but also, for the only time in his career to date, gave himself the leading role. Although a flop on release, it is nevertheless also frequently acclaimed as being among his most accomplished films. It openly borrows from and expands upon themes and techniques already explored in his two iconic 1960s horror films, *Repulsion* and *Rosemary's Baby*, to the extent that it could be viewed as the culmination of a claustrophobic trilogy dealing with interior space mutated by delusional or otherwise agitated subjectivities and the invasion of that space. Yet it also develops upon those films, attaining a level of narrative and emotional complexity (as well as black humour) that Polanski has yet to surpass, deftly underpinning the overt pleasures of a full-blooded psychological shocker with unsettlingly vertiginous narrative ambiguity.

Mild little office clerk Trelkovsky (Polanski) rents a flat that belonged to an Egyptology enthusiast, Simone Choule (Dominique Poulange) who killed herself by leaping from its window. At the time of his first inquiries into taking the rooms, she is still alive in hospital, covered completely in bandages with only a mouth of broken teeth visible. When she spots the visiting Trelkovsky, the otherwise silent patient emits a blood-curdling scream. While in the hospital, he meets Choule's friend Stella (Isabelle Adjani) and a mutual attraction is evident. Upon Choule's death, he moves into the flat and slowly comes to believe that the eccentric, repressively strict neighbours are trying to drive him insane by causing him to believe that he is the dead woman. Assailed by hallucinations, he takes to cross-dressing and eventually throws himself from the same window as Choule did, twice in succession, the first fall having failed to kill him. When he wakes up in hospital, also hidden in a mummy-like covering of bandages, he is confronted by the sight of Stella and himself standing by his bed. He emits the same horrifying scream as Choule did when he visited her, whereupon the film ends.

Repulsion, Rosemary's Baby, The Tenant: the 'apartment trilogy'

The horror of *Repulsion, Rosemary's Baby* and *The Tenant* all stems from the invasion and violation, real or imaginary, of private space and the imposition from outside of an alien idea of a character's identity that, in one way or another, comes to dominate their actions and perceptions. For Carol (Catherine Deneuve) in *Repulsion* it is men's assumption of her sexual availability; for Rosemary (Mia Farrow) it is her coercion into adopting the role of Satan's mother; for Trelkovsky it is his schizophrenic merging with the memory of Simone Choule. The action of all three films is centred on the closed interior space of an apartment, the claustrophobic site of spatial manipulation. Polanski displays a predilection for restrictive spatial unities – the boat in *Knife in the Water*, the island in *Cul-de-Sac*, the house in *Death and the Maiden* and, to a less controlled degree, the sprawling seaside residence in *What?*. But the interaction between character and environment is never as pronounced as in the 'trilogy', especially in *Repulsion* and *The Tenant*. In these films space attains an expressionistic fluidity subject to the protagonists' mental state.

Repulsion presents the viewer with a straightforward phenomenology of pathological subjectivity. As Carol's alienation increases, the normal proportions of her flat become wildly distorted visually in reflection of her unhinged mind. The private space of the apartment is rendered even more 'private' through becoming an extension of her mind. Thus the 'invasions' of this intimate space, whether hallucinated or the product of a reality distorted by hallucination, all occur on the same spatial plane and with the same level of perceptual verisimilitude. *Rosemary's Baby* inverts this relationship between heroine and space. If Carol's flat confirms and externalises her predicament even if only to herself, the horror of Rosemary's apartment is that it denies her problems and forces her to internalise her sense of disturbance. To the last it is a conspicuously bright, clean space, the blandly cheerful vision of a glossy magazine distressingly unmarked by the obscene happenings it is witness to. The matrix of terror is not, this time, the suffering mind but the tortured body, specifically Rosemary's womb which nurtures a growing demon. The constrictive façade of normalcy behind which possibly as great a cataclysm as the end of the world is coming into being, ultimately becomes as much a distortion of reality as Carol's fantasies.

Rosemary's Baby prefigures *The Tenant* in a number of ways, most notably through the introduction of the tropes of 'haunted space' and malevolently intrusive neighbours. For both Rosemary and Trelkovsky, a plot on the part of their elderly neighbours brings about their misfortune. In *The Tenant* the oppressively strict landlord Monsieur Zy (Melvyn Douglas) and other tenants make Trelkovsky's life unbearable by banging on the wall at the slightest sound, scolding him for minor misdemeanours, persecuting him for not signing a petition for the expulsion of one of the other tenants even to the point of lodging a complaint with the police, yet preventing him from going to the law when his flat is burgled. The scene of Trelkovsky's suicide in which grotesque, presumably subjective images of the wicked neighbours chasing Trelkovsky to his fate are intercut with shots of them 'in real' imploring him to see reason and refrain would seem to ultimately clear them of any culpability beyond extreme crankiness in bringing about his death bid. This interpretation would make them appear closer to the well-meaning, if voyeuristically curious, neighbours that pour into Carol's flat at the end of *Repulsion* than to the evil Satanists next door to Rosemary.

Apartments in both *Rosemary's Baby* and *The Tenant* could be designated to varying degrees 'haunted space' in that the history of the building or room as still contained in it is crucial to the plot. In *Rosemary's Baby*, as in *The Tenant*, the previous resident died. Sinister events surrounding this event are implied by clues left in the flat. Most notable of these is a wardrobe pushed up against a door – a wardrobe and that which it covers will take on great importance in *The Tenant*. Unlike the flat in *The Tenant* which remains a veritable shrine to Choule's memory, Rosemary's is completely redecorated by the time she and her husband move in. They subsequently discover disturbing facts about the building's history concerning witchcraft but ultimately the sense of 'haunted space' in *Rosemary's Baby* is little more than conventional narrative exposition. However, it does look forward to the enormous elaboration that the idea of 'haunted space' will undergo in *The Tenant* where traces of previous events as inscribed in space and décor are elaborated into a system that is central to Trelkovsky's plight.

Another progression in the 'apartment trilogy' worth tracing is that of the lead character. The first two films play on the horror staple of the vulnerable female in jeopardy but from two very different angles. The icily beautiful Carol is disturbing in her vacancy, her lack of character, her unformed-ness as a person, veering between insecure timidity and murderous self-defence that never grows into self-assertion. Hardly seeming aware of her own actions, her behaviour is frequently somnambulistic. The stereotype of the dumb blonde sex object is inverted – like them she is governed by one impulse but it is the antithesis of sexual desire, revulsion. Her empty-headedness, rather than making her easily dominated by men, is the locus of an apparently impenetrable (in every sense) psychosis that leads to their deaths. Carol remains beyond the comprehension of those around her, larger than life, a monstrous enigma.

Rosemary, on the other hand, represents a contrasting image of fashionable normality, a character in complete accord with her blandly pleasant taste in interior design. Her desires are for a child and a stable family life. Cryptically expressed feelings of Catholic guilt seem the only ripples in her placid personality. Therefore, unless one is willing to entertain the possibility that the entire satanic drama is nothing more than a projection of these guilt feelings, she embodies traditional domestic 'goodness', albeit with a 1960s style spin, which evil can quite menace without complication.

After these sharply contrasting generic glamour queens, Trelkovsky seems the product of another tradition entirely, perhaps more in line with the literature of Eastern Europe than horror cinema. The figure of the modest office clerk becoming entrapped in a paranoid scenario might suggest Kafka, although the focus on hysterical subjectivity disastrously engaging with normality on its own terms also brings to mind the Dostoevsky of *The Double* which Polanski abortively attempted to film in the mid-1990s.

The most striking difference between *The Tenant* and the earlier 'apartment' films is that while their heroines demanded dignified treatment, the insignificant Trelkovsky ushers in the ridiculous, the absurd. *The Tenant* is full of black humour, often as broad as anything in the overtly farcical *The Fearless Vampire Killers*. Rather than conventionally alternating horror and humour with the latter providing respite from audience tension, *The Tenant* explores the thin boundary between comedy and horror, commenting upon the uncomfortable extent to which they are often separated only by degrees of intensity. Trelkovsky is not ridiculous in himself, but finds himself constantly undermined and humiliated by other people and situations. Even among his boorish, aggressive friends he seems cowed, ill at ease.

When a comedy star like Buster Keaton inevitably finds himself up against a slighting universe, he fights back. Trelkovsky is not 'the little man who fights back'; he is 'the little man who cracks', whose identity crumbles as horror replaces comedy. Alexander Mackendrick famously commented that what interested him about comedy was the 'snarl behind the grin'. *The Tenant* is not so much the snarl as the primal howl of loneliness and terror behind the grin. Much credit for the success of this difficult fusion of laughter and terror must go to Polanski the actor. His perfectly judged performance makes one regret that he has not stepped before his camera more often. His Trelkovsky remains appealing largely because he avoids ever allowing him to become pathetic. He is essentially charming and self-assured, but it is a charm and self-assurance with frayed edges, constantly undermined by anxieties that might be caused by external factors or self-inflicted. If Trelkovsky had been depicted as overtly neurotic, the schizophrenic mystery of where the self ends and the other begins that gives *The Tenant* its power would have been diluted.

One of his anxieties is racial. A Pole, Trelkovsky always hastens to assure whoever he is disclosing his birthplace to, that he is a French citizen. He is also at pains to reassure a suspicious police inspector that he is not Russian. Like the Belgian Carol in London, he is an outsider. Granted, he has none of her unworldliness; he is not objectified as she is in the system of gazes that *Repulsion*'s sexual tensions generate, although foreignness is certainly an important element in their configuration. Yet the outsider status of both characters leaves them with a stigma of suspicion that adds to their vulnerability when they experience a wrenching shift in the fabric of normality that suddenly leaves them not only excluded from normality's new formation but actively persecuted by it, the fate of each protagonist in the trilogy.

This rupture in reality is apparently brought about by mental aberration (although only speculatively so in *Rosemary's Baby*) but historical circumstance can also engender such a crisis, such a viciously, intrusively alienating assault on a person's identity carried out in the name of a 'normality' that renders normality itself monstrous. To suggest that the trilogy drew deeply upon the horror of Polanski's traumatic childhood as a Jew in occupied Poland would, until recently, have been no more than a prime example of the sort of psychologically presumptuous approach to his cinema that he is so notoriously scathing towards. Yet this 'biographical speculation' is worth mentioning, however inconclusively, simply because it is almost impossible that anyone familiar with *The Tenant* could have watched the scenes in Polanski's Holocaust saga *The Pianist*, detailing Wladyslaw Szpilman's period on the run hiding in various flats, without a shock of recognition. These approximately three reels provide nothing less than a sort of Ur-text for the earlier horror films. All the claustrophobia of the 'apartment' trilogy returns in these images of a persecuted man locked in an apartment, obliged to keep silent out of mortal terror of the neighbours, living or dying on the basis of whom he chooses to trust. The uncanniest of many similarities – especially since *The Tenant* originated from Roland Topor's novel and *The Pianist* from Szpilman's memoir, neither original Polanski stories – is that the fugitive piano player is advised to throw himself from the window if the Gestapo raid his flat, which he at one point prepares to do!

Parasitic narrative and interior space as body

The Tenant is – or at least appears to be – the story of a man who is invaded by the story of a recently dead woman, Simone Choule, and whose personality splits in two as a result. The agent of Choule's parasitic narrative is her apartment and the traces of her presence that it retains. During the scene of her funeral, the priest's eulogy transforms into a fire-and-brimstone rant that probably exists only in Trelkovsky's head, accusing him of being an evil sinner and evoking horrific visions of judgement. This would suggest, *pace Rosemary's Baby*, a deep religious guilt at the source of Trelkovsky's instability. Yet, unlike *Rosemary's Baby*, *The Tenant* is otherwise empty of religious reference which makes the scene rather odd or even misleading unless we interpret it as indicative of a general guilt complex. This would tally with the circumstances of his tenancy, taking the flat almost literally over Choule's dead body and flirting with (and lying to) a friend of hers, Stella, that he met beside her deathbed. The fact that during the priest's oration Trelkovsky is staring lustfully at Stella would further support this interpretation. This general sense of guilt is exacerbated to the point of persecution paranoia by the harassment that he receives from his neighbours who complain and bang on the walls at the slightest noise.

The funeral scene – with its seamless, unnervingly ambiguous segue from reality into subjective vision – introduces Trelkovsky's hallucinatory tendency that will come to dominate as his breakdown worsens. It also announces Polanski's technique of oscillating between overtly hallucinatory episodes and reality without announcing the shift. The result is that one is not always granted absolute certainty as to the objective veracity or otherwise of what one observes. Unlike *Repulsion*'s straightforward descent into visionary alienation, *The Tenant* deals with fluctuating degrees of derangement. The space of Trelkovsky's flat, for instance, is subject to expressionistic visual distortion during scenes of crisis reminiscent of *Repulsion*, yet it subsequently returns to its original state only to be distorted again to a different degree when the plot demands.

The ambiguity generated by the shifting perceptual limits imposed on the viewer is analogous to Trelkovsky's anxiety about the blurred limits of his self. He articulates this in a drunken monologue halfway through the film, questioning the boundaries

A suitable case for treatment: Roman Polanski and Isabelle Adjani in *The Tenant*

of the self and the body: if my arm is severed, I say 'me and my arm'; if my intestines are removed I say 'me and my intestines'; but if my head is cut off, do I say 'me and my head'? What right has the head to be considered synonymous with 'me'? This line of questioning examines identity's dominion in terms of diminution and subtraction – I lose my arm, therefore it is no longer me, and so on – whereas what his tenancy in Choule's flat confronts him with is actually the opposite: an identity, Choule's, that has spilled far beyond the boundaries of its body, that has imbued an environment with its presence and is now taking control of another body and another mind.

The main traces of Choule's presence are the wardrobe and the window through which she plunged. The wardrobe contains the clothes Trelkovsky will don when he 'becomes' her and hides a hole in the wall stopped up with cotton wool that holds a human tooth. The tooth is presumably Choule's – this is confirmed by a gap in her mouth visible during the hospital visit. This hidden tooth bestows a creepily organic aspect on her continuing influence over the space, as if it were more extension of body than, as in *Repulsion*, mind.

The window overlooks a conservatory roof with a jagged hole caused by Choule's falling through it in her suicide attempt. Visible across the courtyard is a lavatory window through which Trelkovsky sees strange figures, neighbours and strangers, standing perfectly still for hours. He also visualises Choule standing there, staring at him. During his breakdown, he finds Egyptian hieroglyphs carved into the lavatory wall at which these apparitions were most probably staring.

Trelkovsky's transformation begins with him making use of Choule's remaining personal effects, starting with her nail varnish and proceeding to her clothes. The morning after his first cross-dressing he awakes forgetful of the previous night to the spectacle of snickering workmen finally mending the hole in the conservatory roof. It is as if Trelkovsky's 're-embodiment' of Choule had in some way reversed the event of her death in that the damage she had left is at last fixed, further heightening the impression of a mysterious link between Choule and the building. While again in his Choule persona, he replaces the tooth in the wall that he had discarded with one of his own. The gap in his mouth left by its extraction is identical to that in Choule's mouth. The reinsertion of the tooth in the wall implies that the 'making whole' of the room is as important as his altering his physical appearance in 'reincarnating' her.

As Choule, he states 'I'm pregnant'. Pregnant with the reinvention of Choule or, maybe, with the events of her story? If the flat is somehow an extension of Choule's body, perhaps it could be perceived as a womb preparing to give birth to the 'second' Choule. And perhaps throwing himself through the window is the birth process that the flat prepares Trelkovsky for?

The system of swallowing space

The aspects of the flat that signify Choule's memory – the wardrobe, the window, the broken roof below and the view on the lavatory window – seem, furthermore, to be linked by an occult system of attractions. Throughout the film subtle use is made of the wardrobe mirror and its reflections as focus of Trelkovsky's shifting identity. Polanski chooses the second occasion that Trelkovsky looks into the mirror to articulate the interconnection of wardrobe, window, conservatory roof and lavatory window. Trelkovsky spontaneously moves from studying his reflection to open the cupboard and examine Choule's clothes. As if mysteriously drawn to it, he then approaches and opens the window. He looks out at the broken conservatory roof before shifting his gaze to the lavatory window. A man goes to defecate, the only instance in the film in which we see someone making normal use of the toilet. Trelkovsky turns away from the window into a disturbing off-centre close-up indicating unease, and lights a cigarette.

This prefigures the more alarming events that follow within this geometry of attractions. It is when the cupboard is moved such that the mirror reflects the window opposite and the hole with the tooth behind the wardrobe's first position is revealed that Trelkovsky starts seeing apparitions in the lavatory, as if moving the wardrobe had unleashed them. The first of these is visible as soon as he has finished shifting the mirror, a shadowy woman (presumably Choule) staring straight at him. The other apparitions that appear later all gaze at the hieroglyphs on the wall rather than at his apartment.

If the wardrobe was indeed restraining the power of Choule's influence before it was moved, this is no doubt linked with the mirror as symbol and gauge of identity. In facing the window it no longer reflects Trelkovsky's stable identity image but the fatal abyss into which Choule/Trelkovsky plunge. The third space that it occupies is with its back against the window. It is moved here during an invasion hallucination reminiscent of *Repulsion* in order to hamper entry by unidentified assailants. Thus it is again employed defensively in the hope that it will restrain the intruder as it did the influence of Choule's tooth. This time it is all but futile: it temporarily keeps the invaders out but Trelkovsky's identity has already been irreparably compromised.

The relationship of the mirror in the flat with the lavatory window and its mysterious apparitions is both diagrammatic and the primary site of *The Tenant*'s central trauma – the gaze of the self upon the other that becomes displaced. Trelkovsky gazes across the courtyard at the apparitions which embody the haunted mystery of the building, the obscure other that disturbs his peace of mind. The crucial moment of breakdown when Choule finally begins taking Trelkovsky over is the latter's visit to the lavatory in a feverish state during which he finds the hieroglyphs on the wall and, in looking across the courtyard, sees himself staring out of his flat window. The boundaries of the self have dissolved and drifted beyond the body. Trelkovsky is simultaneously the self and the other; there is no difference between him and that which haunts him. Brilliantly, Polanski does not cut between the two Trelkovskies but pans from the Trelkovsky in the toilet to the window through which the one in the flat is visible keeping the back of the former's head in shot throughout. That both gazes occupy the same space clarifies that the gaze has doubled, not become disembodied.

When he returns to the flat, he sees Choule in the lavatory window laughingly taking off her covering of bandages. As well as dramatically announcing her 'resurrection', this links the gaze upon the self to the film's two most important scenes – those set in the hospital which give the film its vertiginous circularity. In the first, the otherwise silent Choule, just out of a coma, stares at Trelkovsky and emits a blood-curdling scream. The patient, mummified in bandages with only her eyes and mouth (with the prominent gap in the teeth) visible, has apparently never seen Trelkovsky before. At this point in the film the viewer can only speculate as to the meaning of this event: some form of premonition, maybe, or simply another sick gag to heighten Trelkovsky's sense of unease.

The second hospital scene ends the film. It is now apparently Trelkovsky, bandaged identically to Choule and with the same gap in the teeth, who is in the hospital bed. He opens his eyes and sees himself and Stella standing over him. He then emits the same scream as Choule did during his visit. In short, it is a repeat of the earlier visit except that now Trelkovsky is in Choule's place. It is apparently the final stage in three-point identity transference – Trelkovsky looking at Choule in the hospital, Trelkovsky looking at Trelkovsky across the courtyard from the lavatory, now Choule or Trelkovsky-as-Choule looking at Trelkovsky again in the hospital. This is numerically linked back to the spatial arrangement of the building: the mirror (which is also moved so that it occupies three places, each crucial to the story's development) and the lavatory window, representing the self and other, with the broken conservatory roof representing the trauma – suicide – that unites them.

The simplest and most reductive explanation would be that the final scene is simply a hallucination, Trelkovsky having come to completely identify with Choule in his own consciousness. The low lighting in the second scene also suggests that it is not taking place in 'reality'. However, this explanation is rendered ambiguous by the fact that we do not really know who it is behind the bandages – Choule or Trelkovsky? As in the lavatory scene, the terror is derived from recognition of alienation from accepted self. Rather than being specifically either Choule or Trelkovsky, the bandaged creature in the hospital bed is perhaps an abstract embodiment of this sense of schizophrenic otherness that Trelkovsky has been forced to recognise as part of himself, his terror and his madness extending beyond the hitherto dominant Trelkovsky/Choule dichotomy. This 'embodied otherness' is faceless, a scream inscribed in a body stripped of speci-fying features. It is into this scream that Polanski zooms twice, once in each hospital scene, the second zoom being the final image in the film. This zoom takes us beyond even the ambiguous body on the bed into a void of primal chaos and pure terror beyond form, beyond identity.

What the zoom enacts is the broken mouth swallowing the gaze, the plunge of consciousness into the abyss of insanity. The forward motion of this swallowing zoom and the image of the mouth is frequently echoed throughout the film in both décor and *mise-en-scène*, particularly in scenes set around the flat. Most obviously, there is the plunge from the window – the 'mouth' of the window itself and the broken roof of the conservatory below, the jagged edges of which unmistakably resemble the broken mouth. Another 'mouth' is discernable in the low-angle shot of the spiral staircase as Trelkovsky ascends to the flat for the very first time, already being 'devoured' by the building.

Trelkovsky is frequently framed while in the apartment building with deep spaces opening behind him on several planes through doors or other openings, or in reflec-tions. This gives the impression that he is constantly poised on the edge of a void, always vulnerable, always on the point of being swallowed by space. The often-forward prowling camera that Polanski employs in the apartment building heightens this spatialised instability. This, along with the framing, creates the subtle impression of a threatening off-screen. An excellent example of Polanski's management of space is the first scene in the flat, when the concierge (Shelley Winters) shows Trelkovsky around. After gleefully announcing that the previous tenant jumped from the window, she opens it while Trelkovsky stands in the middle of the room, the camera behind him. As she gloatingly beckons for him to look and he moves forward, the camera dollies towards the window behind him as if being sucked into it. As he looks down, Polanski cuts to a point of view shot of the hole in the conservatory roof incorporating a short pan, vertiginously destabilising the image as if Trelkovsky was himself on the point of falling out.

The following shot announces the drama that will unfold between Trelkovsky and his neighbours. Typically, it is structured on three planes, with the bright square of the window in the background, little Trelkovsky next to it in the left-hand corner and the considerable bulk of the concierge dominating the foreground to the right. The depth of field draws the eye towards the window, while Trelkovsky appears trapped between the window and the overbearing concierge. Towards the end of the shot she turns and jovially pushes him to look again out of the window, although the force of her gestures and the angle make it appear that she is actually pushing him out.

Although the only location outside the apartment building where the forward prowling camera is similarly employed in the hospital, many of the other scenes are built around a single discreet camera movement, most often a lateral pan or track that nevertheless echoes the basic forward motion that drives *The Tenant* towards its final terrifying image.

Beyond the double

Had the zoom into the mouth occurred only once, only at the film's conclusion, it could be interpreted as precisely that, a conclusion. Yet its repetition implies a circularity that is cyclical and arguably regenerative. The first scream announces the start of Choule's re-emergence in Trelkovsky. As we noted earlier, Trelkovsky-as-Choule cryptically declares that s/he is pregnant and we suggested that the climactic leaps from the window were as much gestures of birth as self-destruction, giving (re)birth to Choule's narrative if not to Choule herself. Similarly, the zoom into the mouth might not be wholly negative but signify the commencement of another cycle of events.

Choule's parasitic narrative came from the scream and returns to it. The shift from point of view of observer in the first scene to screamer in the second implies that the cycle might be recommencing with the observer. Yet the zoom into the mouth's darkness, a mouth set in a body rendered featureless, moves beyond and abolishes character and even form, returning the narrative to its ontological matrix of raw terror in the camera movement that the entire film has been preparing for visually.

Until this point the audience has most probably considered itself safely tied to the central axis of Trelkovsky's subjectivity, embraced within the shifting, diegetic dynamics of varyingly delusional perception and orientating parentheses of objective perspective (intercutting an imagined assault on Trelkovsky with 'real' images of him alone gripping his throat as if fighting off a strangler; objective images of an innocent visitor knocking at Stella's door with Trelkovsky's vision of the visitor as landlord Zy come to kidnap him; shots of the neighbours trying to persuade him not to jump from the window with subjectified images of them chasing him to his death, and so on) as well as the oscillations between the Trelkovsky and Choule-Trelkovsky identities. Yet the final zoom displaces this axis by placing the audience at the limit of the ultimate of *The Tenant's* dualities, that of birth/death (or birth/suicide, which achieved synthesis in the act of plunging from the window). Beyond this limit, in the howling emptiness of the broken mouth: the conflicts and dichotomies that (un)formed Trelkovsky no longer have any purchase. Both 'Choule' and 'Trelkovsky' have been transcended, which leaves the viewer disturbingly disorientated, adrift beyond the character they have identified with and against. So far one has been led to assume that, as proper to a highly subjective narrative, character generated form. Therefore in moving beyond character we are abandoned in a void of formless emotion. Michelangelo Antonioni goes beyond narrative in *L'Eclisse* (1962) by reducing it to an ultimately dispensable element in a plastic/temporal system and drifting away from it to the benefit of other elements. In *The Tenant* Polanski deconstructs narrative by doing the exact opposite, by concentrating the narrative into its emotional first principle, into its originary impulse which is manifest not, as we might have supposed, in Trelkovsky's psyche but rather in the more abstract locus of the screaming mouth.

Having pulled the rug of character perspective out from under us, Polanski leaves us free to look back over the film in terms other than those dictated by the Trelkovsky/ Choule conflict. It becomes apparent that the aforementioned visual echoes of the mouth, in both the sets and camera movement within the apartment building, rather than simply prefiguring the screaming mouth are perhaps extensions of it, constructs assembled after its own image. Hence the uncanny intelligence that the space of the flat seems imbued with, the strange forces of attraction that operate within it, its active role in Trelkovsky's story. The building is the primal howl of terror inscribed in matter and that which takes place within it an attempt to arrange the howl into events, to give it form in time. This makes it in some ways analogous to the mysterious planet in Andrei Tarkovsky's *Solaris* (1972), which embodies images from human visitors' subconscious minds in a semi-stable matter of its own generation in order to study them. The difference here is that the 'planet' – the building – also creates the 'visitors' (and their minds, subconscious and otherwise) and does so in order to reflect for itself its own formless energies.

This state of things is hinted at in the shot behind *The Tenant*'s opening credits, a mysterious little scene which makes no sense in the context of a narrative of subjective projection. The camera starts on a shot looking through the apartment window of Trelkovsky staring out of it in the frozen poise that will become familiar as that of the apparitions in the lavatory window. Tilt down to the broken conservatory roof and tilt up again to the window to reveal Choule in the same position. The camera, on a crane, then describes a slow 270-degree movement across the courtyard. Most of the windows are empty but Trelkovsky is again visible in the lavatory window and, in one other window, there is a glimpse of what appears to be a tenant making a bed. The camera finally cranes down to the gate leading out on to the street. This opens and Trelkovsky enters, heading straight for the concierge's room to ask about a flat to rent – the story begins. All of this proceeds without a single cut. Trelkovsky and Choule are already somehow present in the building when Trelkovsky first arrives!

How could the building have 'gained possession' of the new tenant before his arrival? If Polanski was truly following Trelkovsky's story, would the logical opening not feature him approaching the building from outside? Other than his workplace, his Polish origin and the cryptic (and not necessarily true) remark that 'a relative' had told him about the vacant flat, we know nothing concrete about Trelkovsky's life and background. Perhaps Trelkovsky is no more than a figment of the building's capacity for creating, altering and combining narratives, one Trelkovsky among countless others enacting parallel variations on a story of identity displacement.

And why just one story? Certain events that occur within the film and might be initially interpreted as Trelkovsky's hallucinations could, in fact, be evidence of parallel dramas unfolding within the same generative space and overlapping temporally. Apart from Choule, the brooding figures in the lavatory window might be subject to a logic governed by a completely different plot, incidentally intruding on Trelkovsky's. Likewise, the woman (Lila Kedrova) with the disabled child who asks Trelkovsky if he signed a petition for her eviction and the woman who brings the eviction petition (Jo Van Fleet) but describes a different tenant might be equally real, but operating in different realities. This might also explain why there is no one in the corridor when Trelkovsky answers a knock on his flat door. And maybe the other tenants' misdirected ire at Trelkovsky's alleged noise might be meant for 'another' Trelkovsky who is, in fact, guilty of making it?

In moving beyond the psychological paradigm of the split personality, the film itself splits open into an exhilarating *mise-en-âbyme* of baroque narrativity that springs from the formless impulse of blank terror at the fragility of identity.

CHAPTER TEN

Polanski's Iconoclastic Journeys in Time: When Angels Fall and Bitter Moon

Izabela Kalinowska

The making and the popular success of *The Pianist* focused the attention of critics and the viewing public alike on one particular aspect of Roman Polanski's life. Just like many other people who trace their origins to the particular place and time of East Central Europe in the first half of the twentieth century, Polanski experienced wartime Poland's extremes of hardship and loss. 'Very specific visual elements of these memories occur in Polanski's films. In general, violence and blood are common, and they almost always erupt suddenly, and unexpectedly', remarks Herbert Eagle (1994: 95). Although the traumas he sustained have left a mark on Polanski's way of interpreting reality, all of his works prior to *The Pianist* have been devoid of any overt references either to his or Poland's traumatic past. With the exception of *The Pianist*, Polanski's films lack any of the retrospection present in the oeuvres of Andrzej Munk, Andrzej Wajda, Tadeusz Konwicki and other Polish filmmakers of the same generation. For Wajda, in particular, the catastrophe of the war provides a caesura, a moment of crisis that has become etched very profoundly in the nation's memory. In Czeslaw Milosz's 1945 poem *In Warsaw*, the poet, faced with the ruins of the known world, resigns himself to the fate of the chronicler of wartime suffering. The same may be said of the stance embraced by Wajda who, throughout his career as a filmmaker, has partaken in the post-war rituals of remembrance. This tendency is quite apparent in both Wajda's continued preoccupation with the subject of the war and in the narrative structure of his films, including their reliance on flashbacks.

A desire to contain the past, to block off the resurgence of personal nightmares, may explain Polanski's reluctance to look back. After all, a 'lack of witnessing, numbing, the unrepresentable, the absence of narrative, and failures in language' (Kaplan & Wang 2004: 4) are well-known factors in the psychology of trauma. The filmmaker's decision to turn down the offer to direct *Schindler's List* as well as some of his comments on the occasion of *The Pianist*'s release suggest a perceived need for a distance towards his own wartime experiences.[1] Significantly, nearly all of Polanski's films, including *The Pianist*, eschew the flashback, the narrative device that best represents the process of remembering. This creative choice hints at a need for distance, or perhaps even a clear break, from the past.

However, such psychoanalysing rests on mere speculation. Instead of analysing the author, my search for the causes of Polanski's disavowal of the flashback focuses on his two films that do actually rely on this device. Only his 22-minute graduation short *When Angels Fall* (*Gdy spadają anioły*) and the star-studded feature *Bitter Moon* use the flashback as a narrative device in its classic form. Although these two films differ sharply from one another in most respects, each of them reveals Polanski's deep-seated mistrust of retrospection. In each case, Polanski finds a way to problematise the flashback and its reliability as a tool that grants the viewers access to the repositories of personal and communal memories. Revisiting the past often implies control, privilege and exclusion. Some people, perspectives and incidents enter the reconstructed picture of events past, while others are either suppressed or entirely excluded. Polanski focuses on this manipulative potential of the resulting figures of memory. Remembrance is linked to interpretation. This nexus leads him to focus on agency: who is doing the remembering and why? Both in *When Angels Fall* and in *Bitter Moon* Polanski emerges as a critic of the potential of cinematic retrospective to create and perpetuate myths that sustain a particular socio-cultural order. Rather than use film as a means to recapture the past, Polanski exposes the constructed character of visual flashbacks. Such reflexivity allows him to maintain an ironic distance towards the cultural mainstream.

In *When Angels Fall*, Polanski enters into a polemic with the mythologising of maternity that lies at the heart of modern Polish culture. In *Bitter Moon*, the flash-back-fueled journey in time reveals the story of a relationship. But the filmmaker simultaneously invites his viewers to travel 'much farther', to quote one of the film's characters. He takes them on a journey through the conventions of cinematic story-telling that leads to the unmasking of the principal storyteller: the male subject of modern Western cultures. The self-conscious character of both *When Angels Fall* and *Bitter Moon* provides Polanski with the means to destabilise a world determined by the mechanism of cultural transmission. The two films flaunt their own constructed-ness thereby bringing into question the cognitive value of other retrospective projects. As a consistent critic of the myth-building potential of retrospection, Polanski resists the temptation to transform the past into a fetish. He sustains this attitude throughout his oeuvres, including, I would argue, the adaptation of Wladyslaw Szpilman's war memoir in *The Pianist*.

When Angels Fall introduces an elderly woman who first feeds pigeons in the street then picks up a discarded sunflower core from the cobbled surface of the road on the way to her job.[2] She descends into the subterranean, windowless interior of her workplace, a baroque men's room, with a line of ornate urinals along one wall, and a row of stalls on the other side.[3] Light streams through the glass-tile ceiling above her. Throughout the film, the woman does not utter a word, but the sounds and images that reach her trigger a series of flashbacks that reveal the course of her life. The flashbacks' chronological progression mirrors the temporal progression of the day. The morning evokes visions of the woman's youth in the countryside. Soon after she arrives in the restroom and sprinkles some powdered soap on the floor, she sits down and hears the footsteps of people walking over the glass ceiling above her. The sound creates an aural bridge to the past. The first of the series of five colour flashbacks (the time-present sequences are black and white) reveals soldiers marching through the country-side. A beautiful young girl (Barbara Kwiatkowska) looks out the window of a country cottage, framed by sunflowers. Polanski cuts back to the restroom. The woman's point of view falls on a drunken young man who is barely standing on his feet. This image sparks a flashback to her intimate encounter with a young soldier. Polanski includes the outcome of this encounter within the same flashback. The next sequence reveals the woman rocking a baby in a cradle, alone in her little house. Outside the house, a man gesticulates and addresses inaudible threats at the woman. The following return to time-present has the restroom lady focus on a boy who brings in a bird in a cage. This image corresponds to the subsequent flashback in which the young woman casts a concerned gaze at a boy using a stick to lash a frog in the meadow outside the house. A situation involving a uniformed policeman triggers the next flashback. He grabs the drunken young man by his arm and escorts him out of the lavatory. In the flashback, a young man, presumably the woman's grown son, struggles against two gendarmes/soldiers who are forcibly taking him away from the house as the woman looks on help-lessly. Back in the time-present of the restroom, a man comes in to read the electrical meter. The woman turns the light on. The prime of her life already behind her, in the next flashback she travels to a city in search of employment. The motif of electricity may be a trigger that differentiates her country existence from life in an urban setting. In the last flashback, the visibly aged woman (Roman Polanski) works as a cleaning lady in a middle-class home. She rushes outside of the house when she sights a column of marching soldiers. She tries and fails to place a package in one of the soldiers' hands. Within the same flashback, the filmmaker has his viewers follow the soldiers to what looks like a First World War battlefield.

The structure of the woman's subjective flashbacks breaks down at this point, as the perspective shifts to one of the soldiers (Andrzej Kondratiuk), who first loses a comrade to an artillery shell and then stumbles into the ruins of a building to discover an 'enemy' soldier hiding there. The only extended human interaction that involves eye contact transpires between the two soldiers. The 'enemy' soldier raises his hand to his coat. He wants to treat 'our' soldier to a cigarette, but the son misinterprets this gesture. The encounter ends tragically when 'our' soldier shoots the other and kills him. The film's two timelines coalesce towards the film's end. The soldier/son crushes through the restroom's glass ceiling, clad as an angel.[4] The old lady kneels down in front of him.

Polanski window shot: Barbara Kwiatkowska in *When Angels Fall*

At first glance, *When Angels Fall* appears to be a masterfully completed exercise in visual flashback and not much more. But closer scrutiny reveals Polanski's engagement with the mythic structures of modern Polish culture and his questioning of historical retrospection's ideological implications. Maureen Turim points out that personal memories accessed by way of film flashbacks 'also give us images of history, the shared and recorded past' (1989: 2). Polanski manipulates the *mise-en-scène* of the flashbacks to accentuate the shift from the personal to the communal dimension of remembrance. The timeframe of the picture extends not only beyond the last day in the life of a restroom attendant, but also far beyond the span of a single lifetime. The realities of the world surrounding the men's room imply post-war (Eastern) Europe, that is, the time and place of the film's making. But other clues substantially broaden the timeframe. The uniforms worn by soldiers in the first two flashbacks suggest Polish soldiers who fought alongside Napoleon's army up to 1813. The two uniformed men who take the woman's son away wear imperial Russian uniforms. The soldiers who march through the city are stylised, judging by the design of their helmets, to look like Prussian troops, as is the adversary/friend of 'our' soldier-turned-angel in the extended flashback. The son/angel, in turn, wears a French-like uniform from the time of the First World War. Modern Europe imagined as a battlefield becomes the stage against which Polanski sets the quiet drama of the restroom attendant.

The focus of Polanski's film falls outside of the scope offered by grand historical retrospectives. In his autobiography, the filmmaker makes the following comment regarding his choice of subject:

My subject was one of those outwardly dull and uneventful lives that never make the average person think twice … To me, a lavatory attendant's life seemed to epitomise vacuity, drudgery, monotony. Nobody would ever look at an old crone in a public lavatory, with her pathetic saucerful of coins and her vacant, impersonal air, and conceive of her having had a life imbued with passion and drama. (1984: 52)

As different armies come and go the nameless protagonist of *When Angels Fall* remains voiceless. Gradually, she becomes entirely transparent to people around her. We can note here that diegetic dialogue is not completely absent from the film. One of the restroom clients speaks to the woman, and the soldier/son emits a cry of warning before he shoots the 'enemy' soldier. But the woman herself remains silent throughout the film. The shift of perspective, from the old woman to the soldier in the film's last flashback, mirrors the dominant culture's preoccupation with the fate of the male subject. In the end, the son's/soldier's story subsumes the story of his mother, albeit Polanski foregrounds this transposition in order to critique rather than to emulate the emerging pattern. The old woman belongs to the nameless and voiceless millions who suffer all kinds of deprivations and who, in spite of their lives' hardships, do not think of themselves as victims. Rather, they calmly accept the fate that has been dealt to them. The often-traumatic life experiences of such people remain outside the purview of historical analysis and outside the mainstream of cinematic representation. They are relegated to a position beyond the horizon of dominant historical and cultural discourse. By bringing this aspect of culture to focus, Polanski situates himself within the tradition of European modernist art. He signals the limits of representation and indicates the oppressive potential of traditional cultural forms. This counter-cultural aspect of his cinema should not be underestimated.

The making of *When Angels Fall* coincided with the period of intensified historical retrospection in Polish cinema initiated by the political changes of the post-1956 thaw. In addition to the European dimension of *When Angels Fall*, the film's military references resonate with specifically Polish connotations. Modern Poland has been the site of many a battle. Poles have served, either voluntarily or as draftees, in various armies, some of which promised to liberate their homeland, as was the case with Napoleon, others subjected it to prolonged periods of occupation (Russia, Austria and Prussia/Germany).

As Tadeusz Lubelski points out, within the movement known as the Polish School (1956–62), the filmmaker often assumes the position of a psychoanalyst, addressing events and subjects pushed into the nation's subconscious. The unmasking that ensues after the overcoming of historical taboos transcends merely descriptive renditions of past events. Films belonging to this group, such as Andrzej Wajda's *Ashes and Diamonds* (*Popiół i diament*, 1958) and *Lotna* (1959), Stanisław Lenartowicz's *Pills for Aurelia* (*Pigułki dla Aurelii*, 1958), Andrzej Munk's *Eroica* (1957), 'activated collective consciousness, provoked, forced [the viewers] to verify [the collective's] axioms. While talking about the past, these filmmakers engaged their audiences in a dialogue about the present' (2000: 143).

'Scholars frequently juxtapose', Marek Haltof writes, 'Wajda's romanticism and Munk's rationalism, comparing Wajda's dramatic characters, torn between their sense of duty to the nation and their personal happiness, to Munk's commonsensical, pragmatic protagonists' (2002: 84). While Wajda, in his war films, especially *Kanal* (*Kanał*, 1957), *Ashes and Diamonds* and *Lotna*, upholds, for the most part, the cultural traditions stemming from nineteenth-century Polish literature, Munk challenges the notions that comprised the patriotic canon. Clearly, in *When Angels Fall*, Polanski comes closer to the questioning attitude of Munk, one of his teachers at the Łódź Film School, and – like Wajda – also a collaborator and a friend. Polanski's use of flashback brings to mind Munk's masterful *Man on the Track* (*Człowiek na torze*, 1957). The flashback-driven narrative of *Man on the Track* seeks to destabilise the dominant discursive practice of socialist realism. Instead of delivering the one and only ideologically correct account of a railroad worker's death, Munk confronts his audience with the event's three conflicting accounts.[5] Maureen Turim's characterisation of Munk's unfinished *Passenger* (*Pasażerka*, 1962) as 'a critique of the self-serving framing and selectivity of memory' (1989: 233) applies to the earlier picture as well. In a similar vein, the flashback narrative of Polanski's *When Angels Fall* questions the structures of the war-induced national martyrology by probing the boundaries of culturally circumscribed tradition.

The visual qualities of the early flashbacks in *When Angels Fall* are reminiscent of the nostalgic symbolism of Wajda's films. Yet Polanski stylises these sequences to the point of an overstatement. He does not follow in Wajda's footsteps. Rather, he challenges the type of mythologising of the past that inflects and characterises Wajda's early work. First of all, instead of presenting a heroic male subject who is tragically trapped in history, Polanski picks a woman whose occupation places her at the rock bottom of the social hierarchy. Wajda's *Ashes and Diamonds* includes a restroom attendant among the gallery of its protagonists. The restroom itself is an important meeting place for the film's main protagonists, but the woman who takes care of it provides merely an element of comic relief.[6] Following the flashback of the son's seizure by the Russians in *When Angels Fall*, Polanski cuts to a medium shot of the restroom attendant, seated at her table. In the background, on the wall, one can clearly make out a saber, hanging on a piece of embroidered white linen cloth of the type that would normally adorn the wall of a peasant kitchen. The cloth connects the woman to her peasant origins. The absurd display of the saber links the picture once more to traditions of the rise and fall of Poland's pre-modern gentry republic and of the heroic struggles that dominated Poland's modern history. The *mise-en-scène* of Wajda's *Ashes and Diamonds* relied on the same prop as a marker of the cultural space of Polishness. While Wajda's film oscillates between a reverence for and the questioning of the heroic national ethos, in *When Angels Fall* Polanski comes very close to ridiculing the same tradition.

The placement of a female figure within such a historically charged context must necessarily evoke associations with the cultural construct known as the Polish Mother ('Matka Polka'). According to Elżbieta Ostrowska, who has analysed the specificity of Polish maternal discourse, in Poland, the mother came to personify the motherland, 'invariably pure and immaculate like the mother of Jesus'. She concludes that this idealisation of woman makes her a perfect but totally one-dimensional figure. She is 'liberated' from taking part in the dramatic conflicts and moral dilemmas of national life – the domain of a residual masculine activity. And yet she provides, whether she wants to or not, an omniscient voice in the domestic sphere. In both cases she is deprived of the right to make a choice, to be herself. By and large, this myth of the Polish Mother with its perfection and infallibility, placed woman in a superior position within Polish cultural discourses yet inevitably repressed her own subjectivity. Polish women became imprisoned in this rigid symbolic image, which necessarily impacted upon their material lives. (1998: 423)

When Angels Fall deconstructs the myth of the Polish Mother by pointing to the icon's oppressive character. Historical and social circumstances determine the life of the paradigmatic Polish Mother and the story of Polanski's restroom attendant conforms to the same pattern. At no point does she control her own life. She fulfills the role first of a sexual object, then of a mother to a son (young males are needed as soldiers). Polanski reduces the traditionally caring role of the Polish Mother to the woman's cleaning duties. She is needed as someone who takes care of the men's room. She disinfects it and turns the lights on. But she is also entirely transparent to the men who rely on her services. Her subjectivity is eclipsed by greater social and historical discourses. Their logic condemns her to the position of an object.

Bitter Moon, Polanski's other flashback-driven film, features a very different type of protagonist. The social position occupied by its principal storyteller Oscar (Peter Coyote) situates him squarely at the opposite end of the spectrum to *When Angels Fall*'s restroom attendant. His discursive mastery, in the most literal sense, is unquestionable. He counters the silence of the woman of the early short with an obtrusive, obnoxious garrulity. The two films differ in other respects as well. The artifice of *When Angels Fall*, a mostly silent film stylised in part to look like a naïf painting, is very evident. In contrast, the seamless realism of *Bitter Moon*'s opening sequence does not indicate the same degree of foregrounding of cinematic form. Yet in both films Polanski uses a conventional, flashback-driven narration to show the limitations constricting this type of linear, retrospective storytelling. In the end, both *When Angels Fall* and *Bitter Moon* are equally reflexive. Despite the differences between the two films, Polanski uses a similar strategy to deconstruct a 'dominant fiction' in each of them.[7]

In *Bitter Moon*, the story's time-present is set on a liner, taking passengers to Istanbul. Fiona (Kristin Scott Thomas) and Nigel (Hugh Grant), apparently a successful British professional couple, are traveling to the East on the occasion of their seventh wedding anniversary. Their lives intersect in a strange way with the journey of two other passengers – a French woman Mimi (Emmanuelle Seigner) and her partner Oscar, an (aspiring) American writer who resides in Paris. While Mimi tempts Nigel with her good looks and the sensuous, erotic movements of her body, Oscar, the story's main narrator, lures Nigel into listening to his confessional narrative.

'This is some sort of a game?' Nigel asks Mimi when she admits that she pretended not to recognise him on the occasion of their second meeting. Indeed, a game involving

Nigel and Oscar begins soon after Oscar approaches Nigel on the ship's deck and begins a conversation. 'Beware of her,' states Oscar, right at the onset of their acquaintance. 'She's a walking mantrap. I am her husband. Look what she did to me.' He removes a blanket from his immobile legs. Oscar and Nigel's conversation begins to set up the frame for the story of the journey within the journey.

Oscar: What do you think of her?
Nigel: Well, if you mean what I think you mean, she is very good
          looking.
Oscar: Good looking? All of that and more ... She gives you a hard-on,
          doesn't she?
Nigel: I beg your pardon?
Oscar: Come on, Nigel. Don't be so British. Would you like to fuck her?
          Admit it, it's not a crime ... You are itching to know some more
          about her, aren't you? Well, aren't you?
Nigel: Yeah.

Oscar establishes that Nigel is 'exactly the listener' who he has been looking for, and he proceeds with the story: 'Eternity for me began one summer day in Paris...'

The darkness shrouding the deck at the time of the two men's encounter; the mention of Oscar's mysterious crippling by a beautiful woman; his insistence on telling the story and the stilted flare of his narration – all of these features point to film noir as *Bitter Moon*'s inspirational source. As in film noir, the narration in Polanski's film draws attention to itself. Jonathan Rosenbaum, one of very few critics who appreciated *Bitter Moon* upon its release, describes Oscar's narration as 'an ornate purple prose that is one of the movie's most useful and ambiguous narrative devices' (1997: 31). 'Once the presence of the voice-over narrator has been established, the entire film serves as a sort of linguistic event', concludes Eric Smoodin about film noir (quoted in Telotte 1989: 41). Language becomes a tool that allows the narrator to assume illusory control over a reality that is slipping dangerously out of control. As J. P. Telotte explains,

> the narration consists of a voice, but it indicates an individual's presence and consciousness, which together motivate all that we see, move our vantage freely about in time and space. That voice, though, stands 'over' all else, signaling its proprietary control over the narrative. (ibid.)

That voice, it has to be added, often comes from someone who is barely holding on to life, as, for example, Walter Neff in *Double Indemnity* (Billy Wilder, 1944), or who is already dead, as with Joe Gillis in *Sunset Boulevard* (Billy Wilder, 1950) (Telotte 1989: 16). The wounded Oscar fits right in with film noir's protagonists/narrators: 'I leave the words to him. It is all he has left,' says Mimi to Nigel.[8]

In film noir and in *Bitter Moon*, the narrator's voice asserts its own subjectivity. Originating on society's dark fringes, the voice-over functions as a subversive element in relation to the dominant culture. It creates its own legend by unmasking the unpleasant truth about the foundations of all human interaction. In *Bitter Moon*, the relationship between Oscar and Nigel embodies the dynamic between the noir-like narrator and the world of the English establishment. Nigel stands for life's proper, public sphere – bond trading and the City. Oscar takes it upon himself to demonstrate to Nigel that this world rests on a very flimsy structure of falsehood and pretense. Nigel is easily lured into admitting that the prospect of getting to know Mimi interests him more than does the mission of revitalising the officially sanctioned relationship with his wife. Throughout the film he confirms over and again how easily corruptible, or, rather, how very hypocritical he really is.

As Oscar plays his game with Nigel, the naïve listener, enticing him to places where Nigel would rather not admit to having ventured, Polanski engages his viewers in a similar manner. Mimi's sexual allure and the enigma of Oscar's disability provide the narrative's bait. A series of four flashbacks exposes the details of Oscar's relationship with Mimi, which progresses from the initial 'innocent' infatuation to an openly sexual obsession that is then transformed into a passionate, several-days-long consummation of the relationship. The next stage presents the couple's search for new thrills that help them sustain the intensity of what is, from the narrator's perspective, primarily a sexual union. Oscar gradually grows tired of Mimi. Since she cannot break her emotional dependence on him, the relationship drifts towards a sado-masochistic scenario. Oscar's inventiveness manifests itself in a rich repertoire of abuses directed at Mimi. His remarks downgrade her intellectually and physically. He flirts with other women in her presence and makes her feel entirely redundant in all facets of their shared life. The psychodrama ends when, following Mimi's abortion, Oscar tricks her into taking a trip to Martinique and gets off the plane just before take off. He is rid of her and he is free to immerse himself in a perversely hedonistic lifestyle. Mimi returns when he is in the hospital recovering from a car accident. She appears to have regained her composure. He is just as verbally abusive and emotionally cruel to her as he was before their separation. She knocks him off the hospital bed and permanently incapacitates him. Turning the tables on Oscar, Mimi declares herself his carer and proceeds to abuse him psychologically and physically in ways similar to the treatment he visited upon her.

As in *When Angels Fall*, the chronologically ordered flashbacks of *Bitter Moon* reveal a personal story. But here again, Polanski plays a multi-leveled game with his viewers. His cinematic language draws attention to itself. The story of Oscar's relationship with Mimi becomes a story about the different ways of telling stories.

Polanski's feat can be compared to the accomplishment of the esteemed nineteenth-century Polish poet Adam Mickiewicz, who authored a famed cycle of love sonnets in 1826. Mickiewicz's Odessa sonnets, so called because of the place that inspired their writing, present subsequent phases of a relationship: from a pure fascination with the love object, through the relationship's ripening and consummation, to eventual disenchantment. At the same time, on a meta-literary level, the cycle evinces a clear progression of literary conventions: from sonnets that borrow from Petrarch, through sentimental poetry and the poetry of Romantic disenchantment, to irony that brings all social forms and literary conventions into question, and then to the sober realism in the sonnets that come near the cycle's end (Zgorzelski 1961: 105). Mickie-wicz emphasises the literariness of his own utterance. Similarly, Polanski endows his love story with a meta-cinematic dimension.

Polanski stylises the flashbacks in *Bitter Moon* to imitate different film schools and a variety of cinematic genres. The initial flashback, when Oscar first notices Mimi on a Paris bus, has a New Wave quality to it, both aesthetically and through the mood of innocent mischievousness that it creates. When Mimi first enters Oscar's apart-ment, at the onset of their sexual adventures, Polanski adopts the aesthetics of the 1970s. The following episodes mock the genre of soft porn. The scene at the breakfast table, when Mimi spits out milk and spreads it over her face, neck and breasts for Oscar to lick, could be taken for a parody of a similar food-and-sex-by-the-refrigerator scene in Adrian Lyne's *9½ Weeks* (1986). The toast that pops out at the moment of heightened arousal provides a purely comic component, and a clear sign of a self-conscious distancing that is at work in Polanski's film. The final phases of the couple's heavily propped-up sex life are bereft of any pornographic quality. Instead, they bring a grotesque distortion of the genre of hardcore pornography. At the end of the road, stripped of the various masks provided by conventional aesthetics, Mimi and Oscar's relationship reveals the common denominator of all human interaction: a struggle for control that leads to exploitation and abuse. Ultimately, as Sabina Spielrein, Carl Jung's frustrated lover who inspired Freud's interest in the death drive, phrased it: 'the life-giving sexual animal becomes the source of death' (1987: 124). Polanski's narrative culminates at the fatal intersection of Eros and Thanatos, of the drive to sexual pleasure and the compulsion to destroy and self-destruct.

As a storyteller, Oscar operates in a way that is analogous to the functioning of the mechanisms of popular cinema. He entices Nigel to listen to him, he incites his curi-osity, he tickles his desire. He wants to win his attention by any means available. 'You would make a great analyst', says Oscar, as Nigel is leaving his cabin after the first flash-back session. But the reversal of their roles is quite clear. Oscar does not really need to unburden himself in order to be able to move on with his life. He talks because he is at the end of the road. He transmits his story to a willing male listener in order to assure its survival and continuity. Well aware of Nigel's weaknesses, Oscar plays the role of his analyst by making Nigel aware of his own desire for Mimi. By foregrounding the generic features of the film's flashbacks, Polanski distances himself from the control mechanisms that operate within culture. He exposes these mechanisms and, at the same time, deconstructs the traditional coding of masculinity.

The film's two side episodes that involve the liner's other male passengers empha-sise Polanski's assault on traditional Western masculinity; one involves an Italian man traveling on the liner, the other centres on an Indian passenger. Nigel abandons Fiona and two other bridge partners at one point in order to meet with Mimi. A handsome, Mediterranean-looking man who has been observing the game takes his place. Later Nigel finds Fiona flirting with the macho Italian. When the same man becomes Mimi's dance partner, Oscar refers to him as the 'Latino lover boy'. A New Year's celebration on the cruise ship terminates in a fistfight. As should be expected of a personification of masculine virility, the 'Latino lover boy' is eager to become involved in the fight.

'Mimi deprives Nigel...': Emmanuelle Seigner and Kristin Scott Thomas in *Bitter Moon*

He assumes a kung-fu posture and is ready to strike when a man dressed in a clown costume walks up to him and easily knocks him down with just one punch.

Mimi deprives Nigel of the dominant position in the relationship by crippling him. Nigel, who is ineffective as a husband, is merely tricked by Mimi into believing that she will have an affair with him. 'Whatever you can do, I can do better', says Fiona at one point. In the end she is the one who goes to bed with Mimi, allowing both Oscar and Nigel to join the long line of Polanski's emasculated male protagonists. Before them came such memorable characters as, among others, the sports writer Andrzej in *Knife in the Water*, George the castle owner and Dickie the robber in *Cul-de-Sac*, as well as the private eye J. J. Gittes in *Chinatown*.

As Rosenbaum observes, 'the way third world exoticism is enlisted to spice up sex, marital and otherwise, is a subtle but telling theme throughout the movie (1997: 30). The trope of a revitalising journey to the East has provided one of the defining moments of modern European literature and culture. In *Bitter Moon* Nigel takes his wife on a trip to Istanbul and India to partake of the reputed benefits of an Oriental escapade. For an Indian gentleman, a fellow passenger traveling with his daughter, this worn plot is only too obvious. He counters the self-centered Western male fantasy with his commonsense advice: 'Children are a better form of marital therapy than any trip to India.' In Pascal Bruckner's novel, on which Polanski based his script for *Bitter Moon*, the Oriental theme lacks the subtlety that it later received in Polanski's treatment. Franz, the crippled narrator of the flashbacks in Bruckner's *Lunes de fiel*, describes the object of his attraction in the following terms:

I learned from Rebecca that she was eighteen, ten years younger than myself. Jewish Arab, originating from Africa, she came from a modest background – her father was in the spice trade at Belleville – when I myself, of distant Germanic background, came from a family of the middle bourgeoisie. (1981: 29)

According to the novel's epilogue, Fiona's literary counterpart ends up a junkie in India, while her partner (Didier) lands in a Turkish jail called 'Sark' ('I asked my lawyer what this meant in Turkish. He responded: the Orient' (Bruckner 1981: 249)). In Bruckner's novel, both the Oriental woman and the Orient itself first entice and then trap the three Western adventurers. Polanski's restraint in employing these stock Orientalist tropes creates a distance not only between the literary original and its filmic adaptation, but also between the film's author and the main currents of Western European culture. What little is left of Bruckner's ornate Orientalism in Polanski's film serves to expose the perfunctory character of European travelers' thirst for the exotic.[9] The figure of the wise Indian gentleman represents this attitude well.

Independently of the cultural context in which he finds himself, Polanski adopts the perspective of an outsider. The examples of *When Angels Fall* and *Bitter Moon*, films whose origins separate them in time and space, illustrate their maker's propensity towards adopting the perspective of a stranger. Such vistas allow him to maintain the position of a critic of dominant fictions. He punctures the balloon of established culture, no matter what presuppositions lie at its base. In both cases, the films' narrative structure engenders a play with conventions that provides Polanski with the means to destabilise a world determined by the transmission of culturally-coded paradigms. His meta-cinematic commentary reveals how cultural forms mediate and direct identity-forming processes within a culture. Temporality carries the mark of the ideologically determined means of representation. More clearly than any other of Polanski's films, *When Angels Fall* and *Bitter Moon* illustrate the filmmaker's skeptical attitude towards retrospection.

Polanski looks at history, its representations, and at all retrospective projects, with the skeptical eye of a Central European, from the distance afforded to him by the bitter experience that stems from having seen the grand narratives of German Nazism and Soviet Communism enforce their all-encompassing visions of humanity's past and future. E. Ann Kaplan and Ban Wang's reconsideration of traumatic narratives gives further theoretical grounding to this type of skepticism:

As a reaction-formation, trauma discourse ... may degenerate into a signature for victimhood, or an unresolved melancholia mired in injured narcissism or national pride, a melodramatic scenario for self-aggrandisement, a paralysis of the mind and the body, and a failure in language, image and narrative. (Kaplan & Wang 2004: 15)

Kaplan and Wang's conclusion may help explain Polanski's guarded attitude towards retrospection. Rather than contribute to the mythologising of the past, his flashbacks assign agency to those excluded from historical retrospectives, as in *When Angels Fall*, or they undermine the authority of the established power brokers, as in *Bitter Moon*. In both cases, the filmmaker's preoccupation with the mechanisms of cultural transmission takes precedence over the compulsion to relive the traumas of his own past.

Notes

1   In television and press interviews Polanski claimed that Szpilman's memoir attracted his attention because it was in some ways similar, but at the same time different, from his own experiences. Szpilman spent most of the war in the Warsaw ghetto. Polanski knew the ghetto of Cracow.

2   Polanski does not provide the name of the elderly woman who played in *When Angels Fall* in the credits. According to his autobiography, she was 'an inmate of a home for the destitute' (Polanski 1984: 153).

3   As Polanski informs in his autobiography: 'In need of an elaborate Art Deco set, I approached a Krakow academy student, Kazimierz Wisniak, whose work I knew and admired. Together we designed the public lavatory for *When Angels Fall*, molded its *fin de siecle* ceramic urinals in plaster, and assembled it on the school's sound stage. Modeled on a lavatory in one of Krakow's historic squares, it had a roof of frosted glass tiles, set flush with the sidewalk, through which those inside could glimpse the tide of humanity flowing overhead, the shadows of anonymous feet coming and going' (1984: 153).

4   In *The Tenant*, Trelkovsky (Polanski) crashes through a similar glass-tile structure after he jumps out the window of his apartment.

5   As Haltof points out, *Rashomon* (*Rashômon*, Akira Kurosawa, 1950) along with *Citizen Kane* (Orson Welles, 1941) were among the films most revered by Polish filmmakers of this era (2002: 67).

6   Wajda's choice of the restroom as the locale for some of the young AK conspirators' meetings may, in fact, foreshadow Maciek Chełmicki's (Zbigniew Cybulski) eventual death on the garbage dump. In both cases the clash between the lofty ideals that the freedom fighters embrace and the profane spaces they occupy has a tragic, ironic resonance. Polanski's relationship towards Wajda's war film is best described as dialogical.

7   I borrow the term 'dominant fiction' from Kaja Silverman who explains that '"Fiction" underscores the *imaginary* rather than the delusory nature of ideology, while "dominant" isolates from the whole repertoire of culture's images, sounds and narrative elaborations those through which the conventional subject is psychologically aligned with the symbolic order' (1992: 54).

8   John Orr has suggested that 'Oscar's prose in overdrive is a parody of the Great American Writer in Paris and indicates a collapse of a played-out idiom.' Orr's observation emphasises a crucial aspect of *Bitter Moon*'s voice-over, one that brings into focus Polanski's preoccupation with both narrative and cultural conventions (personal communication, 12 November 2004).

9   One should note that Polanski does reproduce the structuring of Bruckner's *Lunes de fiel* by incorporating flashbacks into his *Bitter Moon*.

CHAPTER ELEVEN

The Pianist and its Contexts: Polanski's Narration of Holocaust Evasion and Survival

Michael Stevenson

After playing Chopin, I feel as if I had been weeping over sins that I had never committed, and mourning over tragedies that were not my own.
– Oscar Wilde

Whenever I get happy, I always have a terrible feeling.
– Roman Polanski

Polanski's *The Pianist* can be approached in a number of ways. A thoroughgoing auteurist attention to the narrative would yield much in relation to his other work. Here, however, I want to place the film within the context of Holocaust debates and specifically those that have to do with questions of representation. In some sense it is highly significant that Polanski has studiously avoided the historical except in one early short film, *When Angels Fall* (see the chapters by Elżbieta Ostrowska and Izabela Kalinowska in this volume). So I have decided to produce three lines of discussion on *The Pianist*: firstly, to reprise some of the general arguments about Holocaust representation; secondly, to place the entwined narratives of Wladyslaw Szpilman and Polanski in relation to a particular mode of Holocaust narration that includes Primo Levi and Tadeusz Borowski; thirdly, to link these with other issues more directly contextual, the construction of the Warsaw Ghetto and those who survived and hid in the city. In this I am indebted to Gunnar S. Paulsson's *Secret City: The Hidden*

Jews of Warsaw, 1940–1945 (2002). This work begins to address in meticulous detail the 'unexplored continent' of evasion and survival, a neglected aspect of Holocaust Studies.

Paulsson's *Secret City* is joined by Tim Cole's *Holocaust City: The Making of a Jewish Ghetto* (2002) on the history of the Budapest ghetto. The publication of both books in the same year suggests a new direction in Holocaust research. They are both situated somewhere between an ethnography of events in a ghetto (see Dobroszycki 1984) and a detailed analysis of the vagaries of evasion and survival. Paulsson's study provides a useful contextual parallel with *The Pianist*, both with Szpilman's memoir and Polanski's film. This is to be found in its concentration on small everyday processes as well as the shifting and often improvised nature of Nazi oppression that constantly shifted the parameters in the possibilities of evasion and survival.

This is not to claim the film is attempting an unusual strategy for Polanski, a kind of quotidian 'realism', as may be claimed for *Schindler's List* (Steven Spielberg, 1993). This would be quite inappropriate. The film does have a clear sense of documentary drama, but with a striking sense of controlled artifice. There are, also, additional elements not present in Szpilman's memoir that appropriately broaden the historical perspective as well as providing a sharpened representation of the family. Polanski adds explicit scenes of the ghetto uprising and the start of the Warsaw Uprising that go beyond the book.

Paulsson reminds us of the exceptional nature of the Warsaw Ghetto experience and the extraordinary nature of life in Warsaw during the Second World War. To summarise the complex city experience as another key context for the film is important in understanding the reasons for *The Pianist*'s firm sobriety. Paulsson states the reality directly and succinctly:

> Ninety-eight percent of the Jewish population perished ... together with one-quarter of the Polish population ... some 720,000; a number that dwarfs the destruction of life in Hiroshima and Nagasaki combined ... the greatest slaughter in a single city in human history. Warsaw thus had far more Holocaust victims than any whole country save the USSR and Poland itself.

He then notes:

> The flight of twenty-odd thousand Jews ... seems by comparison a negligible phenomenon ... almost unnoticed by historians ... yet it was the greatest mass escape in history ... and the life of these fugitives in hiding for up to four years is a story with few parallels. (Paulsson 2002: 1–3)

This account must be added to in relation to survival figures. Many thousands of Jews hid in cities, towns and villages across Europe. Yet it is surprising, because of continuing presumptions of an overwhelmingly hostile environment outside the ghetto, that Warsaw accounted for by far the largest number of Jews in hiding. Necessarily, therefore, Warsaw also provided the largest number of helpers, institutions of aid and charitable organisations as well as those who preyed on the vulnerability of evaders and survivors. This was Paulsson's 'secret city'.

Yet the book and the film are not at all about direct resistance. Rather, Szpilman with Polanski and others represents a specific type of response to the Holocaust. Raul Hilberg, in his volume *The Destruction of the European Jews*, proposed five categories of response to such genocidal oppression: resistance, alleviation, evasion, paralysis and compliance. Hilberg and others tended to emphasise the latter pair of terms, paralysis and compliance, as most typical (1985: 1030). Earlier writing on the Holocaust stressed these categories although this was swiftly followed by protest and a counter wave of material emphasising resistance (Ainsztein 1974) and alleviation (Trunk 1996). A stress on paralysis and compliance is seen in this response as a slur, a too excessive highlighting of the failure to resist and that there needed to be a counterbalance in which the emphasis should be on resistance. What was left out in both accounts of the Jewish experience until very recently was the fifth category, that of evasion. It is this recent area of debate, what Paulsson calls 'the unexplored continent of Holocaust Studies' (2002: 7) that chimes so powerfully with Polanski's concerns in the film, driven by his reading of Szpilman and his own experience not returned to by him in cinema until 2002. Recent writing on the Holocaust has also stressed different ways of thinking about resistance in order to see evasion as in a continuum with resistance. This is partly evident in Yehuda Bauer's *Rethinking the Holocaust* (2001: 143–66). Though even here evasion, exactly at the heart of Polanski and Szpilman's narratives, is hardly raised. Still, debate on this subject did not exist until *Secret City* was published in the same year as the film was released. Although Paulsson does not mention Szpilman much of his book would be very familiar to a reader of the post-war memoir and the film would seem like a companion piece. In this sense *The Pianist* is quite unlike other Holocaust film and is more akin or related to the experience of Anne Frank.

These revelations of the apparently small experiences of the Holocaust, as with Art Spiegelman's *Maus: A Survivor's Tale* (1986), do not add significantly to explanations, yet they represent material that provides further help in trying to bridge the abyss between despair at never being able to understand and a possible extending of the knowledge that means the task of so doing may continue. The two million or so Jews who fled or went into hiding were driven by 'surely the most reasonable and human of all responses to an overwhelming hostile force' (Paulsson 2002: 9). They are now much more than a footnote in the Holocaust record. This is especially so as these evaders evince characteristics of the continuity between the ordinary and the extreme and the moralities that then become at stake and are questioned (Todorov 1999: 34).

The contextual arguments, introduced above, are supplemented in this chapter with analyses of three scenes from the early part of *The Pianist*. Rather than choosing scenes to represent the processes of the film as a whole, these have been selected to represent a characteristic narrational strategy adopted by Polanski. In them, Polanski's *mise-en-scène* and camera work indicate how he is attempting to grapple with issues of how representation may be able to produce knowledge of this extreme experience. He uses many strategies from his earlier work, especially his mastery of precise, specific placement of camera in relation to the deeply troubling central issue of a scene. He also produces new elements, most particularly a stillness and quietness of means, in narrative and *mise-en-scène* that enable a gap to be opened up between horror and contemplation. The often calm and steady narrative pace thus enables a most profound sense, quieter yet much more troubled, of the frantic experience of attempts at survival.

Analysis 1: Warsaw in late summer…

The film begins with a prologue with three main inflections: immediately, the quiet and calm of the C sharp minor nocturne; no title sequence; twelve fleeting black and white shots, newsreel with scratches, not reconstructed, suggesting urgency, each lasting only two or three seconds. This contrasts with the calm content of the shots: a sunny day, possibly a Sunday, with many walking in the park with prams, flower baskets visible, a great city at rest, peace and leisure. Only the twelfth shot breaks the security of the content. Here a newsboy hurries towards the camera and there is a close-up of his pale, serious face. Immediately the cut takes us to Polish Radio, to the final broadcast on 23 September. Thus the newsreel shots suggest a time before because by the time of the broadcast Warsaw had been under bombardment and siege from the beginning of the month. The film moves across a sharp break into an absolute insecurity. The nocturne plays over all this and even the explosions outside the studio hardly stop Szpilman playing. Indeed at first he refuses, shaking his head. Only the violent incursion of a bomb can finally do that.

Adrien Brody's still and quiet performance gives no answers to our many questions. We have to invest ourselves in a new and far more painful way into these experiences. This performative mode only breaks up at moments of extreme stress, at the Umschlagplatz after being dragged unwillingly from his family, and because he is an artist, at the final moments of realisation signified by his wan smile as he returns to playing the nocturne. If we could identify with Szpilman as active agent in the narrative much would be lost. Our identification with him is rather more distant. Cooler, it is thus more icily terrifying in developing our sense of helplessness in relation to Szpilman, reminding us of the worst nightmares of being lost and with little chance to find a way out. He meanders through the confined space of the ghetto and of Warsaw and as he looks obliquely through windows, small gaps and around corners at the catastrophe, he never quite sees the totality of the action, the complete picture, and neither do we.

Thus Polanski provides a means of helping us to experience the improvisations of terror, played out day by day as oppressors seek to entrap and make the victim passive. In this Polanski follows the events of Szpilman's memoir closely, but often uses an icy and clinically calm *mise-en-scène* that renders the events as near unbearable. In *The Pianist* everything must be at one remove, with no clear linear psychology. Szpilman must wander, hope, evade, make a small move, think that all is impossible and chance-like and yet continue, making the most of the faint and ephemeral chances that come his way. This is a description of a survival strategy.

In 1945, Szpilman will be back in the same Polish Radio studio, apparently picking up exactly where he left off in 1939. This could be seen as a satisfying rounding out, an escape from the darkness. But the gaze by Szpilman's returning musician friend Lednicki through the studio window suggests rather a kind of rebirth amidst great sorrow and knowledge.

The Pianist represents a finally explicit culmination of intersecting discourses that have been a constant troubling undercurrent in Polanski's work, especially of the nameless, faceless everpresent threat that exists just beyond an illusionary zone of security. The lack of reference to his wartime experience has been a significant structuring *absence* for critics of his work. Now, *The Pianist* represents an opportunity grasped to the full, to open up finally to that experience and provide a thoroughly revisionist way of representing it, using all available narrative resources. For many, an initial line of enquiry would lead to the influence on his work of Polanski's childhood in the Cracow Ghetto. In his earlier films this is characterised by a recurrent *mise-en-scène* of entrapment, of steadily increasing pressure, of uncertainty as to its cause and an avoidance of generically familiar closure.

In his autobiography, written some forty years after liberation, Polanski gives some twenty-five pages to his ghetto experience. The general tone of his survivor recounting is sometimes light, with no sense of the Holocaust as inexplicable mystery that has haunted analyses of it since the 1960s. 'I played with Polish, not just Jewish kids', and 'It would be wrong to think that fear dominated our lives during this preliminary period. I had some good times too … playing with my sled in the snow, swapping postage stamps…'. Yet this is after another iconic moment finally to be used in *The Pianist*: '"What are they doing?" I asked. "They're building a wall." Suddenly, it dawned on me: they were walling us in. My heart sank…' (1984: 14–15). The tone of this narrative continues to oscillate between the ordinary life of a child, and isolated moments of realisation that a gradual process of elaborate deception is enveloping the ghetto. Yet even the ghetto is better than outside. On one of his many small escapes from the Podgórze Ghetto, Polanski comments 'It wasn't until I was back inside the ghetto, after slipping through the wire again, that I felt entirely safe' (1984: 19). Other incidents are recounted in Polanski's own short survivor narrative of the Cracow Ghetto that will be used in *The Pianist*. Most notably these:

> Near us, guarding the assembled ghetto inmates, stood a young Polish militiaman … I went up and tried out our story on him. He must have seen through it but pretended not to. His nod of assent was barely perceptible. We started running. 'Walk slowly,' he growled, 'don't run.' We walked. (1984: 23)

And, as his father is being deported, 'glad of any excuse to rejoin him':

> I headed back to the ghetto … I saw a column of male prisoners being marched away … among them was my father. He didn't see me at first. I had to trot to keep up … At last he spotted me … He dropped back with the tacit assistance of others … to be farther from the nearest guard and closer to me. Then, out of the corner of his mouth, he hissed, 'Shove off!' … I watched … then turned away. I didn't look back. (1984: 25)

It is not only that incidents recounted by Polanski are worked into *The Pianist* as are other incidents generically present in Holocaust representation, for example the street executions in *Schindler's List*, but rather the tone of the telling, having in this a significant fidelity to Szpilman's memoir. Laconic, cool and underplayed (yet note the implicit comment of the exclamation mark after 'Shove off') Polanski's account works against the tendency in other memoirs to represent the unspeakable in much more graphic detail. Polanski provides a detailed, if brief, account but avoids any over-arching attempt at interpretation in judging what had happened to him. Again, in this approach to narration he resembles Szpilman and others.

Polanski and Szpilman, in their separate accounts are best seen in relation to a group of survivor narratives of a rather more ambiguous kind (Borowski, Levi, Spiegelman, Charlotte Delbo *et al.*). Their recounting of survival comes from a sensibility aware of the dangers of the corrupting fascination that may be released by their stories if there is any recourse to an excessive *mise-en-scène*. Instead, they want to mark a small, even ironic distance between the events and themselves. This kind of witnessing attempts to mark the dissonance between the extraordinary and the everyday, avoiding an overwhelming clamour of terror in an attempt to find a way of providing space for a specific kind of thought, a distance, a breathing moment, if only slight, on these events. It is worth noting that Alain Resnais also made such an attempt very early on in filmic representation of the Holocaust. In *Night and Fog* (*Nuit et brouillard*, 1955), the oscillation between contemporary colour footage and black and white archive material coupled with Hanns Eisler's contemplative score enables much of the same effect as noted above: not to reflect trauma mimetically, but to attempt to produce it as an object of knowledge and potential transformation.

Analysis 2: a family in the ghetto

Immediately following the bombing at the Radio Station, Szpilman arrives home. Polanski develops as sharply as possible the processes of knowledge production in relation to who knows what about the engulfing events. The family, in 18 shots and two minutes, express a range of contrasting attitudes from passivity to bustling action to evade and survive, to go to the country. Two well-known British actors head the family as Mother (Maureen Lipman) and Father (Frank Finlay). No doubt this brings to a British audience a strong sense of artifice as we see familiar and comfortable faces represent a bourgeois family in an atrocious situation. The interplay between these elements provides a useful distance for the viewer as we oscillate rapidly between familiarity and strangeness. In this way the film uses a range of artifice, in performance and *mise-en-scène*, so that we may see in a new light what has perhaps become too conventional in Holocaust representation. It asks us to try to look again at a family on the edge, to see their uncertainty afresh.

Mother is full of a premonitory trepidation, potentially useful in survival. Henryk (Ed Stoppard), Wladyslaw's brother, is developed rather more than in the book as a knowing and cynical figure, Polanski doubling him with Wladyslaw around the issues of knowing, and who is unwilling however to act through that knowledge that Wladyslaw does not seem to possess. He would rather die in his own home. The family members and the camera slide in and out of exits at speed. Father asks if he should take a particular portrait. Mother looks at him pityingly in his lack of knowledge. Later Father talks about new lines of defence across the Vistula. Regina (Julia Rayner) mocks this. Wladyslaw enters and now the Steadicam holds him central, sliding past and round him as he stares bewildered at the activity. His self-absorption is more evident. Our identification with him is made more complex and troubled by the processes of distanciation these strategies enable.

Finally a calmer centre, an authentic voice of reassurance emerges as Henryk tunes in to BBC news. 'There are other stations than Warsaw you know', he rather condescendingly avers. Britain has declared war and France will soon. Given our perspective on the betrayals of Poland this is not reassuring but Father crows, gurgles with delight. The Polish national anthem plays on the BBC but is interrupted by Hitler's speech on defending the German nation. The radio is firmly knocked and the BBC returns. The whole family gather together with us just outside the ring. They embrace in confidence for the future. They know each other now after the fragmentation of the first shots of the scene. They think they are together again in security. The terrible inklings of doubt are gone. This is a quite spurious coherence, one of an underlying desperation and only a momentary safety.

A special dinner is then held and this begins the theme of food in relation to survival. There will be several more of them before the final meal at the Umschlagplatz. Polanski with spectacular precision here develops his key task, his need to examine, within the specific possibilities of narrative fiction, the ways in which momentary, hesitant and small steps of understanding the engulfing process were gained.

It is useful to group Polanski's attitude with a number of other first-person accounts in order to discern the productivity of these in relation to the meanings of the Holocaust. This is specifically in relation to the 'the question why'. The reference here is to the moment in Primo Levi's account of survival in *If This is a Man*:

> Driven by thirst, I eyed a fine icicle outside the window, within hands reach. I opened the window and broke off the icicle but at once a large, heavy guard prowling outside brutally snatched it away from me. *Warum?* I asked in my poor German. *Hier ist kein warum* (there is no why here) he replied, pushing me inside with a shove … The explanation is repugnant but simple: in this place everything is forbidden, not for hidden reasons, but because the camp has been created for that purpose. If one wants to live one must learn this quickly and well. (1987: 35)

The tone of this passage, from the apparently very small detail, the window and the icicle suggesting a very limited compass of view to the implications of the iconic *Hier ist kein Warum*, is shared in the key survivor texts of Levi, Borowski and Szpilman and in Polanski too without making inflated claims for the latter as literature. Though it should be recalled that even the very possibility of Holocaust narrative as 'literature' is riddled with a certain sense of its impossibility. In Polanski's case it is surely his film of Szpilman's account that is his most felt addition to the clarity in finding possible ways of understanding a little more of these events when 'the very business of rational analysis grows unsteady before the enormity of the facts' (Steiner 1972: 31). Szpilman apparently has had a very different experience from a camp survivor – he moves from ghetto constraint to fugitive isolation. It might be claimed that to compare his experience is somewhat spurious. However, the stages of the experience are in every case similar. The movement is from a search for reassurance coupled with a growing dread then to the point of discovery of the very worst. This is followed by the shock of immediate survival on the ramp or at the Umschlagplatz and then the processes of survival. Again there is much that is similar in the latter experience, whether it was Borowski, Levi or Szpilman. The need to depend upon others was a paramount principle. Anyone who hoped to make it on their own, by whatever means, was likely to fail in the attempt. No matter how small or infrequent, the processes of solidarity and help were crucial, whether from fellow Poles in Warsaw or fellow scavengers in the Auschwitz work details. No matter how cynical, self-serving and demanding of reciprocity such sharing might entail, complete aloneness meant no chance at all.[1] Yet on the whole, we see in these particular modes of Holocaust narration micro-histories rather than anything purporting to have a large analytical dimension. They are written in the hope of understanding for oneself and, in the small detail, for others. In the film of Szpilman's memoir we see a conscious fusing of small detail, with Polanski drawing upon many sources in a mosaic of interweaving detail, unexorcisable memory. In addition it is important to note that they are not accounts of victimhood:

> Victimhood is a powerful, yet contradictory, force. Powerful because, once claimed, it can provide the moral basis for redress, retaliation and even revenge in order to right any given wrong – real or imagined ... Contradictory because, in order to harness that power, one must first admit weakness. Victims, by their very nature, have less power than their persecutors: victimhood is a passive state – the result of bad things happening to people who are unable to prevent it. (Younge 2004)

Szpilman, Polanski, Levi and Borowski in their narratives do not admit this kind of victimhood. All seem to be, in a sense, contemplative of an extraordinary and largely inexplicable event over which it is necessary to bear witness.

In relation to witnessing and the need to continue it as long as is possible, it should not be forgotten that there is an animus against the attempt to counter the *Hier ist Kein Warum* syndrome, most spectacularly by Claude Lanzmann in what Robert Rosenbaum calls his 'War Against the Question Why'.

Lanzmann's positions on the possibilities of Holocaust representation need to be questioned. Rosenbaum notes that in *Shoah* (1985), Lanzmann had 'entered into a holy war against explainers'. One acolyte sees Lanzmann as 'an amazing psychoanalytic presence ... tangible both in the depth of his silence and in the efficacy of his speech, in the success of his interventions in bringing forth the truth' (1998: 252). Most contradictorily, he allows himself the privilege to continue speaking on these matters, uttering, what Rosenbaum calls, 'Sinai-like rhetoric' and that he, 'hurls thunderbolts at those who violate his commandments' (1998: 253). In attacking *Schindler's List* in *Le Monde* on 3 March 1994, Lanzmann proposed that, 'After *Shoah*, certain things can no longer be done' (ibid.). This is not merely an incorrect echoing appropriation of Theodor Adorno's remark that to write poetry after Auschwitz is barbaric, but rather more, that, 'after *Shoah*, after *his film*, certain things are forbidden' (ibid.). Clearly, given Lanzmann's position, a case has to be made that Polanski and others, in making complex narratives of evasion and survival based on first-hand accounts, are not only admissible but essential in developing further an understanding of the minutiae of the events, of the micro processes, in order to both make available memory otherwise to be eventually lost and to prepare and continue analyses of the irrational monstrosity that nearly overwhelmed Szpilman, Borowski, Levi and Polanski. And doing this with a calm and rational curiosity, an aesthetic tact that does not mask a controlled outrage.

Analysis 3: a hot afternoon at the Umschlagplatz…

This scene is very near the centre of Szpilman's account but earlier in the film, as Polanski wants to give weight to later scenes of isolation in peeling and dilapidated apartments, echoing voices and threatening neighbours, with only partial sidelong looks at history unfolding outside (a strong link to previous films). Polanski adheres very closely to the book but with some telling additions. In particular he keeps to the relatively calm tone that Szpilman maintains until the end when he finally understands what is being managed, 'In a flash I realised what awaited the people' (1999: 106). Yet there is a greater sense of uncertainty in the film maintaining the theme noted in Analysis 1. The family enters the Umschlagplatz searching with their eyes as to what may be happening. Despite the immediate killing of the young woman in the previous scene as she asks, 'Where are you taking us?', still, desperately, hope is not completely gone. The scene is poised around this issue as characters variously demonstrate a range of attitudes to this uncertainty. It is here quite specifically a *mise-en-scène* of *demonstration* as Polanski in ten minutes and 46 shots (averaging well over ten seconds a shot) with a quiet and ferocious clarity presents us with Szpilman's precise description. The option might have been to develop the scene as in the selection on the camp square at Płaszow in *Schindler's List*, with racing camera, hysteria and explicit terror. Instead, Polanski, prompted by the chapter in the source memoir, uses calm camera movement and analytical cutting, shot/reverse shot (set-ups) of the most conventional kind as conversations occur. The audience's knowledge is thus added to. In that we see the how of the process in a series of small vignettes, of family, of children. Only near the end does the camera enable a release from this. There is an intense and sharp tilt down as a soldier throws the bolt on the door of the train carriage. Such camera usage allows for a much more developed thinking about the emotional processes of courage, love, despair, of family, of knowledge that we must know but can hardly bear to know.

Polanski concentrates rather more on Szpilman than the book. He is the uncertain centre of the scene, even stumbling clumsily against people. He stares in astonishment as Halina (Jessica Kate Meyer) and Henryk return, desperate to be reunited with the family. 'Stupid, stupid', he mutters to himself both about their bravery and his incomprehension of the events he and the camera pick out.

There are fifteen of these short vignettes all with their specific gestus: the everyday quotidian civility of the man's doffed cap to Szpilman in such contradiction to the audience's knowledge of the terrible inexorability of the events; the story, narrated three times, of the smothered child, contrasting so strongly with the heroic silence of children in *Schindler's List*; the strangeness of the child with the birdcage looking for a lost pet; the fierce argument about resistance between the dentist (who does resist on the behalf of a pregnant woman at the train and is instantly killed), the businessman and Mr Szpilman. The book mentions Henryk reading Shakespeare and Polanski includes this but adds (what else?) lines from *The Merchant of Venice*. This latter addition may be thought gratuitous, over artificial, but is appropriate, given Henryk's ironic distancing of himself from the events, contrasted with Szpilman's mystified uncertainty.

The scene starts to draw to its terrible climax. Father divides a caramel into six small pieces for each member of the family; the theme of food in relation to love and survival is extended. A train whistle sounds as a few dark chords are sounded from Wojciech Kilar's spare, understated soundtrack score. Guards gather round, the emphasis is on the young Jewish Police, with a few Germans and Ukrainians in the background. These well-fed young men know well what is happening. 'Off to the melting pot', is the last line of the scene, delivered by one of them to a German guard. All is being managed effectively. One of the most mysterious moments of the whole film now occurs (and is not in the book). Szpilman says to Halina, 'It's a funny time to say this but I wish I knew you better.' Halina quietly thanks him. Again I can only assume that Polanski, in adding this strange yet deeply touching moment, wants to emphasise the way that all processes of knowing/not knowing are at stake in Holocaust representation, even, perhaps most especially, our knowledge of ourselves and those close to us. Szpilman's last chance to know his sister has gone, echoing in reverse the loving 'shove off' of Polanski's father.

Reviewers many times note the understated tone and imagery of Szpilman's sharp and brief account of his experiences. This fits very precisely with my contention as to the modesty and usefulness of first-hand reportage of evasion and survival. Typical is Lisa Appignanesi's review:

> The grand historical narrative of the Second World War, with its alliances and troop movements, its heroes and villains, is now largely established. Yet 54 years on, the smaller, individual accounts of those who lived through the war's terror continue to shock or surprise by their very particularity … The immediacy of Szpilman's account goes hand in hand with a rare tone of innocence. History has not yet been written, certainly not digested. We are drawn in to share his surprise and then disbelief at the horrifying progress of events. His

shock and ensuing numbness become ours, so that acts of ordinary kindness or humanity take on an aura of miracle. (1999)[2]

I would add that the Szpilman's book has something also of quiet desperation and submerged anxiety in Chopin about it as well. The key piece for the whole film is, of course, the C sharp minor nocturne that Szpilman reports playing at the last broadcast of Polish Radio on 23 August 1939. It is also the piece he plays to Captain Wilm Hosenfeld (Thomas Kretschmann) when they meet late in 1944 (not the Ballade in G minor that is used in the film). This nocturne is deceptive in its simplicity and, in fact, was variously dismissed by some critics. Herbert Weinstock considered it to be, 'ungrateful in performance … without balance or design' (quoted in Bailie 1998: 379), whereas others value it precisely for its modesty and balance, with 'an inexplicable yet compelling unity … as if passing through a dreamlike landscape … with a quiet and solemn expectancy … and having a melody that is one of the most vocal in Chopin' (ibid.).

The coolness and balance of Szpilman's writing can be quite disconcerting even when he recalls *in extremis*, for example when he is starving and visited by the treacherous street hustler and fixer, Szalas (Andrew Tiernan), the only Polish helper who fails him, sharply contrasting with others (cf. Paulsson 2002: 8).[3] A tone is achieved through slight deprecation, wit and a reduction of adjectival possibilities, and even here not wanting to apportion blame:

> Beaming, evidently with his mind on something else, he would always enquire, 'Still alive then, are you?'
>   I *was* still alive, even though the combination of malnutrition and grief had given me jaundice. Szalas did not take that too seriously, and told me the cheering tale of his grandfather, whose girlfriend had jilted him when he suddenly went down with jaundice. (2000: 143)

The film remains largely true to this tone throughout, constantly drawing back in all areas of its construction when there might be a temptation to attempt to impose something more, a point of view allocating explanation of human behaviour and thus the potential for a clear and unambiguous accusation of blame. Only at the very end does Polanski allow himself to break the rule he has imposed upon himself in making the film, that is, to wind his experience into that of Szpilman, to rise to the challenge of making a film recreating a world of evasion that had run parallel to his own. Only then at the end, over the end titles, does he allow an explosion into the exuberance of a concert performance of the Grande Polonaise Brillante.

But Polanski has offered much in this film and thought much. He has delineated another way of handling a narration of the Holocaust through film. Those who know parallel texts such as *Schindler's List* will notice many elements in common, down to particular scenes deemed necessary to include. I have no animus against Spielberg and would defend many of his decisions made in constructing his Holocaust film. But it is Polanski's task to re-focus on these details away from sentiment and melodrama, consoling as these are, and towards difficulty. The difficulty any and all may face when, as Primo Levi's warned, that if 'a conception of the world is carried rigorously to its logical conclusion; so long as the conception subsists, the conclusion remains to threaten us...' (1987: 15).

And, again in *If This is a Man*, when asked as to his method of writing about his experience:

> I prefer the role of witness to that of judge. I can bear witness only to the things that I myself endured and saw. My books are not history books. Remembering is a duty. These experiences were not meaningless. The camps were not an accident, an unforeseen historical accident. (1987: 390–1)

In this Levi is joined with the quiet and just mode of reporting atrocious events that are also the task of Szpilman and Polanski.

My thanks to the film research group (The Sewing Circle) in the Department of Film, Theatre and Television at the University of Reading, who devoted two seminars to The Pianist in the autumn of 2003.

Notes

1   Borowski's accounts of everyday survival are also particularly relevant here. Tadeusz Borowski is certainly as important as Primo Levi among those who have recounted Holocaust survival in the way I describe. Jan Kott's introduction to Borowski's *This Way to the Gas, Ladies and Gentlemen* puts it thus: 'The difference between executioner and victim is stripped of all greatness and pathos' (1976: 7). These stories show atrocious crimes becoming an unremarkable daily routine. Kott continues: 'The narrator is a Kapo, Tadeusz ... the identification of the narrator (with the Kapo) was the moral decision of a prisoner who had lived through Auschwitz – an acceptance of mutual responsibility, mutual participation and mutual guilt' (1976: 9). Borowski himself wrote that 'the first duty is to make clear what a camp is ... and how did it happen that *you* survived. Tell then how you bought places in the hospital ... tell about the hierarchy of fear, about the loneliness of every man' (1976: 22).
2   For more recognition and valuing of the tone of voice in Szpilman, see: http://www.szpilman.net/framebook.html
3   Paulsson has 31 references in his index to these small-time fixers in *Secret City*. He always uses the Polish name for them – 'szmalcownik'.

FILMOGRAPHY

Bicycle (*Rower*) 1955
St. Roman Polanski, Adam Fiut.
Sc. Roman Polanski
Ph. Nikoła Todorow
Pr. PWSF – Łódź,
Colour [never completed]

Murder (*Morderstwo*) 1957
Sc. Roman Polanski
Ph. Nikoła Todorow
Pr. PWSF – Łódź
B&W, 1 min. 30s

Teethful Smile (*Uśmiech zębiczny*) 1957
Starring: Nikoła Todorow
Sc. Roman Polanski
Ph. Henryk Kucharski
Pr. PWSF – Łódź
B&W, 1 min. 27s

Let's Break the Ball (*Rozbijemy zabawę*) 1957
Sc. Roman Polanski
Ph. Andrzej Galiński, Marek Nowicki
Mu. Krzysztof Komeda
Pr. PWSF – Łódź
B&W, 8 min. 49s

Two Men and a Wardrobe (*Dwaj ludzie z szafą*) 1958
St. Henryk Kluba, Jakub Goldberg, Roman Polanski, Stanisław Michalski
Sc. Roman Polanski
Ph. Maciej Kijowski
Mu. Krzysztof Komeda
Pr. PWSF – Łódź
B&W, 15 min.

The Lamp (*Lampa*) 1959
Sc. Roman Polanski
Ph. Krzysztof Romanowski
Pr. PWSFiT – Łódź
B&W, 7 min. 50s

When Angels Fall (*Gdy spadają anioły*) 1959
St. Barbara Kwiatkowska, Andrzej Kondratiuk, Jakub Goldberg, Roman Polanski
Sc. Roman Polanski
Ph. Henryk Kucharski
Mu. Krzysztof Komeda
Pr. PWSFiT – Łódź
B&W/Colour, 22 min.

The Fat and the Lean (*Le Gros et le maigre*) 1961
Co-dir. André Katelbach
St. André Katelbach, Roman Polanski
Sc. Roman Polanski, Jean-Pierre Rousseau
Ph. Jean-Michel Boussaguet
Mu. Krzysztof Komeda
Pr. Claude Joudieux/APEC (Paris)
B&W, 16 min.

Mammals (*Ssaki*) 1962
St. Henryk Kluba, Michał Żołnierkiewicz, Wojciech Frykowski
Sc. Roman Polanski, Andrzej Kondratiuk
Ph. Andrzej Kondratiuk
Mu. Krzysztof Komeda
Pr: Film Polski
B&W. 10 min. 15s

Knife in the water (*Nóż w wodzie*) 1962
St. Leon Niemczyk, Zygmunt Malanowicz (voice: Roman Polanski; uncredited), Jolanta Umecka (voice: Anna Ciepielewska; uncredited)
Sc. Roman Polanski, Jerzy Skolimowski, Jakub Goldberg
Ph. Jerzy Lipman
Mu. Krzysztof Komeda
Pr. ZRF Kamera (Warsaw)
B&W, 94 min.

Amsterdam (*La Rivière de Diamants*) in *The World's Most Beautiful Swindlers* (*Les Plus belles escroqueries du monde*) 1964
St. Nicole Karen, Jan Teulings, Arnold Gelderman
Sc. Roman Polanski, Gérard Brach
Ph. Jerzy Lipman
Mu. Krzysztof Komeda
Pr: Ulysse Prodctions
B&W, 33 min.

Repulsion 1965
St. Catherine Deneuve, Yvonne Furneaux, Ian Hendry, John Fraser
Sc. Roman Polanski, Gérard Brach
Ph. Gilbert Taylor
Mu. Chico Hamilton
Pr. Gene Gutowski
B&W, 104 min.

Cul-de-Sac 1966
St. Donald Pleasance, François Dorléac, Lionel Stander, Jack MacGowran
Sc. Roman Polanski, Gérard Brach
Ph. Gilbert Taylor
Mu. Krzysztof Komeda
Pr. Gene Gutowski
B&W, 111 min.

The Fearless Vampire Killers (aka *The Fearless Vampire Killers or Pardon Me, But Your Teeth Are in My Neck*) 1967
St. Jack MacGowran, Roman Polanski, Jessie Robins, Sharon Tate
Sc. Roman Polanski, Gérard Brach
Ph. Douglas Slocombe
Mu. Krzysztof Komeda
Pr. Gene Gutowski
Colour, 91 min.

Rosemary's Baby 1968
St. Mia Farrow, John Cassavetes, Ruth Gordon, Sidney Blackmer

Sc. Roman Polanski, from the novel by Ira Levin
Ph. William Fraker
Mu. Krzysztof Komeda
Pr. William Castle
Colour, 137 min.

Macbeth (aka *The Tragedy of Macbeth*) 1971
St. Jon Finch, Francesca Annis, Martin Shaw, Nicholas Selby
Sc. Roman Polanski, Kenneth Tynan, from the play by William Shakespeare
Ph. Gilbert Taylor
Pr. Andrew Braunsberg and Roman Polanski
Colour, 140 min.

What? 1972
Starring: Sydne Rome, Marcello Mastroianni, Hugh Griffith, Roman Polanski
Sc. Roman Polanski, Gérard Brach
Ph. Marcello Gatti, Giuseppe Ruzzolini
Mu. Claudio Gizzi
Pr. Carlo Ponti
Colour, 112 min.

Chinatown 1974
St. Jack Nicholson, Faye Dunaway, John Huston, Perry Lopez
Sc. Robert Towne
Ph. John A. Alonzo
Mu. Jerry Goldsmith
Pr. Robert Evans.
Colour, 130 min.

The Tenant (*Le Locataire*) 1976
St. Roman Polanski, Isabelle Adjani, Shelley Winters, Melvyn Douglas
Sc. Roman Polanski, Gérard Brach from the novel by Roland Topor
Ph. Sven Nykvist
Mu. Philippe Sarde
Pr. Andrew Braunsberg
Colour, 125 min.

Tess 1979
St. Nastassia Kinski, Peter Firth, Leigh Lawson, John Collin
Sc. Roman Polanski, Gérard Brach, John Brownjohn, from the novel by Thomas Hardy
Ph. Geoffrey Unsworth, Ghislain Cloquet
Mu. Philippe Sarde
Pr. Claude Berri
Colour, 180 min.

Pirates 1986
St. Walter Matthau, Cris Campion, Damien Thomas, Olu Jacobs
Sc. Roman Polanski, Gérard Brach, John Brownjohn
Ph. Witold Sobocinski
Mu. Philippe Sarde
Pr. Tarak Ben Amarr
Colour, 124 min.

Frantic 1988
St. Harrison Ford, Betty Buckley, Emmanuelle Seigner, John Mahoney
Sc. Roman Polanski, Gérard Brach
Ph. Witold Sobocinski
Mu. Ennio Morricone, Astor Piazzolla
Pr. Tim Hampton, Thom Mount
Colour, 119 min.

Bitter Moon 1992
St. Peter Coyote, Emmanuelle Seigner, Hugh Grant, Kristin Scott Thomas.
Sc. Roman Polanski, Gérard Brach, John Brownjohn, from the novel by Pascal Bruckner
Ph. Tonino Delli Colli
Mu. Vangelis
Pr. Robert Benmussa
Colour, 138 min.

Death and the Maiden 1994
St. Sigourney Weaver, Ben Kingsley, Stuart Wilson
Sc. Rafael Iglesias, Ariel Dorfman, from the play by Ariel Dorfman
Ph. Tonino Delli Colli
Mu. Wojciech Kilar
Pr. Josh Kramer, Thom Mount
Colour, 103 min.

The Ninth Gate 1999
St. Johny Depp, Emmanuelle Seigner, Frank Langella, Lena Olin
Sc. Arturo Pérez-Reverte, John Brownjohn, Enrique Urbizu, from the novel by Arturo Pérez-Reverte
Ph. Darius Khondji
Mu. Wojciech Kilar
Pr. Roman Polanski
Colour, 133 min.

The Pianist 2002
St. Adrien Brody, Thomas Kretschmann, Frank Finlay, Maureen Lipman
Sc. Ronald Harwood, from the book by Wladyslaw Szpilman
Ph. Pawel Edelman

Mu. Wojciech Kilar
Pr. Roman Polanski, Robert Benmussa, Alain Sarde
Colour, 150 min.

Olivier Twist 2005
St. Ben Kingsley, Barney Clark, Jamie Foreman, Harry Eden
Sc. Ronald Harwood, from the novel by Charles Dickens
Ph. Pawel Edelman
Mu. Rachel Portman
Pr. Robert Benmussa, Alain Sarde, Roman Polanski, Timothy Burril
Colour, 132 min.

BIBLIOGRAPHY

Ainsztein, R. (1974) *Jewish Resistance in Nazi-Occupied Eastern Europe*. London: Paul Elek.

Appignanesi, L. (1999) 'Notes from the Warsaw Ghetto'. Book review of *The Pianist*, *Observer*, 28 March. On-line. Available at http://www.guardian.co.uk.

Arendt, H. (1963) *Eichmann in Jerusalem: A Report on the Banality of Evil*. New York: Viking.

Bailie, E. (1998) *Chopin*. London: Kahn & Averill.

Baird, R. (2000) 'The Startle Effect', *Film Quarterly*, 53, 12–24.

Bakhtin, M. (1984) *Rabelais and His World*, trans. H. Iswolsky. Bloomington, IN: Indiana University Press.

Bauer, Y. (2001) *Rethinking the Holocaust*. London: Yale University Press.

Beckett, S. (1968a) *Endgame*. London: Faber and Faber.

____ (1968b) *Waiting for Godot*. London: Faber and Faber.

Benedetto, R. (1999) 'The Two Chinatowns: Towne's Screenplay vs. Polanski's Film', *Creative Screenwriting*, 6, 6,, 49–54.

Bersani, L. (1984 [1969]) *A Future for Astyanax: Character and Desire in Literature*. New York: Columbia University Press.

Bettelheim, B. (1977) *The Uses of Enchantment: The Meaning and Importance of Fairy Tales*. New York: Vintage.

Bird, D. (2002) *Roman Polanski*. Harpenden: Pocket Essentials.

Boothby, R. (1991) *Death and Desire: Psychoanalytic Theory in Lacan's Return to Freud*. New York: Routledge.

Bordwell, D. (1985) *Narration in the Fiction Film*. Madison: University of Wisconsin Press.

_____ (2005) *Figures Traced in Light: On Cinematic Staging*. Berkeley: University of California Press.

_____ (2006) *The Way Hollywood Tells it: Story and Style in Modern Movies*. Berkeley: University of California Press.

Borowski, T. (1976) *This Way for the Gas, Ladies and Gentlemen*, trans. B. Vedder. London: Penguin.

Bresson, R. (1977) *Notes on Cinematography*. New York. Urizen Books.

Brooks, P. (1984) *Reading for the Plot: Design and Intention in Narrative*. New York: Knopf.

Brown, K. (1996–97) 'Repulsion', *EUFS Programme*. Available at http://ww.eufs.org.uk/films/repulsion.html.

Bruckner, P. (1981) *Lunes de fiel*. Paris: Seuil.

Butler, I (1970a) *The Cinema of Roman Polanski*. New York: A. S. Barnes.

_____ (1970b) 'Polanski and Repulsion', in I. Butler, *Horror in the Cinema*. New York: A. S. Barnes, 131–44.

Carroll, L. (1900) *Alice in Wonderland and Through the Looking Glass*. Chicago: Goldsmith.

Cawelti, J. G. (1979) '*Chinatown* and Generic Transformation in Recent American Films', in G. Mast and M. Cohen (eds) *Film Theory and Criticism*, second edition. New York and Oxford: Oxford University Press, 559–79.

Charity, T. (2005) '*The Others*', in J. Pym (ed.) *Time Out Film Guide*, thirteenth edition. London: Ebury, 972.

Chion, M. (1999) *The Voice in the Cinema*, trans. C. Gorbman. New York: Columbia University Press.

Ciment, M. and M. Sineux (1988) 'Entretien avec Roman Polanski', *Positif*, 327, 5–9.

Clover, C. (1992) *Men, Women and Chainsaws: Gender in the Modern Horror Film*. London: British Film Institute.

Cole, T. (2002) *Holocaust City: The Making of a Jewish Ghetto*. London: Routledge.

Cousins, M. (2000) 'Interview with Roman Polanski', BBC *Scene-by-Scene*. 6 March, La Salle des Fetes, Museé D'Orsay, Paris.

_____ (2002) *Scene by Scene: Film Actors and Directors Discuss their Work*. London: Lawrence King.

_____ (2004) *The Story of Film*. London: Pavilion.

Cox, S. (1995/96) 'Repulsion', *EUFS Programme*. Available at http://www.eufs.org.uk/films, repulsion.html.

Delbo, C. (1995) *Auschwitz and After*, trans. R. C. Lamont, intr. L. Langer. New Haven, CT and London: Yale University Press.

De Lauretis, T. (1984) *Alice Doesn't: Feminism, Semiotics, Cinema*. Bloomington, IN: Indiana University Press.

Deleuze, G. and F. Guattari (1977) *Anti-Oedipus: Capitalism and Schizophrenia*, trans. R. Hurley, M. Seem and H. R. Lane. New York: Viking.

DeVore, D. 'Repulsion', *MJ Movie Vault*. Available at http://www.moviejusstice.com/db/index.php?page.

Doane, M. A. (1987) *The Desire to Desire: The Woman's Film of the 1940s*. Bloomington, IN: Indiana University Press.

Dobroszycki, L. (ed.) (1984) *The Chronicle of the Lodz Ghetto, 1941–1944*. London: Yale

University Press.

Doneson, J. (1978) 'The Jew as a Female Figure in Holocaust Film', *Shoah: A Review of Holocaust Studies and Commemoration*, 1, 1, 11–13, 18.

Durgnat, R. (1965) '*Repulsion*', *Films and Filming*, 11, 28–9.

Eagle, H. (1994) 'Polanski', in D. J. Goulding (ed.) *Five Filmmakers: Tarkovsky, Forman, Polanski, Szabó, Makavejev*. Bloomington and Indianapolis: Indiana University Press, 92–155.

Easthope, A. (1992) *What A Man's Gotta Do*. New York and London: Routledge.

Eaton, M. (1997) *Chinatown*. London: British Film Institute.

Ebert, R. (1997) *Roger Ebert's Book of Film*. New York: W. W. Norton.

Elsaesser, T. (1989) *New German Cinema: A History*. New Brunswick, NJ: Rutgers University Press.

Esslin, M. (1969) *Reflections: Essays on Modern Theatre*. Garden City, NY: Doubleday.

_____ (1983) *The Theatre of the Absurd*, third edition. New York: Penguin Books.

Finkelstein, N. G. (2001) *The Holocaust Industry*, second edition. London: Verso.

Fischer, L. (1996) *Cinematernity: Film, Motherhood, Genre*. Princeton, NJ: Princeton University Press.

Fraker, W. A. and P. Edelman (2004) 'Working with Polanski', *Camera*, January, 42.

Frost, R. (1930) *Collected Works of Robert Frost*. New York: H. Holt.

Gledhill, C. (1999) 'Horror', in P. Cook and M. Bernink (eds) *The Cinema Book*, second edition. London: British Film Institute, 194–208.

Goldhagen, D. (1997) *Hitler's Willing Executioners: Ordinary Germans and the Holocaust*. New York: Vintage.

Gombrowicz, W. (1971) *Teatr*. Paris: Instytut Literacki.

_____ (1981) *Ferdydurke*, trans. E. Mosbacher. Harmondsworth: Penguin.

_____ (1985) *Cosmos*, trans. E. Mosbacher and A. Hamilton, and *Pornografia*, trans. A. Hamilton. New York: Grove Press.

_____ (1988) *Diary*, 1, 1953–1956, trans. L. Vallee. Evanstone, Il: Northwestern University Press.

Goodheart, E. (1991) *Desire and its Discontents*. New York: Columbia University Press.

Goodridge, M. (2002) *Directing*. Crans-Près-Céligny: Rotovision.

Gregory, R. L. (1998) *Eye and Brain*, fifth edition. Oxford: Oxford University Press.

Guthmann, E. (1998) '*Repulsion* Makes Deneuve Go Mad. Polanski's 1965 thriller passes test of crime', *San Francisco Chronicle*, 22 May. Available at http://www.sfgate.com/cgi-bin/article.cgi?file=/c/a/1998/05/22/DD6.

Haltof, M. (2002) *Polish National Cinema*. New York and Oxford: Berghahn Books.

Hardy, P. (1985) *The Aurum Film Encyclopedia: Horror*. London: Aurum.

Henley, J. (2004) 'Emigré Jew's wartime book takes France by storm', *The Guardian*, 23 October. Available at http://www.guardian.co.uk.

Hilberg, R. (1985) *The Destruction of the European Jews*. London: Holmes and Meier.

Houston, B. and M. Kinder (1968–69) '*Rosemary's Baby*', *Sight and Sound*, 38, 1, 17–19.

Jankun-Dopartowa, M. (2000) *Labirynt Polańskiego*. Cracow: Rabid.

Jung C. G. (1964) *Man and his Symbols*. London: Aldus Books.

Kafka, F. (1976) *Franz Kafka*. London: Secker and Warburg.

_____ (1988) *The Collected Short Stories*. London: Penguin.

Kandelman, S. (2003) 'Étonnant itinéraire d'un cinéaste', *Voir*, 20–26 November, 57.

Kaplan, E. A. and B. Wang (2004) 'From Traumatic Paralysis to the Force Field of Modernity', in E. A. Kaplan and B. Wang (eds) *Trauma and Cinema: Cross-Cultural Explorations.* Hong Kong: Hong Kong University Press, 1–22.

Kay, K. and G. Peary (eds.) (1977) *Women and the Cinema: A Critical Anthology.* New York: E. P. Dutton.

Kemp, P. (2000) '*The Ninth Gate*', *Sight and Sound,* 10, 9, 45–6.

Kiernan, T. (1980) *The Roman Polanski Story.* New York: Delilah/Grove Press.

Kott, J. (1976) 'Introduction', to T. Borowski, *This Way for the Gas, Ladies and Gentlemen*, trans. B. Vedder. London: Penguin, 11–26.

Lawton, A. (1981) 'The Double … A Dostoevskian Theme in Polanski', *Literature/Film Quarterly,* 9, 2, 121–9.

Leach, J. (1978) 'Notes on Polanski's Cinema of Cruelty', *Wide Angle,* 2, 1.

Leaming, B. (1981) *Polanski. A Biography. The Filmmaker as Voyeur.* New York: Simon and Schuster/A Touchstone Book.

Levi, P. (1987) *If This is a Man*, trans. S. Woolf. London: Sphere Books.

Lubelski, T. (2000) *Strategie autorskie w polskim filmie fabularnym lat 1945–1961.* Cracow: Rabid.

Mansfield, N. (2000) *Subjectivity: Theories of Self from Freud to Haraway.* New York: New York University Press.

Marszałek, R. (1995) 'Polański i kultura masowa', in B. Żmudziński (ed.) *Roman Polański.* Cracow: Instytut Francuski, 46–57.

Martineau, B. H. (1977) 'Documenting the Patriarchy: *Chinatown*', in K. Kay and G. Peary (eds) *Women and the Cinema.* New York: E. P. Dutton, 347–51.

Masterman, L. (1970) '*Cul-de-Sac*: Through the Mirror of Surrealism', *Screen,* 11, 6, 44–60.

McArthur, C. (1968–69) 'Polanski: *Rosemary's Baby*', *Sight and Sound,* 38, 1, 14–17.

Mendoza, P. A. (1988) *The Fragrance of Gueva: Conversations with Gabriel García Marquez.* London: Faber and Faber.

Michalek, B. and F. Turaj (1988) *The Modern Cinema of Poland.* Bloomington and Indianapolis, IN: Indiana University Press.

Mrożek, S. (1975) *Wybór dramatów i opowiadań.* Cracow: Wydawnictwo Literackie.

Mulvey, L. (1975) 'Visual Pleasure and Narrative Cinema', *Screen,* 16, 3, 6–18.

O'Shea, S. (1994) 'Roman Polanski's *Bitter Moon*', *Interview,* 24, 3, 22–3.

Ostrowska, E. (1998) 'Filmic Representations of the "Polish Mother" in Post-Second World War Polish Cinema', *The European Journal of Women's Studies,* 5, 3–4, 419–35.

Parker, A., M. Russo, D. Sanner and P. Yaeger (1992) 'Introduction', in A. Parker, M. Russo, D. Sanner and P. Yaeger (eds) *Nationalisms and Sexualities.* London, New York: Routledge, 1–18.

Paulsson, G. S. (2002) *Secret City: The Hidden Jews of Warsaw, 1940–1945.* New Haven, CT and London: Yale University Press.

Pérez, M. (2002) '*Rosemary's Baby*', in M. Ciment and L. Kardish (eds) *Positif: Fifty Years.* New York: The Museum of Modern Art, 101–5.

Pizello, C. (2000) 'Satanic Verses', *American Cinematographer,* 81, 4, 38–49.

Polanski, R. (1975) '"Landscape of a Mind", from an interview with Roman Polanski by Michael Delahaye and Jean-André Fieschi, *Cahiers du cinéma* in English, February 1966, no 3', in *Polanski: Three Film Scripts.* New York: Icon Editions, 205–14.

_____ (1980) 'Kino według Polańskiego' (fragments of Polanski's interviews), *Film na świecie*, 264–5, 8–58.

_____ (1984) *Roman by Polanski*. London: Heinemann/New York: William Morrow.

_____ (1985) *Roman*. London: Pan Books.

Prokop, J. (1993) *Universum polskie: Literatura, wyobraźnia zbiorowa, mity polityczne*. Cracow: Universitas.

Reeves, T. (2001) *The Worldwide Guide to Movie Locations*. London: Titan Books.

Rich, A. (1986) 'Compulsory Heterosexuality and the Lesbian Continuum', in A. Rich, *Blood, Bread, and Poetry: Selected Prose, 1979–1985*. New York: W. W. Norton, 23–75.

Rockett, W. M. (1982) 'Perspectives', *Journal of Popular Film and Television*, 3, 10, 49.

Romero, G. A. (2002) 'Ten Best Movies of All Time', *Sight and Sound*, 12, 9.

Rosenbaum, J. (1997) 'Polanski and the American Experiment (*Bitter Moon*)', in J. Rosenbaum (ed.) *Movies as Politics*. Berkeley, CA: University of California Press, 28–33.

Rosenbaum, R. (1998) *Explaining Hitler: The Search for the Origins of his Evil*. London: Macmillan.

Różewicz, T. (1972) *Sztuki teatralne*. Wrocław, Warsaw, Cracow and Gdansk: Zakład Narodowy im. Ossolińskich.

Said, E. (1994) *Culture and Imperialism*. New York: Vintage Books.

Sartre, J.-P. (1949) *No Exit and Three Other Plays*. New York: Vintage Books/Random House.

_____ (1972) *The Psychology of the Imagination*. London: Methuen.

Schwarberg, G. (2001) *In the Ghetto of Warsaw: Heinrich Jost's Photographs*. Gottingen: Steidl Verlag.

Silverman, K. (1992) *Male Subjectivity at the Margins*. New York: Routledge.

Skolimowski, J. (1990) 'Rysopis', an interview with Jerzy Skolimowski by J. Uszyński, *Film na świecie*, 373, 3–44.

Solomon, S. J. (1976) *Beyond Formula, American Film Genres*. New York: Harcourt, Brace, Jovanovich.

Spiegelman, A. (1986) *Maus: A Survivor's Tale: My Father Bleeds History and Here My Troubles Began*. London: Penguin.

Spielrein, S. (1987) *Saemtliche Schriften*. Freiburg: Kore.

Stachówna, G. (1988a) 'Heroiczna walka z absurdem, czyli *Matnia* Romana Polańskiego', *Kino* 22, 7, 25–8.

_____ (1988b) 'Heroiczna walka z absurdem, czyli *Matnia* Romana Polańskiego', *Kino*, 22, 8, 19–20.

_____ (1994) *Roman Polański i jego filmy*. Warsaw-Łódź: Wydawnictwo Naukowe PWN.

_____ (1996) '*Knife in the Water*, or how to succeed in the art of moving pictures', in W. Godzic (ed.) *Jagiellonian Film Studies*. Cracow: Universitas, 161–71.

Steiner, G. (1972) *In Bluebeard's Castle: Some Notes Towards the Re-definition of Culture*. London: Faber & Faber.

Szpilman, W. (2000) *The Pianist*, trans A. Bell. London: Phoenix.

Telotte, J. P. (1989) *Voices in the Dark: The Narrative Patterns in Film Noir*. Urbana, IL: University of Illinois Press.

Thompson, M. G. (1985) *The Death of Desire: A Study in Psychopathology*. New York: New York University Press.

Todorov, T. (1999) *Facing the Extreme: Moral Life in the Concentration Camps*. London:

Weidenfeld and Nicolson.

Topor, R. (1997) *The Tenant*, trans. Francis K. Price. London: Black Spring Press.

Truffaut, F. (1984) *Hitchcock: The Definitive Study*. London: Paladin Books.

Trunk, I. (1996) *Judenrat*. Lincoln: Nebraska University Press.

Turim, M. (1989) *Flashbacks in Film*. New York and London: Routledge.

Vauchaud, L. (1992) 'Lunes de Fiel: le couteau dans le plaie', *Positif*, 380, 60–1.

Von Sternberg, J. (1965) *Fun in a Chinese Laundry*. New York: Macmillan.

Wajda, A. (1996) *Wajda. Filmy*, Vols. I & II. Warsaw: Wydawnictwa Artystyczne i Filmowe.

_____ (2000) *Kino i reszta świata. Autobiografia*. Cracow: Znak.

Weinberg, G. (1963–64) 'Interview with Roman Polanski', *Sight and Sound*, 33, 1, 32–3.

Wexman, V. W. (1979) *Roman Polanski: A Guide to References and Resources*. Boston: G. K. Hall.

_____ (1985) *Roman Polanski*. Boston: Twayne.

Williams, L. (1981) *Figures of Desire: A Theory and Analysis of Surrealist Film*. Berkeley: University of California Press.

Williams, L. R. (1995) *Critical Desire: Psychoanalysis and the Literary Subject*. London and New York: E. Arnold.

Williams, R. (1966) *Modern Tragedy*. London: Chatto and Windus.

Younge, G. (2004) 'A hierarchy of suffering', *Guardian*, 20 September. On-line. Available http://www.guardian.co.uk.

Zgorzelski, C. (1961) *O lirykach Mickiewicza i Słowackiego: Eseje i studia*. Lublin: Towarzystwo Naukowe KUL.

Żmudziński, B. (ed.) (1995) *Roman Polański*. Cracow: Instytut Francuski.

INDEX

2006
224 pages
1-904764-77-0 (pbk) £15.99
1-904764-78-9 (hbk) £45.00

The Cinema of Todd Haynes
All that Heaven Allows

Edited by James Morrison

From the trenches of independent American film of the 1990s, Todd Haynes has emerged in the twenty-first century as one of the world's most audacious filmmakers. In a series of smart, informative essays, this book traces his career from its roots in New Queer Cinema to the Oscar-nominated *Far from Heaven* (2002), taking in along the way such landmark films as *Poison* (1991), *Safe* (1995) and *Velvet Goldmine* (1998).

2006
288 pages
1-904764-88-6   £15.99 (pbk)
1-904764-89-4   £45.00 (hbk)

The Cinema of Steven Spielberg
Empire of Light

Nigel Morris

Cinema's most successful director is a commercial and cultural force demanding serious consideration. Not just triumphant marketing, this international popularity is partly a function of the movies themselves. Polarised critical attitudes largely overlook this, and evidence either unquestioning adulation or vilification – often vitriolic – for epitomising contemporary Hollywood. Detailed textual analyses reveal that alongside conventional commercial appeal, Spielberg's movies function consistently as a self-reflexive commentary on cinema.

2004
224 pages
1-904764-14-2   £15.99 (pbk)
1-904764-15-0   £45.00 (hbk)

The Cinema of John Carpenter
The Technique of Terror

Edited by Ian Conrich and David Woods

'The *Directors' Cuts* series adds to its roster of studies on the great helmers of the horror new wave with an analysis of arguably the greatest of them all. After an exploration of the nature of genre, the writers identify the structural tensions that beset his films, eschewing any attempt to seek a unified narrative in his output, instead focusing on his motifs. The essays reveal Carpenter's early creative, as well as his technical, excellence.'
– 'Book of the Month', March 2005, *Empire*

The Cinema of Mike Leigh
A Sense of the Real

Gary Watson

'The time is ripe for a serious critical appraisal of the work of Mike Leigh, one of the most innovative and provocative filmmakers in Britain today. Garry Watson's book fills this gap admirably. He has a rare gift for putting the films vividly before us and then making us reconsider them in a new light.'
– Professor Brian McFarlane, Monash University

2004
224 pages
1-904764-10-X £15.99 (pbk)
1-903364-90-6 £45.00 (hbk)

The Cinema of Nanni Moretti
Dreams and Diaries

Ewa Mazierska and Laura Rascaroli

'This, the first book to be written in English on Nanni Moretti, is an excellent, thought-provoking introduction to the director, and finally presents one of Italy's most important contemporary filmmakers to the English-speaking world … It is an invaluable book not only for undergraduates, but also for researchers looking for a new and stimulating approach to Moretti's cinema, and is therefore highly recommendable.'
– *Italian Studies*

2004
208 pages
1-903364-77-9 £15.99 (pbk)
1-903364-78-7 £45.00 (hbk)

The Cinema of Krzysztof Kieslowski
Variations on Destiny and Chance

Marek Haltof

'Haltof works through an enormous amount of Polish film criticism, all of which will be new and interesting to most English-speaking readers. His readings of the films are clear and convincing … he stakes out well-reasoned points of emphasis from which more complicated readings can begin … Highly recommended.'
– *Choice*

2004
208 pages
1-903364-91-4 £15.99 (pbk)
1-903364-92-2 £45.00 (hbk)

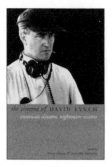

2004
208 pages
1–903364–85–X   £15.99 (pbk)
1–903364–86–8   £45.00 (hbk)

The Cinema of David Lynch
American Dreams, Nightmare Visions

Edited by Erica Sheen and
Annette Davison

'A ground-breaking collection of new essays on one of
contemporary cinema's most tantalising and original
directors. Covering all of Lynch's feature films as well as
his television, this stimulating volume presents a range
of challenging theoretical perspectives on, and insightful
readings of, Lynch's work.'
– Frank Krutnik, University of Sussex

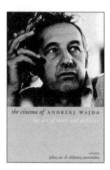

2003
232 pages
1-903364-89-2   £15.99 (pbk)
1-903364-57-4   £45.00 (hbk)

The Cinema of Andrzej Wajda
The Art of Irony and Defiance
Edited by John Orr and
Elzbieta Ostrowska

'The most comprehensive and multifaceted compilation
on Wajda's filmmaking published in English …
A desideratum for anyone drawn to Wajda's films
or Polish cinema in general.'
– Renata Murawska, Macquarie University

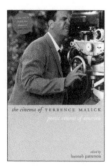

2003
208 pages
1-903364-75-2   £15.99 (pbk)
1-903364-76-0   £45.00 (hbk)

The Cinema of Terrence Malick
Poetic Visions of America

Edited by Hannah Patterson

'Wallflower Press has published several appetising collections
of essays on contemporary auteurs – Lynch, Moretti,
Wenders, Lepage etc – but this is not just a fairly exemplary
study; it's one of the most useful books on film criticism in
a while.'
– Geoff Andrew, *Time Out*

The Cinema of George A. Romero
Knight of the Living Dead

Tony Williams

'This thorough, searching and always intelligent overview does full justice to Romero's "Living Dead" trilogy and also at last rectifies the critical neglect of Romero's other work, fully establishing its complexity and cohesion.'
– Robin Wood

2003
224 pages
1-903364-73-6   £15.99 (pbk)
1-903364-62-0   £45.00 (hbk)

The Cinema of Robert Lepage
The Poetics of Memory

Aleksandar Dundjerovich

'An extremely impressive study … well-informed and very enlightening. Above all, it is excellent at analysing Lepage's creative processes and at conveying the excitement of his genuinely original way of working.'
– Professor David Bradby, Royal Holloway, University of London

2003
192 pages
1-903361-33-7   £15.99 (pbk)
1-903364-34-5   £45.00 (hbk)

The Cinema of Kathryn Bigelow
Hollywood Transgressor

Edited by Deborah Jermyn and Sean Redmond

'The first, long-awaited book-length study of one of the most visionary directors in contemporary Hollywood … This comprehensive, wide-ranging and thought-provoking collection explores Bigelow's controversial and utterly modern work from a variety of perspectives.'
– Laura Rascaroli, National University of Ireland, Cork

2003
192 pages
1-903364-42-6   £15.99 (pbk)
1-903364-43-4   £45.00 (hbk)

2002
192 pages
1-903364-29-9   £15.99 (pbk)
1-903364-30-2   £45.00 (hbk)

The Cinema of Wim Wenders
The Celluloid Highway

Alexander Graf

'Graf has done an excellent job of contextualising and explaining Wenders' views on filmmaking in a way that leads to productive textual analysis of his films. This book is a must for Wenders fans.'
– Julia Knight, University of Luton

2002
192 pages
1-903364-31-0   £15.99 (pbk)
1-903364-32-9   £45.00 (hbk)

The Cinema of Ken Loach
Art in the Service of the People

Jacob Leigh

'Well-researched, informative and perceptive in detail, this book juggles a fair number of theoretical concepts yet the writing remains accessible throughout. It fills a gap in the serious treatment of Loach and should find an appreciative audience among teachers and students of British cinema.'
– *Sight and Sound*

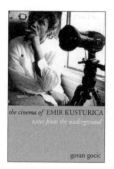

2001
192 pages
1-903364-14-0   £15.99 (pbk)
1-903364-16-7   £45.00 (hbk)

The Cinema of Emir Kusturica
Notes from the Underground

Goran Gocic

'This is a comprehensive and fascinating study of one of Europe's most important film directors. A sharp and perceptive monograph and long overdue as far as English-language film criticism is concerned: this is a must read.'
– Professor John Orr, Edinburgh University

'No.3 in Top Five Film Books of 2001'
– Phillip French, *The Observer*